To John,

Thank you for your thoughts and views for our book.

Very much appreciated and hope you enjoy the book!

Michel

Praise for *Green Gold*

'Through some very robust analysis of the past several years, Driessen and Schmidt have demonstrated the impact of sustainability on deal values, despite recent political headwinds. The book has the facts, figures and case studies to back up their conclusions. They then make some very compelling arguments and recommendations for the near future and beyond, as to why sustainability will remain critical for any investment decision. As an added bonus, Driessen and Schmidt provide several toolkits for the reader to use for their own analysis. No matter what your political persuasion, you would ignore this book at your peril. It should be required reading for any investor today'.

—Professor Scott Moeller, Founder and Director,
M&A Research Centre, Bayes Business School,
City St George's, University of London.

'At last a balanced book with a maximising mindset on sustainability. Refreshes and reinforces the view that sustainability is a driver of financial value as well as enriching societies in so many other ways'.

—Patrick Dunne OBE, Author of Boards

'For many investors today an important question is whether there is a demonstrable positive correlation between a company's adherence to ESG principles and the financial return enjoyed over the long term by that company's shareholders. Or is it the case, as some allege, that investing in an ESG-focussed manner detracts from returns? For their new book *Green Gold*, Driessen and Schmidt have trawled the markets to see whether data from recent deal flow and relevant company performance provides evidence that addresses these questions. Their conclusions may surprise you – in a positive way'.

—James Astor, Private Equity portfolio chair

'A must read and fascinating perspective on a critical question facing business in today's world, on how to create financial value through sustainability, from two incredibly knowledgeable practitioners sharing their experiences and views'.

—Amitava Guharoy, Harvard & INSEAD Alumnus,
Board Director, CEO & Senior Partner in both PwC & EY

'Despite the current geopolitical climate in North America and more widely, ESG remains an important element, and in some cases is the main driver, for corporate strategy, M&A and investment activity'.

—David Petrie, Head Corporate Finance, ICAEW

'Finally a business book which focuses on the financial value through sustainability in transactions from a practical angle focused on value creation. Sharing the different approaches, toolkits and case studies provides a rich and compelling story about the need to include sustainability in capital events. Sustainability is here to stay and the evidence of financial value creation makes this compelling reading for practitioners and senior executives in both corporates and PE'.

—Silvia Rindone, EYParthenon UKI Managing Partner, Strategy and Transactions

'There it is – a simple manual on how to incorporate the complex world of ESG into companies strategic thinking and to make it a driving force for innovation as well as operational excellence. It's an easy read providing clear explanations, practical tools as well as hands on guidance and case studies for all kinds of investors be it Private Equity, Institutional or Corporate. If done right – following an ESG route as integral part of the M&A agenda will be key as is AI – they will both become table stakes!'

—Constantin Gall, Global Leader Aerospace, Defence and Mobility EY

GREEN GOLD

MICHEL DRIESSEN • SEBASTIAN SCHMIDT

GREEN GOLD

HOW SUSTAINABILITY CREATES DEAL VALUE

WILEY

This edition first published 2026

Registered Office(s)
John Wiley & Sons, Inc., 111 River Street, Hoboken, NJ 07030, USA
John Wiley & Sons Ltd, New Era House, 8 Oldlands Way, Bognor Regis, West Sussex, PO22 9NQ, UK

For details of our global editorial offices, customer services, and more information about Wiley products visit us at www.wiley.com.

The manufacturer's authorized representative according to the EU General Product Safety Regulation is Wiley-VCH GmbH, Boschstr. 12, 69469 Weinheim, Germany, e-mail: Product_Safety@wiley.com.

Wiley also publishes its books in a variety of electronic formats and by print-on-demand. Some content that appears in standard print versions of this book may not be available in other formats.

Library of Congress Cataloging-in-Publication Data is Available:

ISBN: 9781394354443 (Cloth)
ISBN: 9781394355945 (ePub)
ISBN: 9781394355952 (ePDF)

Cover Design: Wiley
Cover Image: © ShutterWorx/Getty Images

Printed and bound by CPI Group (UK) Ltd, Croydon, CR0 4YY
C9781394354443_231225

To my late brother Jaco (1967–2024), who was full of life and died too young and to my much loved wife Natalia, for her encouragement and being my sounding board.

—MD

To my family, whose support and love have been my foundation. This book is dedicated to you.

—SeS

Contents

Acknowledgements

WE ARE INDEBTED to several people for developing the idea for this book and producing it. First, Brian Thompson at Beresford Thompson, whose literary and communications expertise was invaluable from beginning to end and everywhere in between.

To our publishers, Wiley, we are grateful for their belief in our idea and the production and editorial support of a big team, but most notably Gemma Valler, Richard Samson and Alice Hadaway.

An important aspect of this book – and, we believe, its unique benefit – comes from the combined wisdom of a large number of senior executives, industry observers and operators who have generously shared their time and views to enlighten and enrich our text. Their names appear in the relevant chapters of the book, but bear repeating here: James Astor, Laurent Bouvier, Amy Clarke, Paul Davison, Amitava Guharoy, Christian Heller, John Hoffmire, Niki Mardas, Rhodri Mason, David Petrie, Henri Servaes and David Stangis.

We would like to thank EY for allowing us the time and editorial freedom to work on this project.

Finally, each of us is grateful to our families for their understanding during the lengthy periods we have spent researching, discussing and writing this book instead of spending time with them.

Introduction

Why We Wrote This Book and Why You Should Read It

Why write a book like this at a time like this? In the first quarter of 2025, global investors withdrew a record amount from sustainable funds (Morningstar, 2025). In the United States, several states are introducing legislation that prohibits the application of ESG considerations when making investment decisions (S&P Global, 2025), and EU policymakers are watering down sustainable finance, disclosure and due diligence rules (The Guardian, 2025). Even Larry Fink, CEO of the global investment firm BlackRock and regarded as a standard-bearer for ESG investing, announced that he will no longer use the term ESG because it has become 'weaponised' (Reuters, 2023).

We believe that these conditions are precisely what make this book so necessary. If the term ESG has, as Fink suggests, become 'weaponised', then even more reason to disarm it by clarifying the financial value of ESG through the lens of the professional investor and deal maker. Can ESG investing create financial value, specifically in transactions? And if so, where can readers find it and how can they realise it?

This book explores how applying Environmental, Social and Governance (ESG) factors can create financial value for corporations, Private Equity firms and other investors during transactions. While we focus solely on the financial benefits of ESG, we acknowledge that there are many other valid reasons for businesses and investors to pursue sustainable practices, whether they are ethical, social or environmental. Our sole focus on financial value does not diminish the importance of non-financial objectives such as reducing the pace of climate change or promoting social well-being. In fact, we believe that financial value can complement and support these objectives rather than contradict them. Ultimately, if sustainable methods of managing and investing in businesses can generate financial value and better returns, they will become more attractive and widely adopted. Consequently, those seeking non-financial benefits can also be rewarded. After all, as one of our distinguished interviewees, Board Member and Amitava Guharoy, Harvard & INSEAD Alumnus commented, 'Without financial sustainability, there is no sustainability'.

Let us set some ground rules before we get into the details. Approaches to sustainability differ depending on geography, industry and organisation. For example, while climate change and environmental sustainability may typically be the primary focus for European and North American investors, those with assets in the Asia-Pacific (APAC) region may prioritise social issues or corporate governance. Similarly, the way sustainable practices create financial value varies significantly across different industry sectors. For instance, consumer goods companies are more likely to step up their sustainability practices in order to meet the expectations of customers (and by doing so, protect or grow revenues). At the same time, those in some non-consumer-facing sectors may see little incentive to do any more than meet minimum regulatory requirements. Therefore, please bear in mind that the lessons we hope you learn along the way may not be universally applicable. As you will already know or soon understand, this is a complex subject full of dead ends and unintended consequences. We will do our best to keep you on track and on target for our destination: financial value.

However, before we begin, let us briefly outline the journey we are taking and introduce you to those driving it.

In Chapter 1, we begin by defining key terms, providing a brief history of ESG and sustainability, explaining the rise of ESG ratings, examining their limitations and then beginning to explore the link between sustainability and financial value. Finally, we examine the recent pushback against ESG and assess its impact on financial value.

In Chapter 2, we examine ESG regulation, exploring the financial value and cost of rules, their relationship to ESG ratings and why some are being rolled back or delayed. Finally, we discuss some of the unintended consequences of regulation and their impact on deals and financial value.

In Chapter 3, we delve into how capital flows support ESG-driven deals and tackle systemic sustainability issues. We begin by sharing our research into more than $6 trillion of sustainability transactions, uncovering key trends and sector stories. We then examine the role of customer sentiment in creating value and driving transactions, before taking a deep dive into how capital flows and transactions address the plastics recycling problem.

In Chapter 4, we return to explore in detail the link between financial value and ESG, surveying the evidence and sharing our research into the cost of capital and price multiples. Finally, we present our approach for creating ESG-driven financial value, expressed in total shareholder return and market capitalisation.

Chapter 5 takes us into the world of ESG due diligence with particular focus on Private Equity. We examine how ESG can be utilised not only to mitigate potentially costly risks but also to identify opportunities to create value. By reviewing their playbook, we reveal which levers Private Equity firms and corporates apply to form and execute ESG value creation plans, from pre-deal to exit.

Chapter 6 provides in-depth real-world case studies revealing what happens when ESG goes wrong and how to put it right. We examine how Boohoo's strong ESG rating failed to shield the company from a scandal, the challenges of rebuilding its reputation and the significant financial impact of major controversies. Finally, in our palm oil case study, we learn that sometimes even the best of ESG intentions can have unintended consequences.

In Chapter 7, we summarise the lessons learned along the way and outline how readers can apply them to spot and create financial value through sustainability.

References

The Guardian (2025). EU Rollback on Environmental Policy is Gaining Momentum, Warn Campaigners. https://www.theguardian.com/environment/2025/jun/26/eu-rollback-on-environmental-policy-deregulation-european-green-deal (accessed 8 August 2025).

Morningstar (2025). Investors Turn Away from ESG Funds in Record Numbers in Q1 2025. https://global.morningstar.com/en-gb/sustainable-investing/investors-turn-away-esg-funds-record-numbers-q1-2025 (accessed 8 August 2025).

Reuters (2023). BlackRock's Fink says he's Stopped Using 'Weaponised' Term ESG. https://www.reuters.com/business/environment/blackrocks-fink-says-hes-stopped-using-weaponised-term-esg-2023-06-26/ (accessed 8 August 2025).

S&P Global (2025). Dozens of New State Anti-ESG Bills Introduced; Federal Legislation Expected. https://www.spglobal.com/market-intelligence/en/news-insights/articles/2025/1/dozens-of-new-state-antiesg-bills-introduced-federal-legislation-expected-87342102 (accessed 17 August 2025).

About the Authors

Michel Driessen is a Professor in the Practice of Finance and the Director of the M&A Research Centre at Bayes Business School. In addition, he is a Chairman, Business Advisor and Board Member. Previously, he was a UK-based Senior Partner in the Strategy and Transaction Group at professional services firm EY, a Partner at Accenture and held senior executive positions at Visa and Rabobank. He is the co-author of two business books, '*Why Deals Fail and How to Rescue Them*' and '*The Deal Paradox: Mergers and Acquisitions Success in the Age of Digital Transformation*'.

Sebastian Schmidt is a Partner at EY Parthenon in its Strategy and Transaction Group based in Germany/Berlin. He was one of the founding members of the decision modelling and economics team in Germany and has led on data analytics and financial modelling projects for corporate and Private Equity clients acting globally. He also led the valuation and business modelling team in Germany and has developed concepts illustrating the connection between ESG measures and enterprise valuation.

We are grateful for the expert input of Priyam Lahiri, a Partner at professional services firm EY. An expert in growth strategy and data-driven decision-making, she combines deep industry knowledge with technological insight. Her analysis of the M&A market appears in Chapter 4.

We are also grateful to Navneet Kumar, Senior Manager at EY in Germany, for his expert guidance on sustainability and his deep commitment to the research, data and analysis that underpin this book. His strategic insights were instrumental in shaping key arguments and significantly enriching the findings.

References

Driessen, M., Faelten, A., and Moeller S. (2023). *The Deal Paradox, Mergers and Acquisitions Success in the Age of Digital Transformation*. London, UK: Kogan Page.

Faelten, A., Driessen, M., and Moeller S. (2016). *Why Deals Fail and How to Rescue Them: M&A Lessons for Business Success*. London, UK: Economist Books.

1

Defining Terms and Exploring the Sustainability/Financial Value Link

Even in our brief introductory statement, we used both the terms sustainability and ESG. This might suggest they are synonyms with nearly identical meanings, but that is not the case. Sustainability is a broad principle that is concerned with balancing environmental, social and economic needs for the long-term benefit of both current and future generations. ESG, on the other hand, is a specific framework used to assess and measure a company's performance against environmental, social and governance factors. What both terms do have in common is that they have come to mean so many different things to so many different people. And by doing so, they risk becoming both essentially meaningless and highly contentious.

Fortunately, this is not a book about definitions, but rather about financial outcomes. However, it is helpful to provide some context to understand how we arrived at our current state in terms of both sustainability and ESG.

So, in our first section, we examine the history of sustainability in all its forms, followed by an overview of the rise of ESG.

In our second section, we take our first steps into exploring the link between sustainability, ESG and financial value.

Thirdly, we examine the recent backlash against ESG and assess its impact on financial value.

A Brief History of Sustainability

Please forgive us for a quick foray into ancient history. If we consider sustainability to revolve around the ability of people and nature to coexist successfully over time, then the concept not only dates back a very long way but has value at its centre. As hunter-gatherers, we lived in a largely harmonious relationship with our environment. Following the agricultural revolution approximately 12,000 years ago, we became farmers, controlling and extracting value from the natural world. The Industrial Revolution, which took place between 1750 and 1900, witnessed both the unprecedented destruction of nature and the unprecedented creation of financial value. Now, we are seeking to reestablish our connection with nature through the development of innovative green technologies. If that is to be the case, there can be little doubt that such technologies will only succeed if they offer the promise of financial value to those who invest in and deliver them.

In other words, the search for value, whether through farming land or harnessing new technologies, is at the heart of the human story, past, present and future. It may even be responsible for the words you are now reading. In his groundbreaking international multi-million-selling book, *Sapiens: A Brief History of Mankind* (Harari, 2015), author Yuval Noah Harari explains how homo sapiens invented the written word some 5,500 years ago to record the ownership of animals and crops. On this basis, Harari believes it is likely that 'the first recorded name in history belongs to an accountant, rather than a prophet, a poet, or a great conqueror'. In this spirit, we will continue our journey to explore financial value and sustainability.

The Modern History of Sustainability

In more modern terms, the history of sustainability can be traced back to the 1950s, with the publication of Howard Bowen's book, *Social*

Responsibilities of the Businessman (Bowen, 1953). Essentially, Bowen's focus is on how an individual business impacts the society in which it operates and how it can take action to reduce harmful aspects and increase positive ones. In the 1960s, anti-Vietnam War activists influenced the investment choices of university endowment funds, leading to the creation of ethical funds, such as the Pax Fund. Pax Fund was the first publicly available US mutual fund to consider social and environmental factors in investment decisions, laying the groundwork for the future of ESG investing. Such funds played a crucial role in assessing the ethical, social and ecological value of their investments and linking these factors to their performance.

Similarly, the anti-apartheid movement's divestment campaigns compelled investors and some companies to sever ties with South Africa, prompting consumers to reconsider the ethics of their purchases. For those old enough to remember, purchasing a South African orange in a UK supermarket became a politically charged act. This early example shows how sustainability-related issues can influence a product's desirability and price point. On the right side of public perception, more significant volumes can be sold at higher prices, adding value. On the wrong side, shunned oranges rot on the shelves at almost any cost, losing value by the hour.

In the 1970s, the focus shifted to the environment, with US Senator Gaylord Nelson organising the world's first Earth Day in 1970. How did he mobilise nearly 10% of the country to attend events nationwide? Due to growing public concern over pollution, environmental damage and health issues resulting from industrial activities, there is a need for action. Public concern may have risen to such levels because of the lack of regulation. It was not until 1972 that the Clean Water Act (CWA) established the basic structure for regulating discharges of pollutants into the waters of the United States and regulating quality standards for surface waters. Until then, there was little to stop factories from discharging toxins into rivers. A decade earlier, the Clean Air Act of 1963 implemented measures to control national air pollution.

It would be wrong to suggest that it was all one-way traffic. Many in the business world, including renowned economist Milton Friedman, challenged the idea of corporate accountability and responsible investment. In his book *Capitalism and Freedom* (Friedman, 1962), he argued that 'there is one and only one social responsibility of business – to use its resources and engage in activities designed to increase its profits'. This idea, known as shareholder primacy, deserves careful consideration.

Shareholder Primacy Versus Stakeholder Capitalism Milton Friedman's faith in shareholder primacy meant he believed that a business executive spending the corporation's money on social causes was essentially operating against the company's interests. Friedman believed that if an executive wanted to make a difference in society and/or the environment, they should do so privately and using their own funds. His argument was financial rather than ethical or political. He believed businesses should focus on their strengths, maximising profits for their shareholders.

The opposing view, most famously espoused much later at the 1987 World Economic Forum's Business Roundtable, is that a business should prioritise the interests of all stakeholders – employees, customers, suppliers, communities and shareholders. The company should ensure it delivers value to all stakeholders, meeting their needs and protecting their interests. Crucially, most exponents of stakeholder capitalism believe that such a stance will not only benefit these individual stakeholders but also ultimately benefit the whole organisation and make it more financially successful. This view is based on the concept of interconnection. Let us take the example of a retailer acting in the best interest of its local community during the COVID-19 pandemic by making free food deliveries to local pensioners. These extra efforts may not appear to be in the direct interest of its shareholders. Still, the stakeholder capitalist would argue that doing so enhances the company's reputation within the community and, through the loyalty and allegiance it fosters, ultimately benefits the company and its shareholders. Note that in this example, the stakeholder capitalist is, in some ways at least, wanting to have their cake and eat it, too. Doing good is not enough. They also aim to establish a connection between doing good and, in the long term, at least, generating financial value.

Just as the opponents of shareholder primacy believe that stakeholder capitalism can ultimately deliver financial value to all stakeholders, Milton Friedman did, in a way, also acknowledge the value of providing value to all stakeholders, writing that, 'it may well be in the long-run interest of a corporation that is a major employer in a small community to devote resources to providing amenities to that community or to improving its government. That may make it easier to attract desirable employees, it may reduce the wage bill or lessen losses from pilferage and sabotage or have other worthwhile effects' (Friedman, 1970). The problem, as we will discover throughout this book, is in measuring the actual financial value of such actions. Consider the example of a company that offers its employees an on-site gym. We could agree on those benefits, such as reduced time off sick and an increased ability to attract and retain talent. We may also see broader social benefits, including healthier populations, reduced need for medical intervention and increased longevity. However, calculating and agreeing on a specific value is a challenge and not always straightforward.

The 1980s and Beyond During this period, multilateral organisations picked up the sustainability baton.

In 1983, the United Nations established an autonomous body to investigate the relationship between human activity and the environment and consider its economic and environmental policy implications.

In 1987, the Brundtland Report 'Our Common Future' formed the basis for the first Conference on Environment and Development, widely known as the Rio Earth Summit, which took place in Rio de Janeiro in 1992. At this groundbreaking event, 154 countries signed the landmark United Nations Framework Convention on Climate Change (UNFCCC) – now more commonly known as the Convention on Climate Change (COP).

Also in 1992, the United Nations Environment Program (UNEP) published the Statement of Commitment by Financial Institutions on Sustainable Development.

The 1997 Kyoto Protocol made curbing greenhouse gas emissions a collective responsibility, reinforcing the integration of environmental considerations into a broader ESG strategy.

In 2000, the United Nations' Millennium Summit established guiding principles on issues including human rights, working conditions, the environment and anti-corruption. Following the summit, the Millennium Development Goals (MDGs) were created, outlining eight international development goals to be achieved by 2015.

That same year, the Carbon Disclosure Project (CDP) was founded, encouraging institutional investors to request that companies report on their climate impact.

The Birth of ESG However, 2004 represents the most significant milestone in sustainability from a business perspective. The term 'ESG' first appeared in a 2004 report titled 'Who Cares Wins' (United Nations, 2004), which was initiated by the UN Secretary General and UN Global Compact in collaboration with the Swiss government. It is interesting to note, in this quote from the executive summary, how much of the focus is on financial value, whether through increasing shareholder returns, boosting company performance or integrating environmental, social and governance (ESG) factors into financial markets. 'The institutions endorsing this report are convinced that in a more globalised, interconnected and competitive world, the way that environmental, social and corporate governance issues are managed is an integral part of companies' overall management capability and quality, required to compete successfully. Companies that perform better in these issues can increase shareholder value by, for example, properly managing risks, anticipating regulatory actions or accessing new markets while contributing to the sustainable development of the societies in which they operate. Moreover, these issues can significantly impact a company's reputation and brand, an increasingly important part of its value'. The report also established a crucial link between ESG actions and financial performance, laying the groundwork for the later development of the UN Principles for Responsible Investing (UN PRI). The same year that 'Who Cares Wins' was published, the UNEP Finance Initiative (UNEP/fi) highlighted the relevance of ESG issues in financial valuation in the Freshfields Report.

The Scandals Trifecta Those seeking further evidence of the need for stronger ESG measures had plenty to consider in the first decade of the millennium. The collapse of American energy company Enron, following widespread internal fraud, led to bankruptcy and the dissolution of its accounting firm, Arthur Andersen. This event raised serious concerns about corporate governance. In 2010, the failure of the BP-operated Deepwater Horizon drilling rig resulted in the largest marine oil spill in history, underscoring the importance of environmental protection. The decade also saw growing awareness of the social harms of company practices, from the use of child labour to the tactics used to sell infant formula milk. While these scandals are rightly remembered for their environmental and social impact, as well as their significant governance failures, their financial impact is also worth noting. In the 40 days following the Deepwater Horizon oil spill, BP's stock price on the New York Stock Exchange fell by more than half, reaching its lowest level since August 1996 (Yahoo Finance, 2014).

The Road to Now In response to growing public concern over environmental damage, new standards emerged, including the Global Reporting Initiative (GRI), founded in 1997, which has become the de facto global standard for transparency on sustainability matters. Additional principles and frameworks were developed, providing further guidance on how companies can integrate and report on ESG factors. Some prominent examples include the Principles for Responsible Investment (PRI), the Climate Disclosure Standards Board (CDSB) and the Sustainability Accounting Standards Board (SASB), which aim to develop accounting standards that reflect the impact of environmental, social and governance (ESG) factors on a company's bottom line within a specific industry. For example, beverage companies must account for water security. Energy firms need to consider the environmental impact of their manufacturing equipment. It was about identifying the risks and opportunities associated with sustainability targets and the start of standardised reporting.

By 2015, the Sustainable Development Goals outlined 17 sustainability targets and set a global agenda for sustainable development. The SDGs, which replaced the Millennium Development Goals, set specific targets with unique indicators to track progress.

Investors continued to demand climate-related financial disclosures from companies, prompting regulators to respond with new reporting requirements. The Task Force on Climate-related Financial Disclosure (TCFD) was established in 2015 and developed a framework to help public companies and other organisations more effectively disclose climate-related risks and opportunities. The TFCD framework is now integrated into its successor: the International Sustainability Standards Board.

New regulations have been established, such as the European Union's Corporate Sustainability Reporting Directive (CSRD), accompanied by the European Sustainability Reporting Standards (ESRS), which require businesses to report on the environmental, social and governance impacts of their business activities.

As we will see later in the chapter, concerns over the complexity and cost of EU reporting and other requirements led to some rules being delayed or rolled back through the EU Omnibus announcement in early 2025.

Short-term Profit Versus Long-term Value Most studies of sustainability eventually confront the need to balance short-term targets with long-term objectives. Simply put, the argument is that the quarterly financial reporting cycle and the long-term needs of people and the environment/planet can create a challenge. Suppose a soap manufacturer decides to meet its sustainability targets by committing to using only recyclable packaging materials in the future. Such an initiative may require new machinery, new suppliers and storage requirements. As a result, the company's current-year profits will decline. An advocate of shareholder primacy might conclude that such an initiative, unless mandated by regulation, was not in the best interest of shareholders. The stakeholder capitalist would be more likely to argue that, while the shareholder may suffer in the short term, other stakeholders would gain value immediately and, in any case, the shareholder would get their returns in the end as, for example, the reputation of the company, its attractiveness as an employer and its ability to maintain market share among eco-conscious consumers would eventually pay off. This general argument gives rise to the concept of long-term value (LTV) which, in the broadest terms, believes focusing on a broad set of stakeholders, with a distinct purpose in mind, is the best way to sustain a business for the long term. Note the role of purpose here. The LTV vision serves as a guiding principle, akin to a North Star, that directs current actions towards long-term objectives.

Shareholder primacy advocates might say this neatly sidesteps the need to fully quantify the value created in favour of a greater, unspecified future financial benefit. Detractors might liken this 'purpose promise' to the proverbial pot of gold at the end of the rainbow; investing today to create more value in the future is hardly alien to the business world. The continual trade-off between present inputs and future outcomes is at the heart of any commercial activity. It is also crucial to investors, who typically seek assets that can provide income and/or growth over an extended period.

Alternatively, perhaps this binary choice between immediate and delayed financial gratification is not entirely accurate. In Alex Edmans' article, Applying Economics – Not Gut Feel – to ESG (Edmans, 2023a), he argues that 'Shareholder value is an inherently long-term concept. It is the present value of all future cash flows, from now until the end of time'. This fits nicely with the broad definition of sustainability as 'the ability to maintain or support a process continuously over time'. Astute readers will immediately spot that this could equally well apply to a planet, a society or a business. You may also note that such a broad and ambiguous definition does not necessarily help the promotion and positioning of sustainability in a financial context.

In the context of this discussion, it is often noted that family-owned businesses appear more able to balance long-term versus short-term challenges than publicly traded companies. The received explanation is that family-owned businesses are more focused on passing on the company to the next generation, so they naturally have a very long-term focus. In contrast, a publicly traded company is more naturally focused on meeting the expectations of the financial analysts and the quarterly reporting cycle.

The continued relevance of the long-term versus short-term debate is evident to this day in publications such as *The New Nature of Business: The Path to Prosperity and Sustainability* by businessman Andre Hoffmann and journalist Peter Vanham (Hoffmann and Vanham, 2024). Their book presents a template for creating what the authors describe as 'sustainable prosperity', which provides a way out of long-standing dilemmas such as how to balance business needs with impact on nature, shareholders with stakeholders and short-term versus long-term profits. As a more modest contribution to this debate, in Chapter 4, we present our research on how sustainability initiatives can create not only social and environmental value but also add financial value. This is because, although not all the benefits of, for example, improving air quality or mitigating climate change will create internal value (by which we mean direct benefits to the individual company rather than to broader society or the environment), some, like reducing energy use, improving compliance or speeding up innovation, may do. This, in turn, will add financial value in terms of both present value and retained earnings, as well as equity value.

The Rise of ESG

Since the 'Who Cares Wins' report (United Nations, 2004) was mentioned earlier in this chapter, ESG has not only become synonymous with sustainability but has also largely replaced it as a term. How did ESG become so dominant?

As we have covered above, the early days of ethical investing began with saying 'no' – whether to tobacco, weapons, South African oranges or any other product judged morally questionable. With the first links established between sustainable investing and performance came the idea that, rather than just excluding certain investments, there may be value in seeking out companies that actively 'do good', not just avoiding those that harm.

Businesses, always eager to attract capital (and, potentially, ESG-motivated customers and employees), now have an incentive to earn and show their 'good' credentials. They may even be willing to spend money and time proving these credentials, provided they have not already done so during their regular business practices.

For investors, there is now a clear need to identify and monitor the investee company's credentials to ensure they meet the required standard.

At the same time, regulators, increasingly globally, were looking to set boundaries and enforce rules on companies regarding their sustainability performance.

In summary, institutions measuring the sustainability of investments, companies seeking to attract and access capital and regulators seeking compliance, all need concrete forms of measurement in a world where, as we have already discussed, much is open to debate and assumption.

ESG became a solution because its three pillars, as shown in Figure 1.1, provided the best available framework for measuring and comparing using standardised methods and metrics.

Even at the level above (in reality, each of these bullets has several subcategories), it is clear that there is potential for these factors to be examined by the company, its investors and regulators against specific criteria. Given a clean bill of health, the company has the green light for investment or regulatory compliance. Better still, if all similar companies undergo a parallel examination, the company can be rated and ranked against its peers.

Even better, if independent third parties conduct those ratings, the risk of bias or self-interest is reduced. This pressure for clarity and metrics led to the rise of the ESG ratings agencies like MSCI, Refinitiv and others.

ESG Ratings – The Pros and Cons As outlined above, the comprehensive and measurable nature of each ESG factor and sub-factor provided a basis for investing trillions of dollars while contributing to

Environmental

- Biodiversity
- Carbon emissions
- Circular economy
- Clean energy and technologies
- Climate risks
- Energy efficiency
- Pollution and waste management
- Use of natural resources

Social

- Child labour
- Community roles
- Diversity, equity and inclusion
- Health and safety
- Human capital
- Human rights
- Labour relations
- Product safety

Governance

- Anti-money laundering
- Board diversity
- Business ethics
- Compensation policies
- Corruption and bribery
- Escalation protocols
- Governance or performanc effect
- Risk tolerance

Figure 1.1 Overview of the three pillars of ESG.

Source: Industry Research

national and supranational sustainable development goals. Customers and employees could also be guided in their choice of where to shop and work. Such a framework could also help to avoid the disastrous environmental, financial and other impacts seen when 'unchecked' corporate actions lead to scandals like Enron or Deepwater Horizon. In short, an ESG rating would mean happy investors, governments, regulators, supranational organisations and companies. As ever, it is not quite that simple.

The first potential issue is that there are multiple providers, each of which publishes its own individual ratings based on its methodologies. However reliable the data – and it should be pointed out that many of the ratings providers are highly respected sources of such data – if the methods differ, so will the underlying basis of the ratings. We have already outlined how much approaches to sustainability can differ, so it should come as no surprise that this is reflected in the approaches of ESG rating agencies. For example, while some place more focus on the impact of the company on the environment, others give more prominence to the impact of the environment on the company, in terms of factors such as climate change risks. Each of the different rating agencies requires slightly different inputs and weighs them differently to calculate their rating. Even where there is apparent standardisation, variations may occur. For example, all ratings providers may collect data on workplace injuries. However, they may use that data differently. Some may base their ratings on the overall number of accidents, while others may consider the severity of any injuries or the trend over time.

Variations extend to the 'scores' awarded to companies undertaking the evaluation process. Some ESG ratings provide companies with a score from one to one hundred, others mimic the credit agencies' CCC to AAA ratings and others follow the educational world's A+ to D scoring methodology. Other quirks include the tendency for larger companies to receive better scores, mainly due to their ability to supply more data and thereby leave fewer blank spaces on the forms. Significantly, in the context of this book, the ratings agencies provide a single consolidated score for a company as a whole, rather than for its individual business units as well. Given that transactions often involve buying only one part of a company and its operations, the single ESG consolidated score is not always sufficient to dealmakers. As we will see in Chapter 5, rather than relying solely on ESG ratings, corporates and Private Equity typically apply their own ESG lens during the due diligence process to assess the financial implications of ESG factors on the target company they are interested in investing in or acquiring.

In summary, whilst recognising that ESG ratings have their strengths, we believe it is fair to say that the current system, which utilises multiple scorekeepers, approaches and methodologies at an aggregated company level, lacks the granularity and detail necessary for a reliable measure of financial value, particularly when applied to a division or business unit within a large corporation.

Despite the limitations described above, there is one crucial aspect in which ESG ratings have immense and unquestionable financial value: many investors and lenders rely (not solely, but to a significant extent) on ESG ratings to make decisions on the cost and availability of funding. This alone means that ESG ratings have significant financial value.

The ESG Investor Universe Having highlighted the link between investing and ESG ratings, it is worth briefly examining the different types of investors and the ESG lens through which they approach decision-making.

The first group consists of large institutional lenders, commonly referred to as banks. We know that many such banks, particularly in Europe but increasingly globally, consider ESG factors when approving loans. The logic for doing so may be purely financial. For example, the bank believes that lending to a company that has fully considered its environmental footprint, social impact and governance quality is less risky than lending to one that has not considered these factors. The lending decision may also be based on broader reasons, such as the bank having signed up for multilateral pledges to slow climate change, speed the transition to green energy or advance progress to one or more of the UN sustainability goals. Whatever the driver, the reality is that a bank will rely on external ESG ratings alongside its internal credit scoring methodologies, addressing ESG to filter its approval process.

Another type of central financial institution is the insurer. The principal role of such an institution is to protect customers against certain risks. Let us take the example of protection against fire risk. It is easy to see why an insurer may, for purely financial reasons, be interested in how climate change might influence the likelihood of such a risk and, therefore, the premium charged. While insurers may have their own models for such specific risks, they may also rely on external ratings to ensure that an organisation has considered these risks and has the necessary governance in place to manage them properly. Insurers may also rely on ESG ratings when choosing where to invest their reserves, which have been built up from past and current premiums. Again, many insurers will utilise ESG ratings to inform their investment decisions.

The final type of financial institution to consider is pension funds, which have a slightly different take on ESG. Firstly, because they are investing to meet the financial demands of workers upon retirement, their focus is long-term. Secondly, as stewards of those workers' monies, the pension fund is obligated to act responsibly, accountably and to the highest standards. This combination of long-term thinking and responsible investing naturally leads them towards what might broadly be called sustainability. This, in turn, makes them naturally inclined towards the use of ESG ratings.

One thing all these institutions have in common is that they are large and typically have multiple customers or borrowers. That makes ESG ratings an attractive proposition, because each institution doing its own thorough ESG analysis of every potential client is likely extremely challenging, fuelling the complexities we have highlighted about such measurements.

Coincidentally, all these institutions share another common element: they all invest in Private Equity funds, which are the next stop on our journey around the ESG investor universe. Given the situation described Private Equity funds may find it helpful to attain a strong ESG rating to attract capital from the institutions we have just described. However, when making their investments, Private Equity funds will not rely solely on the ESG rating of a target. Instead, this type of player in the ESG investor universe will also rely on their expertise and due diligence to identify and rapidly create financial value through applying a distinct ESG lens, while perhaps using the ESG rating as a cross-check or starting position. That is why Private Equity is such a fascinating player in the ESG world and why its approach is central to our book's theme, and why we explore it in detail in Chapter 5.

The Reality of ESG Let us step back from the metrics and measurements to examine ESG in terms of how a company operates and creates value. While the three pillars of ESG are clearly defined on paper, it becomes apparent that they are interlinked in practice. For example, a steel company whose manufacturing processes create high pollution levels will impact the health of the local community and the planet. Therefore, reducing pollution will also improve social conditions, which will have a positive impact across both the E and S pillars. However, there can also be conflict. For example, a food producer decides to stop using palm oil in its products because it has proven harmful to the environment. However, ceasing palm oil procurement has a negative social impact because the thousands of small-scale farmers who have dedicated their land to palm oil production do not have the means to shift to an alternative crop, resulting in potential loss of business, poverty and community breakdown. A clean, green steel plant requires significant investment, but this may be combined with substantial job losses. A local community may see more social value in keeping a polluting steel plant open because they favour jobs over health or environmental improvements. As these examples illustrate, trade-offs and unintended consequences are often inherent in the process and, indeed, the investment thesis of a transaction.

It is also important to note that ESG considers not only the effect of that steel factory on the local environment but also the impact of the environment on the current prospects of the steel plant. How will changes in climate, water availability and other factors impact the plant's ability to operate in the future? Although it may be challenging to capture and calculate the physical and transitional risks accurately, it is clear how much they could impact the company's financial value or viability over the next decade. Without sufficient answers, it would be entirely understandable for any investor to pass on the opportunity. Even a cursory look at the news will demonstrate how extreme climate events are having a tangible impact on the value of company assets. While some of these may be obvious, such as rising sea levels threatening property values or manufacturing facilities, others are less so. For example, the glue in the window frame of a high-speed train may no longer be able to hold the glass in place when temperatures exceed a certain level.

There is also the added need to consider not only all the factors within the company's direct control but also those of third parties. If our fictional steel factory were bringing in key components that were made using slave labour on the other side of the world, this could undermine any claim to sustainability.

For those involved in transactions, this means that the situation is rarely clear-cut, with numerous factors to consider when deciding to acquire or not to acquire. This is why, as we have already explained, the professional investor carefully assesses the individual ESG factors of the specific business rather than solely relying on a generalised rating. Figure 1.2 shows how the economic and financial models on one side, and vulnerability, exposure and climate hazard on the other, are used as inputs to assess the climate-related risks (whether physical or transitional), opportunities (in terms of resource efficiency, products/services, markets, resilience) and financial impact (in terms of income statement, cash flow statement and balance sheet).

Looking at it through that lens (i.e., as an integral part of decision-making for ESG-related investments), it is easy to see how ESG has moved businesses from a world where corporate sustainability was typically the responsibility of a small team working outside the main corridors of power to a position that involves almost every aspect and every executive of a business. That involvement extends from the board level to every department to become an integral part of the business and at the heart of its decision-making. Crucially, businesses must then be able to articulate how sustainability relates to financial value, whether to investors, customers or financial markets. This ability to communicate a coherent and persuasive ESG story to financial analysts is often lacking but can be crucial to creating financial value.

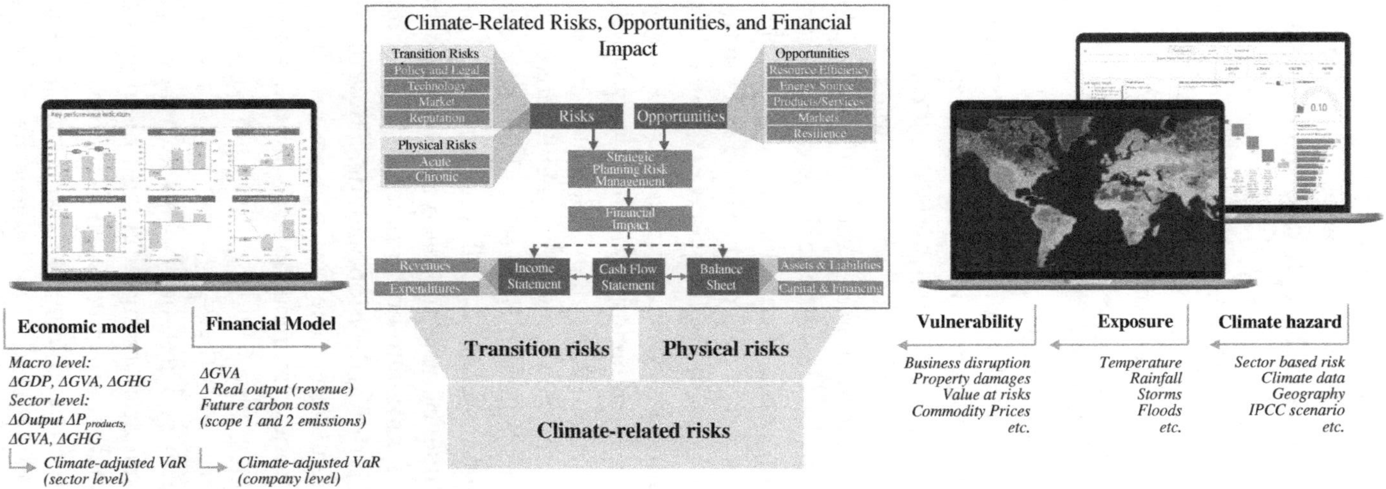

Figure 1.2 **Overview of ESG risks related to climate risks and investment decisions.**

Source: Industry Research

Expert Views on ESG Alex Edmans, whom we also mentioned earlier in this section, is a Professor of Finance at the London Business School and the author of several widely read and highly readable articles. In 'The End of ESG' (Edmans, 2023b), he argues that ESG has become overly focused on labels and compliance, rather than on creating long-term value. That value, he believes, is found by identifying the sustainability factors that are most material to a specific company and addressing them in a way that drives both financial and social benefits.

This is a topic we will continue to explore in the book, and it reveals a recurring tension: ESG is about universal frameworks and metrics, yet creating financial value is about understanding the specific ESG-related factors that can drive financial performance, often within an individual industry, company or business case.

Concerns that ESG has become overly complex, moralistic and philosophical were shared by many of our interviewees. Several felt that the term needed to be 'depoliticised' and seen for what it is, an integral aspect of business. Laurent Bouvier, Global Head of ESG Advisory at UBS believes that 'You need to build ESG in the same way as you do with R&D. Spending money as a percentage each year to build a portfolio of initiatives which you track. Some may prove valuable others may never pay off but as you learn more you will get better at selecting the right projects and initiatives, so it is an iterative learning process'. John Hoffmire, former investment banker and current Chair of the nonprofit Center on Business and Poverty, explains that 'Issues involving the environment, social concerns, and governance all influence financial value. So, the approach around ESG should be to integrate discussion of corporate environmental, social, and governance issues in normal business decision-making. These discussions and analyses should be articulated to the City analysts on a financial basis. For many industries, honest financial analysis around long-term environmental issues, for example, would position companies for the future and set an example for many others'.

Niki Mardas, Executive Director of Global Canopy, a data-driven international environmental organisation, also highlights the lack of integration: 'There is a disconnect between the company and the City/Wall Street, in the sense that the metrics companies are using for ESG do not fit in the financial models and spreadsheets of the analysts.

That's why initiatives like the Taskforce for Nature-related Finance Disclosures (TNFD) are so important, in bringing scientific frameworks and rigour to claims, while aligning them with global political targets, but crucially also with the investor-eye view'. We hope that as readers progress through this book, they will find ways to align these disconnects better and integrate ESG with the financial value of the business case.

Section Summary

From that necessarily brief introduction to sustainability, we can draw the following conclusions:

- Sustainability encompasses several definitions and, as a result, has different meanings for different people.
- ESG has emerged as the clear winner because its framework provides a unified and comprehensive basis for measures and metrics.
- However, it is essential to recognise that ESG factors are about universal frameworks and metrics, whereas creating financial value is about understanding the specific ESG factors that drive financial performance and value. ESG factors are complex, interconnected and multilayered in practice, and despite the clarifications and common standards established, several significant questions remain unanswered: How effective are the metrics? Do they focus too much on risk over opportunity? How does an ESG score relate to financial value?

The Link with Financial Value

Given the complexity and difficulties that we have outlined, why, as deal makers and value creators, should we bother with ESG? The most obvious reason is the extensive and legally binding regulations around ESG reporting and performance. Failure to comply carries considerable risks to financial value, ranging from fines and reputational damage to the loss of a license to operate. However, that is the subject of our next chapter, so we will proceed to the second most apparent reason businesses must pay attention to ESG.

Please note that in this section, we provide an overview of the links between financial value and ESG, then briefly discuss their merit. In the following chapters of this book, we will take a more detailed and scientific approach to specific areas.

Financial Performance and ESG

As mentioned earlier in the chapter, the first sustainable investment funds were established primarily for ethical reasons. However, it was not long before investors became interested in the financial performance of these funds relative to other non-ethical investment vehicles. As ESG frameworks developed, many argued that better governance, improved environmental risk management and social considerations could also boost financial performance. Finding this connection between ESG and financial value soon became the objective of several high-profile surveys and research papers between 2020 and 2025.

'ESG and Financial Performance' (NYU Stern Centre for Sustainable Business, 2021) found a positive relationship between ESG and financial performance by drawing on over 1,000 research papers.

'Does a company's ESG score have a measurable impact on its market value?' Deloitte (2023) showed that, on average across their sample, 'a 10-point difference in an ESG score is associated with an approximate 1.2× higher EV/EBITDA multiple'.

'MSCI ESG Ratings in Global Equity Markets: A Long-term Performance Review' (MSCI, 2024) found that companies with higher MSCI ESG Ratings outperformed their lower-rated counterparts across both the MSCI ACWI Index and the MSCI World Index over the study periods. However, it is only fair to mention that not every survey finds a positive correlation between ESG and financial value. 'Drawing Up the Bill: Are ESG Ratings Related to Stock Returns Around the World?' (Alves et al., 2023) found very little evidence that ESG ratings are related to global stock returns.

Even so, the overwhelming evidence from studies is that ESG appears to have a positive link with financial performance and should therefore be of great interest to investors and dealmakers. However, we must also acknowledge that these studies are based on ESG scores and ratings that, as discussed in this book, have some shortcomings. Despite those shortcomings, these studies do summarise the key trends and implications of ESG to financial value, and as such will to some extent support the due diligence process of investors on individual target companies.

Access to Capital

Another clear link to financial value, which we will examine in greater detail in Chapter 4, is access to capital. Put simply, our research finds evidence that companies with high ESG scores typically experience lower capital costs than companies with poor ESG scores. Given that any company that can raise money at a lower cost has a greater chance of making a profit, this is a significant advantage.

One of the drivers for this advantage is that many providers of capital, from banks and pension funds to so-called green funds, only invest in companies that meet their ESG requirements. This means that high performers have greater access to funding, typically at a lower cost, which can translate directly into improved financial performance.

Climate and Financial Value

Most people intuitively understand that there is a relationship between climate and financial value. Rising sea levels destroy property. Floods harm crops and lead to higher food prices. Quantifying this can be challenging, particularly when such calculations require projections based on often-disputed climate data. However, the insurance industry allows us a clear window into cause and effect. Bloomberg Intelligence estimated the bill for US spending on climate-related damage in the 12 months at nearly $1 trillion, representing 3% of national GDP (Bloomberg, 2025). Insurers bear a significant part of this. According to figures from the National Centres for Environmental Information (NCEI), there were 27 individual weather and climate disasters with at least $1 billion in damages in 2024 alone (NCEI, 2025). While this is not the subject of our book, it is only right to acknowledge that this is an area of sustainability with a direct relation to financial value. As we will explore in Chapter 4, company-specific risks and mitigation measures are embedded in their forecasts and cash flow projections, which investors will weigh according to their individual risk appetite and return expectations. Also, as climate-related risks are an integral part of the operational risks of a company and its peers, they are considered by investors and lenders and thereby influence the cost of capital. We discussed how externalities like climate change can impact the value of a company with Christian Heller, CEO of the Value Balancing Alliance, an organisation dedicated to creating a globally applicable and comprehensive accounting methodology. He explained that 'External effects – the value to society and nature – might have a substantial financial effect on companies' financial performance – business value – as soon as they are internalised through, for example, taxes, certificates, or cost of capital'. Christian added that, 'Businesses that can demonstrate how they integrate externalities in decision-making, controlling, steering, and performance monitoring will see company value increase', before concluding that, 'Environmental risks are quite transparent nowadays. Suppose management boards can demonstrate, based on priorities, how they mitigate and adapt to those risks. In that case, they will secure or even increase company value if investors are receiving transparent information on transition strategies and corresponding financial impact'.

Stakeholder Pressures

Businesses do not act in isolation. They are increasingly subject to changes in the outside world that affect everything from consumer demands to worker needs and the availability of raw materials. In the past, business owners could disregard ESG frameworks and the prospect of climate change, while also largely ignoring the concerns of groups other than shareholders. However, this is unlikely to be the case today. The pressures causing this shift vary from investors who move capital away from poor ESG performers, regulators imposing fines or removing licenses, banks restricting capital, insurance companies withholding or repricing policies and consumers changing buying decisions if their expectations are not met (see Boohoo case study in Chapter 6). Figure 1.3 shows the stakeholders and forces that impact the financial performance of the company, each with its value drivers.

Figure 1.3 Overview of stakeholders and forces and their impact on value.

Source: Industry Research

Stakeholder Value

In many respects, the stakeholder value versus shareholder value conflict outlined earlier in this chapter has been resolved, with most businesses now acknowledging the need to consider how their operations impact key stakeholder groups carefully. One stakeholder group that a business can never ignore is its customers. A comprehensive 2023 joint study from McKinsey and Nielsen, 'Consumers care about sustainability – and back it up with their wallets' (McKinsey & Company 2023), found that products making ESG-related claims averaged 28% cumulative growth over the past five years, compared to 20% for products that made no such claims. Conversely, anything that damages customer sentiment regarding a company's sustainability performance can, as we will see throughout this book, erode financial value.

ESG and Risk Management

Sustainability, and its application through the ESG framework, has traditionally been seen as a risk mitigation or hygiene factor. What will happen if I inadvertently use a supplier with poor employment practices? How will global warming impact my operations in Southern Europe? What happens if an accidental leak damages a nearby water system? These concerns deserve attention, particularly in a world where the penalties for such transgressions can be severe. For example, in Germany, a corporation found to be in breach of supply chain transparency and due diligence requirements may be required to pay fines of up to 2% of its annual revenue and, in some cases, may also be prohibited from bidding on government projects for up to three years (German Supply Chain Due Diligence Act GSCA).

Fines can also be levied in cases where companies have failed to meet their sustainability claims. In 2025, German prosecutors fined asset manager DWS 25 million euros ($27 million) after a lengthy probe found the firm guilty of making misleading statements about its environmental and social investing credentials (Reuters, 2025a). More broadly, by better understanding the environmental, social and governance risks to a company, costly mistakes can be avoided. In all cases, there is a clear link between managing ESG risks and protecting financial value.

ESG and Opportunities

But what about the positives of ESG adoption? The opportunities can be summarised as follows:

- Create new sources of revenue
- Increase operational efficiency
- Drive innovation in products and services
- Create a price premium and boost brand value
- Improve resilience
- Build trust/customer loyalty

Value creation can be incremental, as in the case of a company that improves its office insulation, thereby reducing heating costs and carbon emissions. It may represent a significant step forward, as seen in the case of a technology company utilising solar panels or wind turbines to power its servers, enhancing its ESG rating, reducing costs and improving energy security.

However, the move to sustainable solutions can also be transformational. We will examine one example in detail later, but many more well-known cases warrant brief mention. Market disruptors like Netherlands-based Tony's Chocolonely, which is on a mission to end exploitation in cocoa production, saw revenues exceed €200m by February 2025 (Confectionery Production, 2025). Note how its success has come not despite its strong ethical sense but because of it. In this case, progressive ESG policies do not need to be balanced against short-term profit because they are its most significant differentiator and value creator.

Such highly ethical companies can soon become M&A targets, unlocking immense financial value for both buyer and seller. In 2017, Pukka Herbs, whose website states that 'We are passionate in our determination to do things differently to minimise our impact on our beautiful planet' (Pukka, 2025), was acquired by global consumer products giant Unilever for an undisclosed sum. Through this acquisition, Unilever established a stronger foothold in the growing herbal tea market, where provenance and integrity are highly valued. Pukka gained access to Unilever's extensive global distribution and marketing channels. Interestingly, Pukka co-founder Sebastian Pole explained that he agreed to sell to Unilever because he perceived it as 'a leader in calling for business to act as a force for good. It welcomes our herbal knowledge and wants us to influence positively from within'. This suggests that companies may not always be able to acquire sustainability unless they can demonstrate it to the target company themselves. That links an acquirer's ability to create value to their ESG credentials. As Pole referenced, Unilever has long been a pioneer in environmentally sensitive business practices. However, Pukka has several advantages over its giant rival. Firstly, it has a compelling story to tell as an independent brand with founders who are personally committed to its cause. Secondly, it only sells sustainable products from sustainable sources, eliminating any conflict of interest between its operations. Finally, its small size meant it was agile enough to adapt, while Unilever was at the opposite end of that scale.

Is ESG Value Creation Only an Opportunity for Startups?

There is ample anecdotal evidence that small startups have a competitive advantage in creating transformative financial value from sustainability. At the same time, larger companies must exert significant effort to achieve even incremental gains, especially with integrated (cross-border) supply chains. This is evident in the challenges major consumer goods companies face as they transition to greener processes. What may seem a relatively straightforward task, like stopping the use of microplastics, can be a massive challenge for a large global organisation. This entails significant changes to everything from packaging to supply chains.

True transformation can, therefore, be a cliff face. A good example here is deodorants. A typical spray contains environmentally harmful propellants, and the container used is complex and even dangerous to dispose of and recycle. Startup Wild developed a stick deodorant from natural ingredients and encased it in a reusable container. No gases, no plastic, and it is available at your local supermarket or via an online subscription service. Although Wild's sales are a tiny fraction of those of a major global brand, that small slice will be enough to leave plenty of room for profit and make it a hot target for M&A, which happened in April 2025 when it was acquired by consumer products giant Unilever.

It is easy to conclude that while a large, long-established global company may have to invest millions to effect incremental change, only a startup can deliver something transformative. However, this is not necessarily the case. Consider how the major automotive internal combustion engine (ICE) companies have pivoted to electric vehicle production and begun to adopt new ownership models. The counterargument is that by doing so, they are merely following the lead of the startup leader in electric vehicles, Tesla. However, there is another angle, which argues that the so-called first-mover advantage can be illusory. It is the second mover who can learn from earlier refinements, cheaply acquire companies that are tech-smart but short of capital, and rapidly build scale. The ESG world is a particularly fertile one for savvy acquirers, but also potentially a graveyard of value for those who make the wrong move.

Turning the Tanker

For value hunters, the prospect of an existing, large and struggling business that can be transformed through sustainability is tempting. Let us examine two examples: one fact and the other fiction.

Some readers may have had the experience, perhaps in their youth, of being so cash-strapped that the only way to keep their jalopy on the road was to visit a scrapyard in the hope of getting the required spare part more cheaply. Having negotiated with the often-surly attendant, it was up to the customer to remove the part from a rotting automotive heap and pay the price demanded, with no guarantee that it would work when and if the buyer could successfully install it. Dirty, oily and dodgy, it was hard to imagine anything less clean or green.

In 2022, a leading UK-based salvage and vehicle dismantling company was snapped up in a deal that valued the company at over £200m. The reason for this apparent transformation? The ability to plug into two key trends: sustainability and the rising costs associated with car repair. By reframing the scrapyard, the target company became part of the shift from the 'take, make, throw away' cycle of a linear economy to a more circular model, as shown in Figure 1.4. Keeping reusable parts in circulation in the salvage yard also helps cut repair costs. The unique selling position for reusable parts, the reissuance of parts into the supply chain and capabilities covering the entire salvage journey were the main ESG drivers in this deal whereas their unique positioning combined with high growth ambition, innovative solutions that differentiated their services amongst peers and addressing of customer behaviour and stakeholder needs by the company were the main valuation drivers in this transaction.

Another way of seeing this type of transformation is through a fictional example. Suppose a long-established light bulb manufacturer realises its current high-volume, short-life products are no longer viable in a more regulated, environmentally aware world. In response,

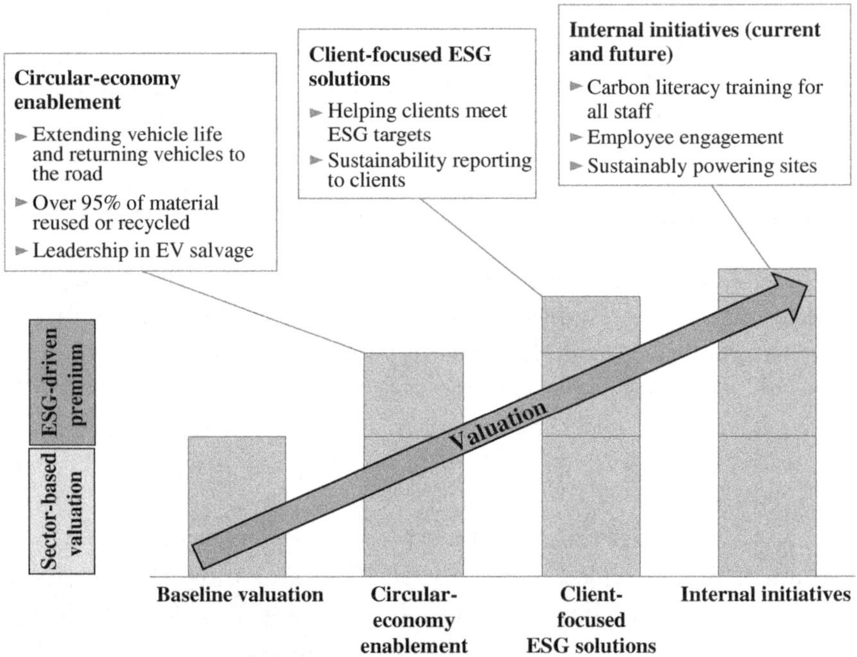

Figure 1.4 Sustainability as a value driver.

Source: Industry Research

it decided to make the bold move of selling lighting as a service rather than selling light bulbs. The incentive now shifts from the need to continually create and sell more low-price light bulbs to supplying fewer, more durable ones that keep customers' homes and offices lit as long as possible. Now, being much closer to the customer, they are also better positioned to leverage their relationship and expertise to sell complementary products and services. A real-life case study mirrors this fictional example. The lighting division of Dutch multinational lighting corporation Philips (now Signify) shifted its business model from selling light bulbs to offering Lighting-as-a-Service (LaaS), through which customers, including the sustainability-oriented Schiphol Airport near Amsterdam, pay for the light instead of buying the light bulbs or fixtures. LaaS was reported to reduce lighting energy consumption by over 50% in 2019 compared to the previous lighting arrangement for the airport lounge (Signify, 2019). Other benefits cited by the customer were lower capital expenditure and greater reliability. Philips/Signify reportedly also benefited from long-term service revenue and stronger customer relationships while being incentivised to innovate and produce longer-lasting, higher-quality components.

The Circular Economy – Value Creator or Destroyer?

In the United States, the term circularity is a long-established synonym for sustainability. Its proponents argue that it is a highly effective means to minimise waste and pollution, keep products and materials in use for as long as possible and regenerate natural systems. Its detractors argue that its radical approach undermines the capitalist system by radically reducing consumption and potentially increasing prices. As is often the case, the truth lies somewhere between the two extremes. On the one hand, circularity is a common-sense approach that even our most conservative grandparents would happily sign up to: 'waste not, want not', as they might say. On the other hand, the ambitious young entrepreneur might worry that money could never be made in a world where nothing was ever thrown away, but instead was repaired, repurposed, recycled or shared. For example, if everyone on your street owns a garden spade that needs replacing every couple of years, that is a significant amount of work for spade manufacturers and marketers. If, instead, the spades are made to last longer and be easily repairable, that picture changes. Worse still, in terms of spade sales, if the neighbourhood starts sharing the new, made-to-last spades instead of buying their own, it could lead to a decline. However, the capitalist system is not about to collapse, because the smart spade maker or seller will find a way to facilitate that system and take a cut.

Sustainability Entrepreneurs Ride the Circularity Merry-Go-Round

The fashion world is almost the epitome of the take-make-break linear economic model, as millions of people buy new outfits, then discard them after just a few weeks. According to research, the average number of times garments are worn decreased by 36% between 2002 and 2017, to an average of less than 10 times (Ellen MacArthur Foundation, 2017).

However, it is the urge to buy new things frequently that creates value for the fashion industry.

In 2008, a young woman in Lithuania was about to move from her hometown to the capital, Vilnius. She decided to slim down her wardrobe by offering unworn garments to her friends through a custom-built online platform, which later became Vinted (The Guardian, 2024). In 2019, Vinted became Lithuania's first tech unicorn after raising €128 million in a funding round at a valuation of €1 billion. A subsequent funding round two years later raised €250 million, valuing the company at €3.5 billion. Vinted acquired Dutch competitor United Wardrobe in 2020, German rival Rebelle in 2022 and Dutch delivery company Homerr in 2023. In 2023, Vinted Group 1 posted €596.3 million in revenue, an increase of 61% since 2022 (€370.2 million). Let us pause for a moment to take that in. A desire to give away unwanted clothes to friends became a multi-billion-dollar company. Talk about value creation.

The following example demonstrates how even long-established companies deeply rooted in the linear fashion economy can benefit from forming partnerships with new and seemingly contradictory business models.

H&M is a global fashion giant with over 4,000 stores in more than 79 markets and 140,000 employees. Sellpy is a Swedish business dedicated to sustainability. To quote their website, 'Sellpy was born from the idea of making it possible for everyone to live circularly. Because the easiest way to reduce emissions is to make better use of what already exists'. They propose that 'By buying and selling second hand, we can save millions of litres of water, avoid tons of emissions, and give clothes and things a longer life'. Aware that sustainability was becoming a key issue for the fashion industry, its customers and shareholders, H&M first invested in Sellpy back in 2015 and has supported every subsequent financing round. As explained on the website, 'At the time of our first investment, H&M did not have a second-hand proposition. However, the signs were clear that the growth of this segment of the fashion market would only accelerate in the coming years. We knew our customers were actively looking for a way to extend the lifecycle of their H&M products, and working with Sellpy allowed us to explore ways to launch a second-hand proposition'. H&M is now the majority owner of Sellpy, which has expanded to 24 markets, helping it become one of the most prominent players in the second-hand fashion market in Europe.

In both cases, financial value has been created from propositions that, at first glance, appeared to be socially and environmentally worthy but without any apparent monetary value. If this teaches us anything, it is to dismiss no idea and thoroughly question our assumptions. It also powerfully illustrates how sustainability can create financial value. Now we will look at the three stages of doing so.

The Three Stages of Financial Value

Let us examine those individual examples through the lens of the three stages of financial value.

The first stage illustrates that there is a baseline of ESG activity that primarily focuses on mitigating risks (compliance) and thereby protecting margins (financial protection). As an organisation steps up its approach from that baseline, it can respond to consumer needs and desires more effectively (customer requirements and protection) and, by doing so, deliver innovative, value-generating solutions (value creation/growth). These three stages are mirrored in the three categories in Figure 1.5 in which we categorise companies regarding their position on the sustainability-to-value journey: Reacting, Optimising and Leading.

Reacting	Optimising	Leading
No previous focus on sustainability, now seeking to meet minimum regulatory/lender standards.	There has been a previous focus on sustainability, but now the focus is shifting from risk protection to value creation, with ESG cascading across the portfolio and into the organisation.	Progressives with a strong sustainability pedigree are seeking to strengthen and further embed their approach.

Figure 1.5 The three stages of the sustainability journey.

Source: Industry Research

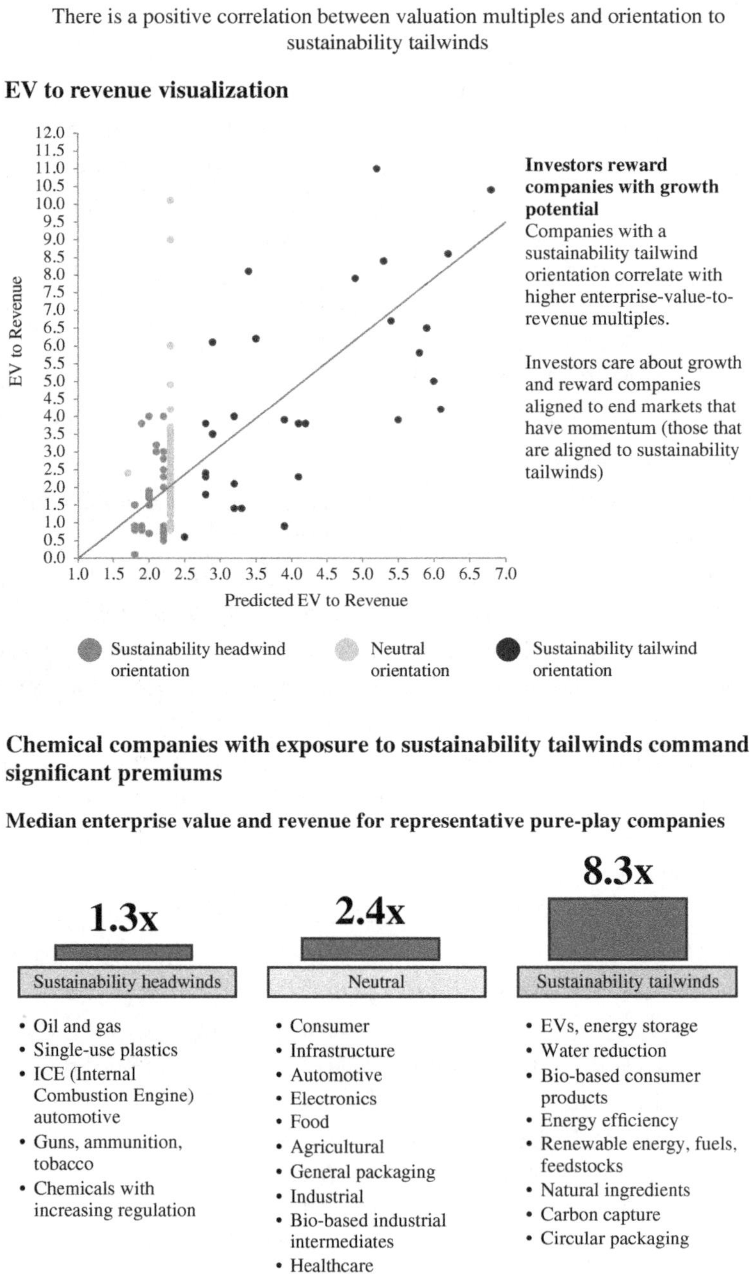

Figure 1.6 Correlation between sustainability focus and valuation multiples.

Source: Adapted from McKinsey

It is now easier to see how the links we highlighted between ESG and financial performance play out in practice. This is also reflected in valuation multiples, as illustrated in Figure 1.6. In essence, the heat map and valuation multiples reveal that companies facing sustainability headwinds – typically those in high-carbon, environmentally harmful industries – earn significantly lower multiples than those benefiting from sustainability tailwinds – usually those involved in clean, efficient energy and the use of natural or biodegradable solutions.

It is fair to acknowledge that, in general, the sustainability headwind category tends to capture older, larger and more asset-intensive companies, which may exhibit lower multiples anyway due to the sector they operate in, lower annual growth rates and the view of financial analysts. However, it is also fair to say that such companies are often more exposed to ESG risks that threaten to erode their financial value and that their asset-heavy businesses face a longer and more challenging transition path towards a more sustainable business model. In Europe, particularly, ESG laggards are likely to find it more difficult to find sources of capital and pay higher interest rates when they do so. To some extent, this split between ESG laggards and leaders reflects the differences between industries, with some well-positioned to realise the financial value of ESG and others less so. In Chapter 4, we explore these variations across sectors and the underlying drivers for these differences.

Integration and Organisation

Like any critical value driver, sustainability must be applied and integrated across all the critical functions and components of the business. Figure 1.7 illustrates that realising value from the sustainability strategy means integrating and implementing ESG across the business. This includes having a clear business strategy, narrative and communication strategy (one that is easy to understand for investors and financial analysts and links to financial metrics) as well as sufficient transparency and visibility in management, financial and operational reporting. With all these elements in place, decisions can be aligned with strategy, ensuring clear accountability and responsibility at the executive level (and immediately below) towards achieving the defined goals and fostering a culture that rewards, reflects and encourages positive employee behaviour.

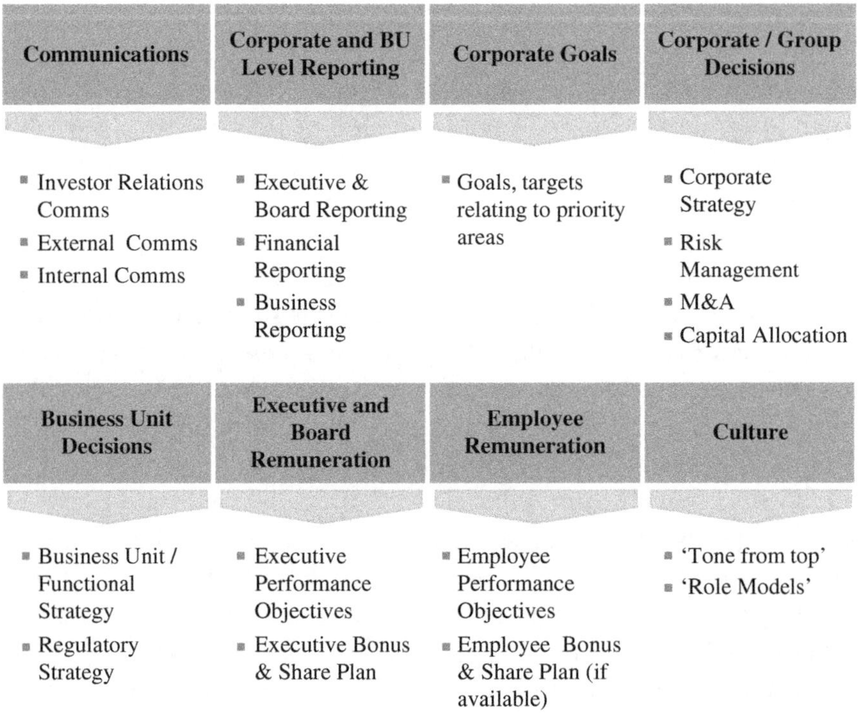

Figure 1.7 Realising the value from a sustainability strategy involves integrating ESG across the business.

Source: Industry Research

Section Summary

- Despite the complexity and occasional confusion around terminology and metrics, ESG can demonstrate a link to financial value.
- That link is shown in two ways. Firstly, through the weight of research evidence that links ESG data to financial performance. Secondly, through real-life examples of individual businesses that have created value through leveraging sustainability and, in many cases, realised that value through M&A.

Does the ESG Pushback Impact Financial Value?

We have gotten this far in the book without terms like 'woke' or 'politically correct' appearing. However, we now raise them because sustainability, in general, and ESG, in particular, have become political touchstones. This is regrettable because, as business professionals searching for value, anything that gets in the way of that quest is a distraction. So let us try to put this shift into perspective and navigate it.

We are writing this book in the first year of President Donald Trump's second term. In his first weeks alone, President Trump withdrew from sustainability pledges, exited the Paris Accord, ended wind energy permits and cut clean economy spending. However, viewing this pushback as a purely US phenomenon would be incorrect. In Europe, the European Union Omnibus Directive is extending compliance dates and narrowing the scope of some of its sustainability regulations (see Chapter 2 for more details).

Interestingly, even before the Trump presidency began, signs emerged that some large investors, who had traditionally been advocates for environmental, social and governance (ESG) principles, were starting to have reservations. Since 2014, professional services firm EY has published an annual Institutional Investor Survey to measure the response of financial institutions to ESG. Until last year, this trend had remained unbroken as investors increasingly considered ESG factors in their decision-making, encouraging and rewarding companies that acted and reported sustainably. However, the EY 2024 Institutional Investor Survey saw a change. Two-thirds of respondents stated that their institutions were likely to decrease consideration of ESG in decision-making, and 92% expressed concern that ESG-related initiatives could harm short-term corporate performance. Yet, we would suggest that other factors may have contributed to this turnaround. In our experience, many investors have not rejected sustainability as such but have become more sceptical about the claims being made about it. One classic example is the tendency for companies to set ambitious targets for the year they aim to reach net zero, but without properly considering how they will achieve them. In other words, investors were perhaps reacting to a certain amount of overreach, rather than fundamentally shifting their position.

This 'reset' is probably familiar to any stock market investor. Markets tend to overreact to positive sentiment, with valuations often overstepping the real-life foundations for outperformance. Once this gap between expectations and action becomes clear, sentiment quickly sours. However, the reality is that the company in question is often judged not by its actual performance but by outside expectations. The fundamental value case remains sound. We believe this is the view to adhere to.

Take, for example, the global banking giant HSBC. In early 2025, it announced its decision to push back its 2030 target to achieve net-zero emissions in its operations and supply chain by 20 years (Reuters, 2025b). While this made headlines, few paid attention to the underlying and arguably more important fact that HSBC continued its commitment to the climate transition, 'by providing and facilitating between $750bn and $1trn of sustainable finance and investment by 2030' (HSBC, 2025).

Similarly, while politicians, including UK Chancellor Rachel Reeves, have toned down their support for green initiatives in the face of more demanding economic or geopolitical pressures, the reality of climate change has never been more apparent. Nor have the financial consequences – for example, the California wildfires of 2024 cost Lloyd's of London £1.8bn (City AM, 2025). Insurers in the UK paid out a record £585 million for weather-related damage to homes and possessions in 2024, according to the Association of British Insurers (ABI).

In another parallel, while the political winds may be blowing back in favour of fossil fuel production, given Trump's famous 'drill, baby, drill' mantra, the overall trend remains essentially unchanged. Green energy continues to develop rapidly, driven by new technologies and the need for clean and cost-effective power. While fossil fuel prices rose following Russia's invasion of Ukraine, supporting new production and emphasising the importance of energy security, those higher energy prices also helped to make green power a more attractive investment.

A notable example is the oil-producing state of Texas, which is also among the nation's top producers of renewable energy. Although there was a backlash against renewables as they began to compete more fiercely with coal and gas-fuelled power, and as part of a broader anti-green political agenda, this was pushed aside by good old-fashioned pragmatism. Texas, facing a massive surge in electricity demand due to population growth, extreme heat and crypto mining, needed all the generation it could get from every source. Having increased its energy supply by 35% between 2020 and 2024, 92% of that new supply came from solar, wind and battery storage (The Texas Tribune, 2025). This is an example of how practical considerations often outweigh politics and perceptions.

The Turning Tide – From Greenwashing and Greenhushing to Greenhiding

The story of 21st-century sustainability could be summed up in those three words. The term 'greenwashing' became prominent as companies sought to advertise their green credentials without backing up those claims with actual actions. As some organisations were called out for greenwashing and faced legal fines and consumer backlash, companies grew more apprehensive about making green claims, opting instead to 'greenhush'. That is, avoid making any sustainability promises for fear that they may be called out and found wanting. Finally, in light of the 2025 sustainability pushback, which legally questions the application of ESG policies and practices, some companies, for fear of being judged harshly, may begin deliberately keeping those policies away from public view ('greenhiding').

The Cost of Controversy

There is an old saying in England that today's news is tomorrow's fish and chip paper. This references the thankfully long-gone habit of wrapping a portion of fish and chips in newspaper to soak up excess frying oil and keep the food warm. The true meaning of the saying, however, is that what seems new and essential today is quickly forgotten. However, in the world of sustainability at least, this is often not the case, as we will evidence later in this book. We will share our research into how negative headlines and consumer sentiment around ESG can impact a company and its financial value. The case studies we feature in Chapter 6 and elsewhere in the book will also highlight how ESG-related scandals may not only impact individual companies for many years but also reshape industries and supply chains.

What Do You Fink?

This yin and yang between stepping forward and pushing back is exemplified by Larry Fink's annual letters to investors, which are read by CEOs of S&P 500 companies and Europe's largest corporations. As chairman and CEO of BlackRock, the world's largest investment manager, Fink oversees over $11 trillion in assets.

In 2016, Fink's letter first mentioned the need for companies to look outside their own four walls and consider environmental and social factors in their decision-making.

Larry Fink's 2018 letter emphasised the need for businesses to align with the interests of external stakeholders and to serve a broader purpose in society. 'Without a sense of purpose, no company – whether public or private – can achieve its full potential', he wrote.

In 2019, he explicitly called for companies to lead in resolving social and environmental issues. He also argued that putting purpose at the heart of business drives profitability and long-term growth.

In the 2020 and 2021 letters, Fink requests disclosure and data from businesses on their climate change impact and clear plans towards achieving net-zero emissions. He also calls for improved disclosure and transparency through adherence to frameworks such as the Sustainability Accounting Standards Board (SASB) and the Task Force on Climate-related Financial Disclosures (TCFD).

Fast forward to 2024, and Fink avoids the phrase 'ESG' altogether, in line with his 2023 statement that it had become too politicised. However, the letter's focus on long-term investing, particularly in infrastructure, as well as societal concerns around ageing demographics and the disillusionment of younger Americans, suggests that a stakeholder lens is still present, albeit without much of the associated terminology.

However, it would be wrong to suggest that, despite the change in tone, nothing has altered. In January 2025, BlackRock withdrew from the world's largest investor climate coalition, the Net Zero Asset Managers (NZAM) initiative, citing that it 'caused confusion regarding BlackRock's practices and subjected us to legal inquiries from various public officials'. This move is part of a broader concern over the legality of US companies spending money on 'non-pecuniary' (i.e., sustainability-led) investments. In this respect, the pendulum has swung back firmly in the direction of Milton Friedman's shareholder primacy. There is also evidence that a combination of political pushback and investor concern is reducing inflow into sustainability funds. The first three months of 2025 saw net outflows of $8.6bn from ESG funds globally. Even Europe, by far the biggest continent in terms of ESG funds, saw negative flows for the first time since Morningstar started tracking this data in 2018 (Financial Times, 2025).

However, for dealmakers, the most significant risk associated with perception is that it could divert the value hunter's attention and focus away from the prize. Opportunities could be missed by going with the flow of negative news on ESG. With that in mind, it might be better to risk being called woke than ending up broke.

Chapter Summary

We can derive two key lessons from this final section of Chapter 1.

- First, the route to sustainability is not linear. There will be challenges and setbacks along the way, but if the fundamentals we have highlighted remain, so will the direction of travel.
- Secondly, while readers would be foolish to ignore media and political perceptions, a relentless focus on financial value will likely prove more fruitful.

References

Alves, R., Krueger, P., and van Dijk, M.A. (2023). Drawing Up the Bill: Are ESG Ratings Related to Stock Returns Around the World? *Swiss Finance Institute Research Paper* No. 25–41. http://dx.doi.org/10.2139/ssrn.4674146

Bloomberg (2025). US Spending on Climate Damage Nears $1 Trillion Per Year. https://www.bloomberg.com/news/articles/2025-06-17/us-spending-on-climate-damage-nears-1-trillion-per-year?embedded-checkout=true (accessed 8 August 2025).

Bowen, H.R. (1953). *Social Responsibilities of the Businessman*. New York: Harper.

City, A.M. (2025). Lloyd's of London Expects £1.8bn Hit from Californian Wildfires. https://www.cityam.com/lloyds-of-london-expects-1-8bn-hit-from-californian-wildfires/ (accessed 8 August 2025).

Confectionery Production (2025). Tony's Chocolonely Annual Report Reveals Revenue Upturn and Progress Tackling Child Labour. https://www.confectioneryproduction.com/news/51488/tonys-chocolonely-annual-report-reveals-revenue-upturn-and-progress-tackling-child-labour/ (accessed 24 November 2025).

Deloitte (2023). Does a Company's ESG Score Have a Measurable Impact on its Market Value? https://www.deloitte.com/ch/en/services/consulting-financial/research/does-a-company-esg-score-have-a-measurable-impact-on-its-market-value.html (accessed 8 August 2025).

Edmans, A. (2023a). Applying Economics – Not Gut Feel – to ESG. *Financial Analysts Journal* 79 (4): 16–29.

Edmans, A. (2023b). The end of ESG. *Financial Management*, 52: 3–17. https://doi.org/10.1111/fima.12413

Ellen MacArthur Foundation (2017). A New Textiles Economy: Redesigning Fashion's Future. https://www.ellenmacarthurfoundation.org/a-new-textiles-economy (accessed 8 August 2025).

EY (2024). How Can Investors Balance Short-term Demands with Long-term Value? https://www.ey.com/en_uk/insights/climate-change-sustainability-services/institutional-investor-survey (accessed 8 August 2025).

Financial Times (2025). Making Sense of a Rough Quarter for ESG Funds. https://www.ft.com/content/142eb9ee-7b20-4308-9d13-38613af58ea1 (accessed 8 August 2025).

Friedman, M. (1962) *Capitalism and Freedom*. Chicago, IL: University of Chicago Press.

Friedman, M. (1970). A Friedman Doctrine: The Social Responsibility of Business Is to Increase Its Profits. The New York Times Magazine (13 September).

The Guardian (2024). The Vinted Phenomenon: How One Woman Sold her Clothes – and Created a Billion-dollar Company. https://www.theguardian.com/fashion/2024/jan/09/the-vinted-phenomenon-how-one-woman-sold-her-clothes-and-created-a-billion-dollar-company (accessed 8 August 2025).

Harari, Y.N. (2015). *Sapiens: A Brief History of Humankind*. New York: Harper.

Hoffmann, A., and Vanham, P. (2024). *The New Nature of Business: The Path to Prosperity and Sustainability*. Hoboken, NJ: Wiley.

HSBC (2025). Financing Net Zero. https://www.hsbc.com/who-we-are/our-climate-strategy/financing-net-zero (accessed 8 August 2025).

McKinsey (2023). Consumers Care About Sustainability – and Back it up with their Wallets. https://www.mckinsey.com/industries/consumer-packaged-goods/our-insights/consumers-care-about-sustainability-and-back-it-up-with-their-wallets#/ (accessed 8 August 2025).

MSCI (2024). MSCI ESG Ratings in Global Equity Markets: A Long-Term Performance Review. https://www.msci.com/downloads/web/msci.com/research-and-insights/paper/msci-esg-ratings-in-global-equity-markets-a-long-term-performance-review/MSCI-ESG-Ratings-in-Global-Equity-Markets---A-Long-Term-Performance-Review---FINAL2.pdf (accessed 8 August 2025).

NOAA National Centres for Environmental Information (2025). U.S. Billion-Dollar Weather and Climate Disasters. https://www.ncei.noaa.gov/access/billions/ (accessed 8 August 2025).

NYU Stern Centre for Sustainable Business (2021). ESG and Financial Performance: Uncovering the Relationship by Aggregating Evidence from 1,000 Plus Studies Published between 2015 and 2020. https://www.stern.nyu.edu/sites/default/files/assets/documents/NYU-RAM_ESG-Paper_2021%20Rev_0.pdf (accessed 8 August 2025).

Pukka Herbs (2025). Impact. https://www.pukkaherbs.com/uk/en/impact (accessed 8 August 2025).

Reuters (2025a). Deutsche Bank-owned Asset Manager DWS Fined $27 Million for Greenwashing. https://www.reuters.com/sustainability/german-asset-manager-dws-fined-25-mln-eur-greenwashing-case-2025-04-02/ (accessed 8 August 2025).

Reuters (2025b). HSBC Delays Net-Zero Emissions Target by 20 Years. https://www.reuters.com/sustainability/hsbc-pushes-back-climate-emissions-target-review-policies-2025-02-19/ (accessed 8 August 2025).

Signify (2019). Case study: Schiphol Airport Amsterdam. https://www.signify.com/global/case-studies/schiphol-airport (accessed 17 August 2025).

Texas Tribune (2025). With Texas Facing Soaring Electricity Demand, the Politics of Energy Quietly Shift at the Capitol. https://www.texastribune.org/2025/03/06/texas-legislature-energy-renewables-power-grid/ (accessed 8 August 2025).

United Nations and Financial Institutions. (2004). *Who Cares Wins: Connecting Financial Markets to a Changing World.* New York: United Nations.

Yahoo Finance (2014). BP lost 55% Shareholder Value After the Deepwater Horizon Incident. https://finance.yahoo.com/news/bp-lost-55-shareholder-value-225105539.html (accessed 17 August 2025).

2

ESG and Regulation – The Hidden Value of Rules

In this chapter, we begin with an overview of the impact of regulation on financial value, then summarise the history and scope of sustainability-related regulation.

Next, we examine the role of ratings agencies in relation to regulation.

Then, we consider whether the recent rollback of regulations has any impact on financial value.

Finally, we explore some of regulation's unintended consequences – good and bad.

The History of Sustainability Regulation

Whether a business embraces or dismisses ESG, it must still comply with the demands of sustainability-related regulation. Failure to do so risks financial penalty, reputational damage and, in the worst case, loss of the company's license to operate.

For dealmakers, any non-compliance issues related to the target company will likely become serious obstacles, complicating the due diligence process and negatively affecting deal completion or purchase price. These problems may not even end there. In 2016, Marriott

International acquired rival operator Starwood Hotels & Resorts in a US $12.2 billion deal (BBC News, 2020). By 2024, Marriott faced multi-million-dollar fines for a 2014 cyberattack on Starwood Hotels & Resorts. In other words, the acquirer was held responsible for regulatory breaches that pre-dated the deal. Applying that principle to the wider world of ESG, the benefits of acquiring a company with a proven 'clean bill of health' are clear. There are risks involved in purchasing a company with extensive and costly ESG issues and/or a history of insufficient regulatory compliance. James Astor, Portfolio Chair in Private Equity, whom we spoke to during the writing of this book, puts it in elegantly simple terms: 'As an investor, I want to buy a compliant company'. Dave Stangis is Partner and Chief Sustainability Officer at Apollo Global Management, an American asset management firm with assets under management of over £750 billion at the end of 2024. He agrees that it is vital to identify any potential ESG issues early but also thinks it is important to spot ESG opportunities that can generate, rather than protect value.

To sum up, even the 'box-ticking' aspects of regulatory compliance have value in their ability to reassure investors or acquirers who are anxious to avoid hidden liabilities and risks and therefore potential value leakage. However, by capitalising on the data generated and procedures established during the compliance and reporting process, it may be possible to identify risks and opportunities that can protect and grow financial value.

The Regulation Timeline

The origins of sustainability regulation can be traced back to the introduction of landmark legislation, such as the UK Clean Air Act of 1956, which was enacted to address pollution from coal-burning and industrial activities. In the United States, the 1972 Clean Water Act (CWA) established the basic framework for regulating discharges of pollutants into the nation's waters. These types of regulations not only set simple, clear and enforceable rules for businesses, but their impact is also easily visible to the public. A clarity that many regulations lack today, due to their greater complexity.

Apart from these landmark laws, and despite a notable increase in awareness about the adverse effects of business on society and the environment, the path to action was rarely through regulation. Instead, grassroots activist movements aimed to influence the investment choices of financial institutions and the purchasing decisions of consumers in response to issues such as the Vietnam War and Apartheid. Corporates began to realise the importance of demonstrating their environmental and social credentials to avoid activist attention and to position their organisation as a force for good. With no established standards for measuring or reporting these factors, the common approach was a few lines in the front section of an annual report describing support for local community organisations, charitable donations and efforts to reduce energy consumption.

From National to Multinational

We can trace the origins of modern sustainability regulation back to the growing realisation by governments that significant environmental challenges, such as protecting the ozone layer, required multinational agreements and action. This led to a groundbreaking series of summits, beginning with the UN Summit on Environment and Development in Rio de Janeiro in 1992. These summits resulted in the adoption of the United Nations Framework Convention on Climate Change (UNFCCC) in 1992 and the Kyoto Protocol in 1997, which committed industrialised countries to stabilise their greenhouse gas (GHG) emissions through national strategies. This, in turn, required a commitment from businesses, and thus, the modern world of sustainability frameworks and regulations was born.

Businesses now needed to balance their environmental and social responsibilities with their economic goals, looking to novel concepts such as Elkington's triple bottom line (Elkington, 1994). Elkington believed that businesses need to measure their success not only by the traditional bottom line of financial performance (most often expressed in terms of profits, return on investment or shareholder value) but also by their impact on the broader economy, the environment and the society they operate in. In conducting their businesses, companies use not only financial resources (such as investment dollars and sales revenues) but also environmental resources (such as water, energy and raw materials) and social resources (such as community employees' time and talents, and infrastructure provided by governmental agencies). According to Elkington, a sustainable business ought to be able to measure, document and report a positive ROI on all three bottom lines – economic, environmental and social – as well as the benefits that stakeholders receive along the same three dimensions.

Around the same time, some companies began to embark on what would later become sustainability and ESG reporting. In addition to their standard annual reports, these pioneering companies started to publish separate environmental reports. As more corporations did so, the need for a framework and set of standards against which companies could report became clear. The Global Reporting Initiative (GRI) was founded in 1997 as the 'first accountability mechanism to ensure companies adhere to responsible environmental conduct principles' (GRI, 2025).

From Voluntary to Mandatory

The landscape of sustainability reporting underwent significant changes with the EU's adoption of Directive 2014/95/EU, also known as the Non-Financial Reporting Directive (NFRD). It sought to establish rules for disclosing non-financial information for 'public interest entities', including listed companies, as well as banks, insurers, and asset managers and owners. The Directive set the first legally binding obligation for corporations to report on concepts, risks and performance for material non-financial matters, such as environment, workforce, human rights, social aspects, anti-corruption and bribery. Just as financial reporting had been subject to regulation for many years, the directive sought to regulate the reporting of sustainability information. The aim was for sustainability reports to become more comparable and transparent, thereby providing investors and other stakeholders with critical and reliable information on sustainability issues.

The NFRD was subsequently amended and became the Corporate Sustainability Reporting Directive (CSRD), introducing several new requirements, including the assurance of certain information, digital tagging of reports and detailed mandatory reporting requirements, to further increase the comparability of sustainability reports. The term 'non-financial' was replaced with 'sustainability reporting'.

The trend towards mandatory reporting, more robust frameworks, increased standardisation and greater disclosure has continued ever since, not only in the EU but worldwide. The number of companies within the scope of sustainability regulation has also broadened, with more companies moving towards these reporting frameworks in much the same way they currently report on their financial accounts.

Materiality

A company may find that certain aspects of sustainability are critical to its operations while others are less relevant. The concept of materiality enables companies to focus their efforts on the sustainability elements most relevant to their business and its stakeholders, including regulators. By focusing equally on all factors, as illustrated in Figure 2.1, a significant amount of time would be wasted, and little insight would be gained.

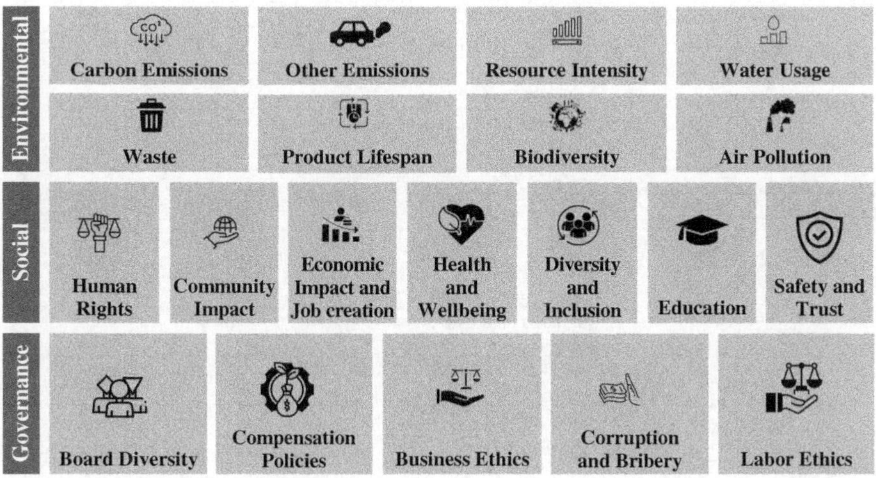

Figure 2.1 Overview of ESG factors.

Source: Industry Research

The Materiality Assessment

Organisations use a materiality assessment to identify and prioritise ESG issues that are most significant to their business operations and stakeholders. The goal is to focus on the topics that significantly impact the organisation's long-term success, financial value and sustainability. However, it also addresses the concerns and expectations of key stakeholders, including regulators. This excerpt from the German multinational chemical and consumer goods company Henkel provides a snapshot as shown in Figure 2.2.

Regulation is a vital part of the materiality assessment. Those conducting the evaluation will carefully scrutinise how the company's

Environmental topics			
European sustainability reporting standard			
Topic (ESRS Code)	**Sub-Topics**	**Impact Materiality**	**Financial Materiality**
	Climate change adaptation	☐	☐
Climate Change (ESRS E1)	Climate change mitigation	☑	☑
	Energy	☑	☐
	Pollution of air	☐	☐
	Pollution of water	☐	☐
	Pollution of soil	☐	☐
Pollution (ESRS E2)	Pollution of living organisms and food resources	☐	☐
	Substances of concern	☐	☐
	Substances of very high concern	☐	☑
	Microplastics	☐	☐
Water and Marine Resources (ESRS E3)	Water	☑	☑
	Marine resources	☐	☐
	Direct impact drivers of biodiversity loss	☑	☐
	Impacts on the state of species	☐	☐
Biodiversity and Ecosystems (ESRS E4)	Impacts on the extent and condition of ecosystems	☑	☐
	Impacts and dependencies on ecosystem services	☐	☐
	Resource inflows, including resource use	☐	☑
Circular Economy (ESRS E5)	Resource outflows related to products and services	☑	☑
	Waste	☑	☐

Figure 2.2 Henkel materiality assessment – overview.

Source: Adapted from Henkel sustainability report 2024

operations align with relevant rules, such as those related to carbon emissions. As readers will discover in Chapter 5, materiality assessments are also essential during the due diligence process, allowing the buyer to thoroughly investigate the ESG-related risks and opportunities of the target company. Here, those conducting the assessment will utilise regulatory frameworks as a key element of their evaluation. We cover the Materiality Assessment in more detail in Chapter 5.

Double Materiality

The concept of 'double materiality' not only recognises that a company's actions impact society and the environment but also acknowledges that the same social and environmental issues will also impact the company's financial performance. A simple example is that a company's carbon emissions contribute to global warming, and the rising temperatures associated with this phenomenon also affect the business's ability to operate and, therefore, its profits. The European Union has dubbed this concept 'Double Materiality' and, like the materiality assessment described previously, it is at the heart of the regulatory process.

Where We Are Today

In recent years, some pushback against sustainability regulation has occurred, which we will examine in detail later in the chapter. However, the overall trend towards greater regulation is shown in Figure 2.3.

The International Sustainability Standards Board (ISSB)

The ISSB establishes a comprehensive global baseline for sustainability-related financial disclosures, enabling companies to provide consistent and transparent information on their sustainability-related financial activities. Organisations must report on significant sustainability-related risks and opportunities, tailored to their sector. These disclosures must cover governance structures, sustainability-related risk management and the financial impact of sustainability-related financial information on business operations.

After a period of slow and steady activities, we have seen unprecedented standard setting initiatives in recent years.

- GRI: Global Reporting Initiative
- CDSB: Climate Disclosure Standards Board
- IR: Integrated Reporting Framework
- SASB: Sustainability Accounting Standards Board
- SDGs: Sustainable development goals
- TCFD: Task Force on Climate Related Financial Disclosures
- SEC: Securities and Exchange Commission
- CSRD: Corporate Sustainability Reporting Directive
- ISSB: International Sustainability Standards Board
- SB 253: California Climate Corporate Data Accountability Act Senate Bill 253
- SB 261: California Greenhouse gases: climate-related financial risk Senate Bill 261
- AB 1305: Voluntary carbon market disclosure Assembly Bill 1305

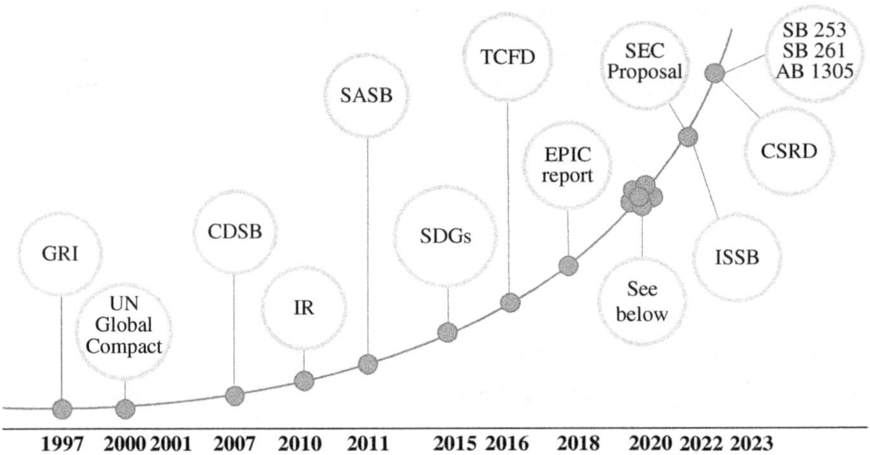

Reporting Activity in 2020

- January 2020: World Economic Forum (WEF) International Business Council (IBC) consultation released. February 2020: EU Non–financial reporting consultation released
- August 2020: Climate Disclosure Project (CDP), CDSB, GRI, International Integrated Reporting Council (IIRC) and SASB Paper released. Also, the WEF- IBC Paper released
- September 2020: IFRS Foundation Consultation released IAASB Climate Alert. October 2020: Financial Reporting Council (FRC) Consultation released
- November 2020: IIRC and SASB announce intention to merge into the VRF

Figure 2.3 Timeline of sustainability reporting activities.

Source: GRI, UNGC, CDSB, IIRC, SASB, UN SDG, TCFD, EPIC, SEC, ISSB, CSRD, California Air Resources Board, IBC, CDP, WEF

The ISSB collaborates with the International Financial Reporting Standards (IFRS) to establish key accounting and reporting standards, including IFRS S1, which requires the disclosure of sustainability-related risks and opportunities. IFRS S2 sets standards on climate-related disclosures.

ISSB aims to deliver positive impacts on company governance, business strategy, access to capital, reputation and employee and stakeholder engagement. Applying IFRS S1 and IFRS S2 is designed to help companies streamline their sustainability reporting processes, providing investors with more accurate information to make informed investment decisions.

Task Force on Climate-Related Financial Disclosures (TFCD)

The International Sustainability Standards Board (ISSB) standards align with the recommendations of the Task Force on Climate-related Financial Disclosures (TCFD). The idea behind the TCFD recommendations is to increase consistency in the reporting of climate-related financial information, guide companies on how to communicate their climate action plans to stakeholders and enhance market transparency, as shown in Figure 2.4. While the TCFD is not a traditional ESG framework, it complements ESG reporting by providing specific guidance on climate-related financial disclosure. By doing so, it can also create a better understanding of where climate-related risks lurk within the economic system and help financial markets optimise capital allocation. While many businesses and governments worldwide have publicly and voluntarily committed to reporting in alignment with the TCFD, regulators are increasingly moving towards making TCFD reporting mandatory for publicly traded companies. For example, the UK's Financial Conduct Authority has made it compulsory for premium-listed companies to disclose in alignment with the TCFD since 2021, as shown in Figure 2.4.

Corporate Sustainability Reporting Directive (CSRD)

The Corporate Sustainability Reporting Directive (CSRD), enacted in 2023, extends reporting requirements to a broader spectrum of companies, aiming to enhance data quality to match financial data standards,

	TCFD	CSRD
Climate risks and opportunities	✓	✓
Risk management/resilience	✓	✓
Climate targets and progress	✓	✓
Governance	✓	✓
Scopes 1,2, and 3	✓	✓
1.5 degree Celsius transition compatible		✓
Stakeholder consideration		✓
Double materiality		✓
Actions to mitigate impact		✓
Strategy implementation		✓
Information on intangibles (e.g. human and social capital)		✓
Third-party insurance		✓

Figure 2.4 Comparison disclosure requirements TCFD and CSRD.

Source: TCFD, CSRD, Industry Research

standardise sustainability disclosures for transparency and increase the accountability of the board of directors by providing investors and stakeholders with insights into companies' social, environmental and governance impacts.

The implication of this Directive, as shown in Figure 2.5, includes a substantial change in how companies prepare and disclose sustainability information. For management this includes: providing additional disclosures (quantitative and qualitative; short-, medium- and long-term

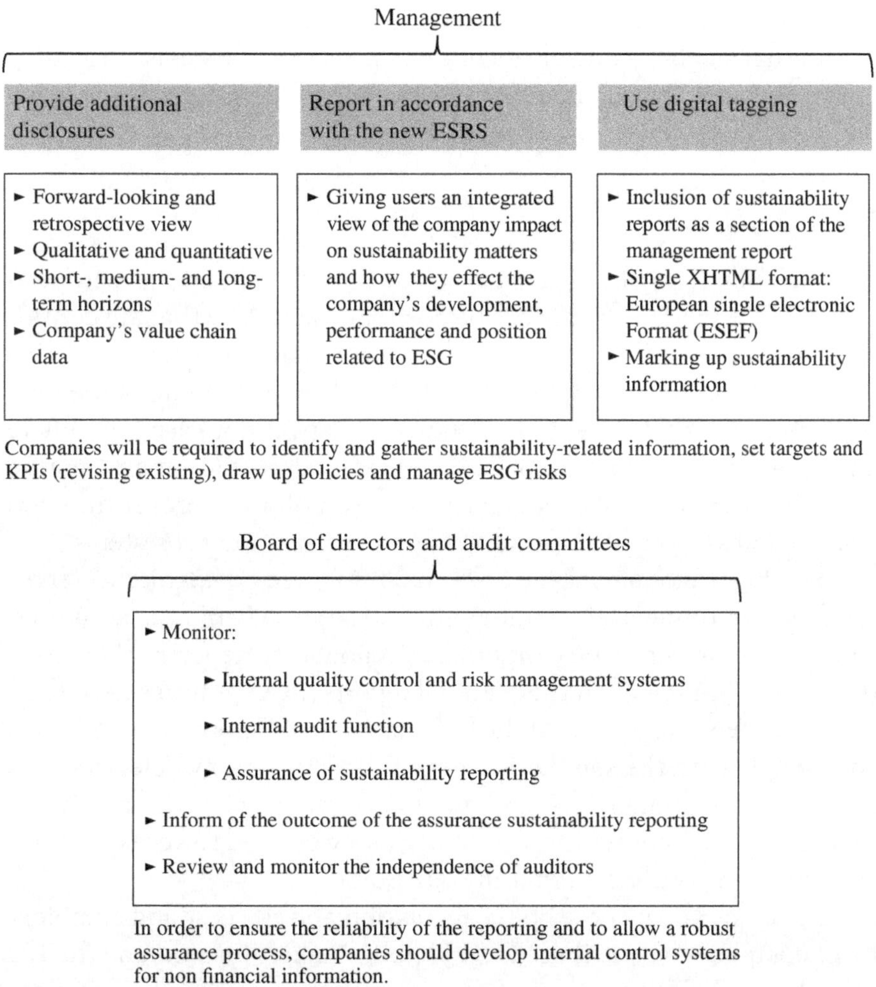

Figure 2.5 CSRD and its main implications for companies.

Source: CSRD, Industry Research

horizons; and the company's whole value chain), reporting by the latest European Sustainability Reporting Standards (ESRS) (providing an integrated view of the company's impact on sustainability matters and how they affect the company's development, performance and position related to ESG); and the use of digital tagging (including the sustainability report as a section of the management report). For the Board of

Directors and the Audit Committees, requirements include monitoring of internal quality control and risk management systems, providing information on the assurance of sustainability reporting and reviewing and monitoring the independence of the auditors.

EU Taxonomy

The EU Taxonomy is a classification system created by the European Union (EU) to identify and define economic activities that are considered environmentally sustainable. It offers a framework for evaluating how much an economic activity contributes to one or more of the EU's six environmental objectives: climate change mitigation, climate change adaptation, sustainable use and protection of water and marine resources, transition to a circular economy, pollution prevention and control and safety and restoration of biodiversity and ecosystems.

The EU Taxonomy Regulation requires large companies to report on the environmental sustainability of their economic activities. Companies subject to the Corporate Sustainability Reporting Directive (CSRD) must include in their annual reports the extent to which their activities meet the criteria of the EU Taxonomy (Taxonomy-eligibility) and comply with the standards set out in the Taxonomy delegated acts (Taxonomy-alignment). Companies not covered by CSRD can choose to disclose this information voluntarily; for example, to access sustainable financing or for other business reasons.

Concerns about the scope of regulation and the cost and complexity of compliance contributed to EU policymakers introducing the EU Omnibus in 2025, a package of proposed regulations aimed at simplifying existing EU legislation, particularly in the area of sustainability reporting and due diligence. The primary goal is to reduce the administrative burden on businesses, enhance their competitiveness and ensure the EU remains a leader in sustainability.

US Regulation

At the federal level, the Securities and Exchange Commission (SEC) has been at the forefront of introducing regulations to enhance transparency and accountability in corporate ESG disclosures. In 2022, the SEC proposed a rule to strengthen the disclosure of ESG metrics, aiming to standardise how companies report their climate-related risks and impacts. SEC regulations also emphasise the importance of climate-related disclosures, equipping companies to manage climate-related risks and meet investor demands for transparency in ESG practices. This includes scenario analysis to assess the impacts of climate-related risks and the effects of severe weather on financial statements and performance. Additionally, GHG emissions metrics under SEC regulations are categorised into defined scopes for reporting purposes, ensuring a comprehensive and consistent approach to ESG reporting.

While federal regulations provide a broad framework, state-level ESG legislation adds another layer of complexity. In 2023, 22 states implemented some form of ESG-related laws, with 18 states focusing on anti-ESG legislation. The evolving state laws on ESG are primarily influenced by the political leanings of the states' legislatures. Companies operating in these states face challenges in navigating business and politics due to the complexity of state measures concerning ESG regulations. Despite these challenges, the overarching goal of ESG regulations and compliance is to ensure that companies substantiate their sustainability claims with concrete actions. We will examine how some US states are leading the pushback against ESG later in this chapter.

Cutting Through Complexity

According to sustainability organisation Plan A, there were over 2,400 ESG regulations worldwide in 2024 (Plan A, 2024). Rather than attempting to list them all, the previous section covers only the principal frameworks and their impact. Figure 2.6 highlights other key frameworks and standard setters while also highlighting the 'cut-through' issues.

What we can conclude from even this simplified approach is that sustainability regulation is complex and that the compliance process is time-consuming and therefore expensive. On the surface, that might suggest that regulation is detrimental to financial value for an individual company. However, this does not factor in the risk mitigation element, avoiding fines or loss of license to operate, and the broader

Figure 2.6 Overview of standards, frameworks and their main implications for companies.

Source: Industry Research

benefits of companies 'doing their homework' on ESG in order to be compliant. Returning to Figure 2.6, it establishes that there are four essential requirements for companies:

- Report on the most material sustainability areas and disclose performance, targets and actions against these
- Disclose and quantify climate-related risks and opportunities relating to the business and their impact on financial statements
- Assess the level of assurance to be obtained, considering regulatory requirements for each of the business's key non-financial reporting metrics
- Ensure there are adequate processes and controls in place for those metrics disclosed

ESG Ratings and Their Relationship to Regulation

ESG ratings are scores or assessments of a company's performance on environmental, social and governance issues. They assess a company's impact on environment, society and governance as well as its exposure to risks associated with those three areas. However, as we outlined in Chapter 1, there are weaknesses in how the ratings process is conducted and in the differences between the methodologies used by each ratings provider. Despite these shortcomings, ESG ratings have significant influence. This is in large part because they affect a company's ability to access capital and the cost of that capital (see Chapter 4).

Given the important and financially valuable role of ESG ratings, it is perhaps surprising that those who provide them are not subject to any regulation, and are therefore able to set their frameworks, assessment processes and methods of scoring companies.

In the EU, ESG rating providers are not currently subject to authorisation or supervision. This is despite several issues emerging, primarily related to the lack of transparency and accuracy in ESG rating methodologies, the presence of conflicts of interest and concerns about greenwashing. As early as 2021, the International Organisation of Securities Commissions (IOSCO) published a final report highlighting shortcomings. The same year, a European Commission study highlighted conflicts of interest and the lack of transparency and accuracy in ESG rating methodologies. A 2023 progress report on greenwashing published by the European Securities and Markets Authority (ESMA) identified ESG ratings as a primary channel for misleading sustainability-related claims and called for regulatory action in the industry. Also in 2023, S&P Global dropped the environmental, social and governance (ESG) scores from its credit ratings with immediate effect, citing technical reasons, but interpreted by many in the ESG universe as a sign of growing uncertainty about the validity and efficacy of ESG scores.

At the time of writing this book, the prospect of regulation is still a live issue. Tulip Siddiq is an MP and former Economic Secretary to the Treasury & City Minister. In the foreword to a 2024 consultation paper on the Future regulatory regime for environmental, social and governance (ESG) ratings providers, she stated that, 'Bringing ESG ratings providers into regulation will boost investor confidence, reduce greenwashing, and address the lack of transparency highlighted in responses to the government's consultation. This will help drive investment, support innovation, and ensure that companies in critical sectors are not penalised by opaque ratings'.

Also in 2024, the Council of the EU adopted a new regulation on environmental, social and governance (ESG) rating activities. The new rules aim at making rating activities in the EU more consistent, transparent and comparable in order to boost investors' confidence in sustainable financial products (Council of the EU press release, 2024). Additionally, international bodies such as the World Economic Forum are working towards creating a universal standard for ESG ratings. It is the authors' opinion that the regulation and standardisation of ESG ratings providers would make ESG ratings not only more credible to the public at a time when the value of sustainability is being challenged, but also to professionals seeking to identify and realise financial value.

It is only fair to point out that, even in their present form, ESG ratings can serve as a valuable source of information to support wider disclosure requirements under regimes such as the Sustainable Finance Disclosure Regulation (SFDR), the Corporate Sustainability Reporting Directive (CSRD) and the Taxonomy Regulation by building on and complementing other existing data sources. Therefore, while ESG ratings alone are not sufficient to satisfy regulators, achieving a rating requires a level of company scrutiny, measurement and reporting that supports regulatory compliance. In other words, the process of attaining a positive ESG rating and gaining regulatory compliance overlaps significantly.

The Impact on Financial Value

Although complying with numerous sustainability regulations and achieving good ESG scores from rating agencies that employ different methodologies can be frustrating and time-consuming, the hard work does appear to have financial value. That is because a 'clean bill of health' in compliance and positive ESG rating scores can make a company more attractive to investors, enjoy a higher valuation (thanks to the link between ESG and financial performance highlighted in Chapter 1 then explored in detail in Chapter 4) and satisfy regulators.

Anecdotal evidence suggests that highly regulated environments can spur, rather than stifle, growth. Sweden was the first country in the world to pass an environmental protection act (1967), hosted the first

UN conference on the global environment in 1972, and has remained in the top 10 of the respected Environmental Performance Index produced by Columbia and Yale universities for more than a decade. Rather than stifling growth, Sweden's highly regulated ESG environment appears to have provided a fertile ground for homegrown and world-leading companies, including Ikea and Spotify.

Wider Benefits of Regulation

It is not hard to be critical of the regulatory burden, so this section provides an antidote by examining the general, positive business outcomes that can result from fair, effective and 'light touch' rules:

1. **Reducing Business Costs and Risks**
   Effective regulation can minimise unnecessary compliance burdens and transactional costs while mitigating risks. In this case, regulators enable businesses to adopt tailored compliance strategies that safeguard reputations and reduce operational friction. For example, processes such as emissions permit trading utilise market mechanisms to achieve environmental goals at lower costs than prescriptive rules. Neglecting ESG considerations often leads to underappreciating the investment risks, which can threaten long-term returns. The question of the financial impact of ESG controversies is key, given that any dollar used to compensate for destructive externalities or litigation cannot be used for reinvestment purposes or returned to investors, thereby impacting value creation.
2. **Enhancing Market Confidence and Stability**
   Regulation underpins trust in financial systems, attracting investment and enabling competitive markets. For example, transparent frameworks cemented the UK's reputation as a safe investment destination. Similarly, consumer protection regulation can encourage both responsible consumption and long-term investment.
3. **Fostering Competition and Innovation**
   Regulation can level the playing field and drive efficiency. Standardised cross-border rules can unlock global investment opportunities.

4. **Enabling Long-Term Growth**
   By addressing market failures, regulation supports sustainable economic activity. Environmental and social regulations create stable conditions for businesses to plan effectively.
5. **Realising Wider Economic Benefits**
   Regulation contributes to broader societal outcomes that indirectly bolster financial value. Public health and safety standards reduce workplace disruptions and healthcare costs, enhancing workforce productivity. Consumer rights protections maintain market integrity, preventing fraud and fostering repeat transactions.

While regulation is vital, its design must avoid unintended constraints. Overly restrictive rules can hinder innovation or disproportionately increase compliance costs. An approach that emphasises proportionality, international alignment and partnership with businesses can maximise value creation while minimising drawbacks. For sustainability regulation specifically, Figure 2.7 neatly summarises this virtuous circle.

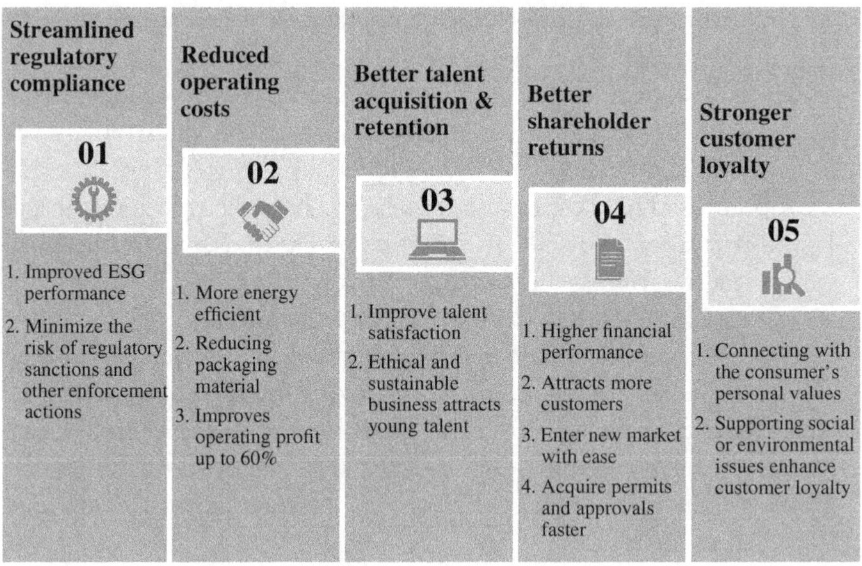

Figure 2.7 The virtuous circle – from regulation to value generation.

Adapted from https://plana.earth/academy/role-of-esg-in-facilitating-climate-action

Regulatory Rollback, the Real Impact

It is only fair to acknowledge that not everyone views regulation in such a rosy light. The pushback against ESG, as detailed at the end of Chapter 1, has been reflected in the rollback of specific sustainability regulations.

One clear example, as mentioned previously, is the European Commission's Omnibus package, which seeks to adjust, ease or postpone sustainability rules in order to unlock growth and ease trade within and beyond the European Union. Ursula von der Leyen, President of the European Commission, said of the Omnibus, 'Simplification promised, simplification delivered! This will make life easier for our businesses while ensuring we stay firmly on course toward our decarbonisation goals. And more simplification is on the way'. Some groups have welcomed it as a boost to competitiveness and adaptability. Others feel it goes too far, potentially weakening environmental and human rights commitments and outcomes.

The pushback is more pronounced in the United States, both politically and principled, with legal challenges against the US Securities and Exchange Commission's (SEC) climate disclosure rule. Initially approved in March 2024 under the Biden administration, the rule was designed to enhance climate-related disclosures by requiring public companies to report material climate-related risks, including Greenhouse Gas (GHG) emissions and their potential financial impacts. Private litigants, state attorneys and other government officials in the United States have increasingly scrutinised the ESG-related decisions of corporate boards, investment managers, pension fiduciaries and funds. There are legal challenges to the use of non-pecuniary factors in investment decisions.

As the proper scope of incorporating ESG into business and investment decisions continues to be debated and the current political environment remains unsettled, the risk of litigation and state inquiries is likely to continue, if not expand. In this environment of competing demands from various regulators and investors, corporate boards and investment managers will face increasingly difficult choices regarding the consideration of ESG factors.

This already has serious consequences for sustainable investing. In January 2025, BlackRock withdrew from the world's largest investor climate coalition, the Net Zero Asset Managers (NZAM). BlackRock commented that being part of NZAM 'caused confusion regarding BlackRock's practices and subjected us to legal inquiries from various public officials' (BlackRock, 2025).

In addition to undermining the confidence of major fund and asset managers about ESG, the pushback may also be impacting global inflows into sustainable funds. In the first quarter of 2025, investors withdrew a record amount from sustainable funds (Financial Times, 2025).

It can be an uncomfortable position for those whose methodologies are under attack from politicians or even subject to legal challenge. However, as we described in Chapter 1, it is essential to maintain a clear head and a sharp focus on financial value. Detractors may argue that the apparent ESG-driven financial value uplift and cost reductions were based on investor fads supported by questionable ESG scores. However, suppose the ESG value identified is based on a deep understanding of how a company can create financial value through sustainability, such as by meeting consumer needs or reducing energy costs. In that case, the basis for investment remains solid. Better still, any pushback may take the froth out of the market and leave ESG leaders better priced.

Double Down or Step Back?

Should dealmakers welcome the easing of regulatory pressures on sustainability? The answer depends on whether or not the company's approach to sustainability truly adds financial value (in other words, the sustainability actions are articulated and financially defined, tracked and monitored). If so, the dealmaker will want to protect that value from accusations of greenwashing and ensure it is included in the valuation and pricing, so they may prefer a tighter regulatory environment that raises the bar for competitors. Accurate data, strong (financial) metrics and the ability to meet the most rigorous standards will be essential tools and data points for making the value case and confirming the investment thesis to investors. On the other side of that argument, unconvincing data and a lack of rigour will likely see investors and customers question the actual value of the company's ESG credentials, and therefore the risk of potential gaps/issues that can lead to reputational loss and/or value loss/leakage.

Weaknesses in areas such as financial metrics and ESG ratings are sometimes used to discredit regulatory frameworks and suggest that rules need to be reduced. However, the counterargument is that reduced standards allow companies to claim good practice without having the real evidence to back it up. This is a potential problem for dealmakers because getting the accurate ESG picture is vital. This suggests that perhaps more, not less, regulation is needed to ensure that a company's ESG credentials stand up to scrutiny. On the flip side, any opacity does give the professional investor with their analytical tools an advantage over those who take ESG ratings and claims at face value.

Taking Action

In such a challenging environment, the investor or CEO can do the following to maximise value:

1. **Make Sure Reporting Requirements Are Transparent and Clearly Understood**

   With the introduction of mandatory reporting and external assurance, it is vital to establish a baseline for what information must be reported and its significance to the company's operations. Collecting the required evidence for assurance, particularly from third-party manufacturers, can be a complex and time-consuming task. Deciding on the format and level of detail for acceptable evidence, as well as the collection method, should be determined early. Prepare for external assurance by implementing stronger controls over day-to-day business information not directly generated for ESG reporting, such as packaging specifications and invoices for raw materials. Additionally, use the information gathered to highlight the financial advantages and implications of ESG investments and initiatives.
2. **Get the Correct Data at the Right Time**

   Sales volumes, packaging components and purchase orders for raw materials are just some of the data elements needed to calculate environmental KPIs. There will also be variations across sites and markets that must be taken into account.

Understanding the origin of the data is essential for achieving a positive assurance outcome. A lot of relevant data often resides with third parties, such as contract manufacturers. Engage with them by creating data collection tools and incorporating reporting obligations into contract renegotiations. Be very clear about which data is needed and where it is located. This is especially important in transactions when decisions are being made about the purchase price.

3. **Build a Digital Sustainability Reporting Capability**

   Establishing a capability that ensures auditability from start to finish, covering raw activity, calculations and disclosures, is crucial for effective sustainability reporting. Anchor the capability around a single source of truth, on which all KPIs are calculated, and integrate both internal and external data sources. This approach helps to eliminate manual workarounds and enhances the potential for automation throughout the process lifecycle. Developing a digital sustainability platform allows for more accurate and consistent reporting while also meeting assurance requirements. Building report portals on the platform enables internal and external stakeholders to scrutinise the data in real time. In our discussions with Dave Stangis, Chief Sustainability Officer at the leading asset management firm Apollo Global Management, he emphasised the importance of having 'platforms and capabilities which make it easier to identify and signal potential issues'.

Unintended Consequences

As sustainability regulation has developed, it has resulted in several significant and sometimes unintended value creation consequences:

The Data Dividend

Stricter regulations demand improved and more standardised data. Producing this data offers benefits beyond merely satisfying regulators. It not only helps identify and mitigate risks but also reveals opportunities by providing insights into performance and peer rankings. For dealmakers, this can be useful for target screening and justifying investment cases. However, these benefits must be weighed against certain data weaknesses. As discussed in this chapter, inconsistencies in ESG ratings and a focus on the organisation as a whole rather than individual business units mean that not all data should be regarded equally.

The Growing ESG Role of the CFO

Another key consequence of tighter regulation is the increasing role of the CFO in sustainability issues. In the early stages of sustainability, ESG-related reporting was usually prepared by a small, dedicated team working independently of the rest of the organisation. The result of this separation was that the CFO did not get involved in the preparation or assurance of those figures. Today, the requirements of regulators, stakeholders and, in some cases, ESG rating agencies, compel CFOs to endorse non-financial metrics. This means the CFO has much greater involvement in collecting, verifying and calculating such data. Consequently, the CFO now holds responsibility for both financial and non-financial reporting, providing an unprecedented view of how both can work together to generate value.

This trend is backed up the findings of the 2024 EY Europe Long-term Value and Corporate Governance Survey (EY, 2024), which revealed that that increasing regulatory scrutiny on sustainability reporting is causing 92% of European companies to make either 'significant changes to optimise' or 'bold changes to transform' their approach, with the CFO at the centre. In the process, the CFO may finally be able to balance better the need to deliver short-term performance with the typically longer-term outcomes from sustainability investments. The same EY survey reveals that 80% of institutional investors agree that CFOs play a crucial role in challenging CEOs and executive teams to adopt a long-term perspective over quarterly earnings performance. They appear to be justified in doing so, with 78% of finance leaders supporting significant sustainability investments, even if it means the company misses quarterly earnings targets. Additionally, the survey finds that a similar proportion of institutional investors support strategic investments in sustainability, even if they result in quarterly earnings targets being missed.

Chapter Summary

- Regulation is complex, and as a result, compliance is time-consuming and costly. However, even a 'box-ticking' approach to regulatory compliance has value in reducing the risk of financial penalties or reputational damage. The compliance process can also contribute to achieving a positive ESG rating, which can help reduce capital costs and unlock investment opportunities.
- Dealmakers can utilise the data and processes associated with regulation and ratings during target screening and due diligence. They also use it to optimise investment in sustainability-related initiatives, thereby unlocking greater financial value. This is supported by the increasing role of the CFO in sustainability-related matters, forging a closer connection between economic and non-financial performance.
- Despite the current pushback against ESG regulation, companies with sustainability programmes backed by a sound investment thesis will continue to create financial value.

References

BBC (2020). Marriott Hotels Fined £18.4m for Data Breach that Hit Millions. https://www.bbc.co.uk/news/technology-54748843 (accessed 8 August 2025).

BlackRock (2025). Excerpt from Letter to Clients on BlackRock's Decision to Leave NZAM. https://www.blackrock.com/corporate/newsroom/announcement/blackrock-withdraws-from-nzam (accessed 8 August 2025).

Council of the EU (2024). Environmental, social and governance (ESG) ratings: Council greenlights new regulation. Press Release (19 November).

Elkington, J. (1994). Towards the sustainable corporation: win-win-win business strategies for sustainable development. *California Management Review* EY (2024). How Can Boards Convert Sustainability From a Wish to a Winning Reality? https://www.ey.com/en_ee/insights/long-term-value/europe-corporate-governance-survey-findings (accessed 8 August 2025).

Financial Times (2025). ESG Fund Outflows Hit Record as Sustainable Investing Backlash Grows. https://www.ft.com/content/9f425c25-4fc3-45de-bcc5-e9c75d6d14d3 (accessed 8 August 2025).

GRI (2025). Our Mission and History. https://www.globalreporting.org/about-gri/mission-history/ (accessed 8 August 2025).

Plan A (2024). All 2025 ESG and Non-financial Reporting Regulations in the EU. https://plana.earth/academy/eu-esg-regulations (accessed 8 August 2025).

3

Capital Flows – How ESG Drives Deals That Create Value

HAVING EXAMINED THE broader ESG context, we now turn our attention to how ESG influences capital flows and impacts dealmaking. We approach this subject from three angles.

Firstly, we share our deal research to reveal the more than $6 trillion flow of capital into sustainability-led transactions.

Secondly, we examine how one single aspect of sustainability – namely, the demand for greater recycling of plastics – drives deals that create financial value.

Thirdly, we demonstrate how consumer sentiment is becoming increasingly central to the investment thesis, creating value and driving transactions.

What Do Deals Tell Us About the Financial Value of ESG?

Before sharing our research, which is based on publicly available information, let us establish the key assumptions and definitions underlying our findings:

What constitutes a sustainable transaction? We define these as transactions involving companies that provide sustainable products, services, software or technologies. This encompasses areas such as positive environmental impact, green infrastructure, responsible supply chains, social responsibility, circularity, energy transition, decarbonisation, blockchain, sustainable finance, sustainable agriculture and green technologies.

What do we classify as M&A? We define M&A as transactions that involve acquiring a majority stake in a company or merging with another. We include buyouts, leveraged buyouts, asset acquisitions, mergers and acquisitions, as well as other types of acquisitions.

What do we classify as a Private Placement (P)? This encompasses transactions that provide funding to a company in exchange for a minority stake in the company. It includes angel and seed investments, crowdfunding, incubator/accelerator support, grant funding, bridging rounds, series A, B, C, D, E+, recap rounds, corporate investments, growth equity, Private Equity, post-IPO equity, private investment in public equity (PIPE), convertible notes, secondary transactions and undefined, unattributed or undisclosed funding rounds.

The Headline Picture – How ESG Created $6.4 Trillion in Deal Value

Using the definitions and assumptions described above, we found that over the five years from January 1, 2020, to March 31, 2025, $6.4 trillion was invested in 226,000 sustainable transactions, comprising one-quarter M&A transactions and the remaining three-quarters private placements, as shown in Figure 3.1.

How does this compare to overall deal volume and value? During the research period, there were 1,222,000 deals, meaning that 19% of the total were sustainable transactions. The value of sustainable transactions accounted for 16% of the total deal value during the research period.

It is interesting to note in passing that, from small startups to multi-billion-dollar deals, sustainability was often a crucial and publicly stated deal driver. For example, announcing the £20bn merger between French water and waste giants Veolia and Suez, Antoine Frérot,

Deal volume and value	2020	2021	2022	2023	2024	YTD Mar'25	Total
Sustainability deals - volume ('000)	40	50	50	44	37	5	226
Total deals - volume ('000)	216	269	262	229	203	44	1,222
% of sustainability deals by volume	19%	19%	19%	19%	18%	12%	19%
Sustainability deals - value ($t)	1.0	1.7	1.4	1.1	1.1	0.2	6.4
Total deals - value ($t)	7.2	10.6	8.0	6.0	6.4	1.8	39.8
% of sustainability deals by value	14%	16%	17%	18%	17%	12%	16%

Note: Value based on disclosed deals

Figure 3.1 Volume and value of sustainability-linked deals.

Source: Pitchbook

the Chairman and CEO of Veolia, said: 'This agreement represents a giant leap for Veolia, for the French approach to ecological transformation, and the preservation of the environment' (Reuters, 2021a). The link with financial value was also clear: in an increasingly regulated world where growing populations require more water and generate more waste, consolidation offers greater opportunities to focus investment, improve efficiency and build scale.

Looking Behind the Headlines: Key Trends

Closer examination of the numbers and the wider business and economic context in which the deals took place makes it possible to identify several key trends, which we present chronologically.

COVID-19 Blocks Deals but Drives Change The years immediately preceding our research period saw consistent growth for most types of transactions, including those involving sustainability-focused companies. However, the COVID-19 pandemic of 2020 and changing geopolitical situations saw deal activity slow down significantly due to rising economic uncertainty and the practical difficulties of conducting deals during a time of social isolation and governmental restrictions. The first year of our research period saw transactions at a rate below trend. However, despite these headwinds, sustainable transactions worldwide in 2020 still topped $1 trillion in value, with 40,000 transactions completed. Of these, 9,000 were mergers and acquisitions (M&A) deals, and 31,000 were private placements.

Post-pandemic Bounceback Let us begin with the anecdotal impact of the COVID-19 pandemic on sustainability and then quickly move on to the facts. A commonly held view is that the pandemic's lockdowns and stay-at-home measures increased public awareness of their local environment and communities as they relied on both more than ever. Another theory is that, just as the role of governments increased during the pandemic, their sense of responsibility and control extended into the post-pandemic recovery period. For example, in late 2020, UK Prime Minister Boris Johnson launched the Ten Point Plan for a Green Industrial Revolution, with the objective of 'Building back better, supporting green jobs, and accelerating our path to net zero' (Gov.UK 2020). The European Green Deal marks a bold commitment to making Europe climate-neutral by 2050, combining a clear roadmap of 50 actions with a new growth strategy rooted in sustainability, innovation and fairness. It aims to transform how we produce and consume, ensuring the transition benefits all – especially the most vulnerable – while positioning Europe as a global leader in green industries. While finding results that match this rhetoric is challenging, we can see evidence that regulatory bodies, particularly in Europe, stepped up their requirements immediately following the pandemic, in 2021 alone.

The EU Sustainable Finance Disclosure Regulation (SFDR) in the EU aimed to standardise ESG disclosures and increase transparency in financial markets.

The Environment Act 2021 was a landmark in UK environmental legislation, setting ambitious new targets and policies to safeguard the environment.

The Financial Reporting Council (FRC) published its first Statement of Intent on Environmental, Social and Governance (ESG) in 2021, which identified underlying issues with the production, audit and assurance, distribution, consumption, supervision and regulation of ESG information.

Add to this the need to comply with governments' net zero ambitions, and there was further pressure on companies to improve their sustainability performance.

All these factors helped to make 2021 the high-water mark for sustainable transactions, with deal volume reaching 50,000 transactions at a total value of $1.7 trillion. Between 2020 and 2021, the total value of sustainable transactions increased by 70% (from $1 trillion to $1.7 trillion), while the overall transaction deal value rose a more modest 47% ($7.2 trillion to $10.6 trillion). The following year, 2022, saw this elevated level of deal activity maintained. Deal numbers stayed the same as in 2021, while deal value slipped slightly from its 2021 high.

ESG Pushback Begins, Both Economic and Political We concluded in Chapter 1 that progress towards sustainability is not a linear path, even if the overall trajectory remains consistent. In 2023, some of the more idealistic and ambitious elements of the 'Build Back Better' philosophy came up against the more pressing, short-term economic realities. Massive government injections of capital during the pandemic, along with fractured supply chains and pent-up consumer demand, all contributed to a spike in inflation and consequent fiscal tightening. This combination of higher borrowing costs, economic uncertainty and geopolitical conflicts dampened deals. As shown in Figure 3.2, sustainability transactions were no exception, with deal numbers dropping from their 2021 high of 50,000 sustainable transactions to a total of 44,000 in 2023 and 37,000 in 2024. The total deal value for both 2023 and 2024 was $1.1 trillion, well below the $1.7 trillion high of 2021. It is worth noting, however, that the share of sustainable transactions held steady between 2020 and 2024, at 19% of total deal volume. Sources within the dealmaking community have voiced the opinion that the headwinds just described shifted the benchmark for sustainable transactions. Investors continued to back innovative companies with high growth potential but demanded a solid investment thesis based on clear evidence of consumer demand or the ability to meet corporate needs. In other words, the financial value story needed to be even more pressing.

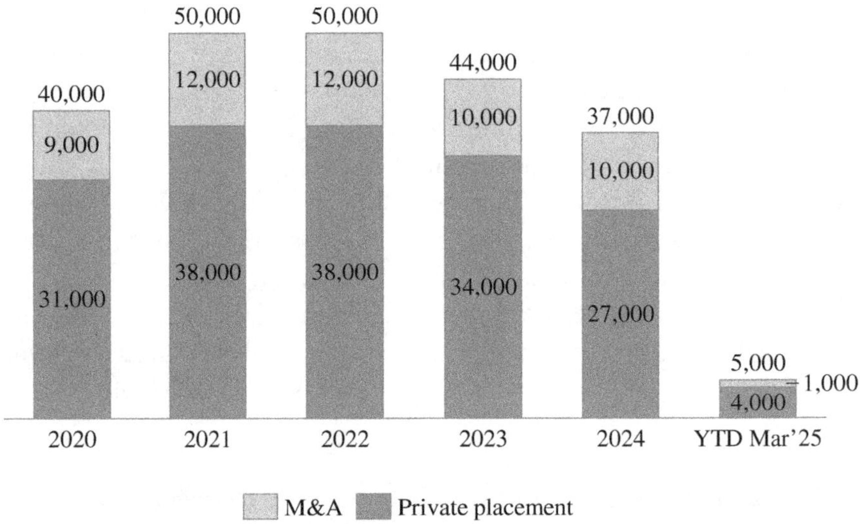

Figure 3.2 Overview of annual sustainable transactions period 2020 to Q1 2025.

Source: S&P Capital IQ

The first quarter of 2025 marks the last period of our research, but it is a highly significant one. It captures the first few weeks after President Trump began his second term in the White House, but before the tariff announcements of 'Liberation Day' in April 2025. As we explored in Chapters 1 and 2, this period is marked by regulatory pushback due to increasing anti-ESG sentiment and some frustration over the lack of clarity regarding aspects of sustainability measures and metrics. This quarter saw a deal value of $0.2 million for Q1 2025, with a total of just 5,000 deals. While it is unwise to extrapolate too much from just one quarter, it is fair to say that the downward trend of 2024 continued into Q1 2025.

That, however, does not tell the whole story. As readers will know, late 2024 and early 2025 saw some of the most significant advances and greatest 'mainstreaming' of AI. Dealmakers quickly grasped how this emerging technology could be a vital tool in the ESG world. The transaction rationale ranged from leveraging AI to optimise resource use to improving ESG metrics and meeting the green power needs of the digital infrastructure on which AI relies. Figure 3.3 highlights the deals in 2024 that centre around the use of AI to accelerate ESG applications.

Shift in CEO's prioritisation of Sustainability, as AI, inflation & geopolitical, uncertainties now atop of their agendas	Atlas Metrics Germany	Sep '24	$13M	AMMC, Redstone, Cherry Ventures	► Series A funding to scale its AI-driven ESG compliance platform and performance management offerings, supporting over 62,500 European companies in meeting stringent ESG reporting by 2025
	briink Germany	Sep '24	$4M	EquityPitcher, Merantix, x3books	► Seed funding to develop specialized AI tools that assist ESG teams in efficiently verifying and benchmarking sustainability data, addressing the increasing demands of regulatory compliance across Europe
	United Kingdom	Sep '24	$5M	YFM Equity Partners	► Private placement to enhance AI-driven ESG data insights platform for asset managers, addressing the growing demand for transparent and timely ESG data, driven by regulatory and sociopolitical pressures
	Daato Germany	Mar '24	$5M	Kopa, Neosfer, IBB Ventures	► Seed funding to enhance its ESG management platform, aiming to simplify compliance for ~60,000 EU companies under new ESG reporting requirements

Figure 3.3 AI-related ESG 2024 deals.

Source: Pitchbook

AI and ESG – A Dynamic Duo

AI plays a crucial role in enhancing environmental, social and governance (ESG) practices by improving data analysis, risk management, reporting and driving progress on ESG targets. It can source, analyse and manage large amounts of data, automate tasks, identify trends (including climate data and energy consumption) and risks and provide insights that lead to more informed and effective decision-making across all three pillars of ESG. The process of developing and implementing an ESG strategy is very data-driven, as is the GAP analysis and compliance workflows. Here, AI technologies can be a powerful tool to enhance the accuracy and efficiency of ESG data management, enabling entities to understand better and address their environmental and social impacts and performance. We also see companies applying ESG principles to govern AI development and ensuring transparency, fairness, environmental responsibility and accountability, using terms like responsible or ethical AI. This is no longer primarily focused on environmental concerns, but also about capturing and improving social outcomes such as equity, inclusion and community well-being. In this context, it is important to note that AI itself is under regulatory scrutiny, with, for example, the EU Artificial Intelligence Act 2024 being introduced to promote responsible AI aligned with fundamental rights and safety.

The Sector Story

Most readers will probably have a mental picture of what a sustainable transaction typically looks like. Perhaps what comes to mind is the acquisition of a company that makes health-enhancing food products from innovative natural ingredients or a building supplier that makes a green alternative to concrete. Think again, because the hottest sector for sustainable transactions, as revealed in our 2020–2025 research, as shown in Figure 3.4, is the ultra-modern and increasingly tech-driven Industrials and Mobility sector (IaM), which saw both the most significant number of deals and the highest total deal value. IaM's deal

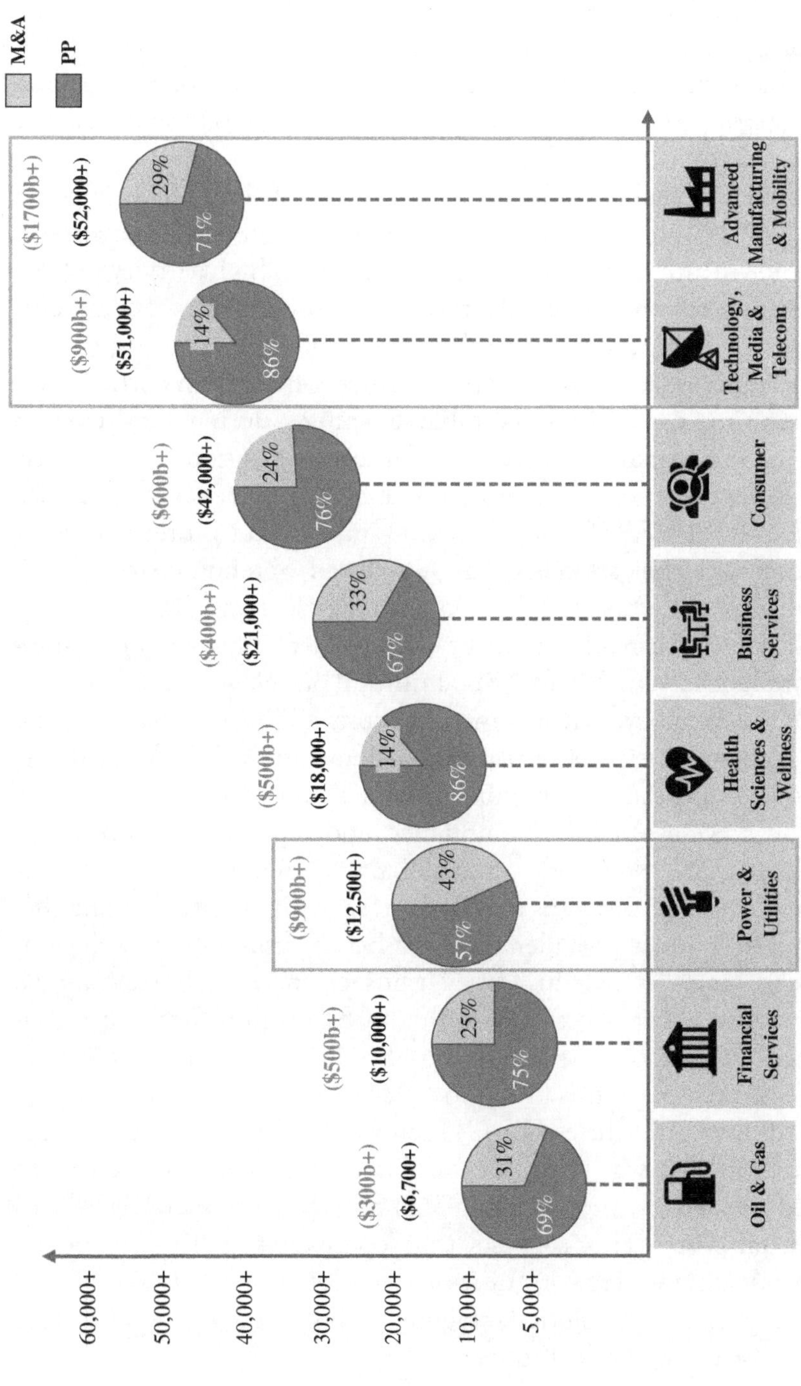

Figure 3.4 Sustainable transactions by sector Jan 2020–March 2025.

Source: Pitchbook

volume of 52,000 transactions narrowly edged out its nearest rival, Technology Media and Telecommunication (TMT), which saw 51,000 sustainable transactions. However, its total deal value of $1.7 trillion vastly outstripped the TMT total deal value of $900 billion during the same period from 2020 to 2025.

So, what is making IaM so hot in terms of deals? The ongoing demand for technological advancements and the growing focus on sustainability within the mobility sector have driven high activity in IaM. For example, advanced manufacturers may support new energy efficiency or recycling advances, while the electrification of transport systems and individual vehicles supports growing interest in cutting-edge manufacturing capabilities. Notable examples during our research period include Amazon's 2020 $1.3 billion acquisition of Zoox, the US-based developer of autonomous ride-hailing vehicles (Forbes, 2020). In 2021, SoftBank paid $2.8bn for a 40% stake in Autostore, a Norway-based company that specialises in automated warehouse storage and order picking (Reuters, 2021b). On a smaller scale, in 2024, Siemens acquired Heliox, a Netherlands-based provider of fast-charging solutions for electric vehicles, for $300 million (Bus News, 2024).

The Technology, Media and Telecom (TMT) sector was the second-largest in terms of transaction volume and value. A key driver was the demand for sustainability software and technology services, including SaaS-based ESG compliance and reporting solutions. For example, in 2022, New York-based global sustainable investment platform Energy Impact Partners invested, along with others, $35m in UK-based ESG Book, a provider of cloud-based sustainability solutions (UK Tech News, 2022). In a 2024 transaction, venture capital firm Redstone and other investors acquired a $13 million stake in Atlas Metrics, a Germany-based developer of ESG reporting and sustainability management platforms (TechEu, 2024).

The Power & Utilities (P&U) sector ranked second in deal value ($900 billion) but was last in deal volume (12,500). This sector also recorded the highest proportion (43%) of M&A transactions for sustainable purposes. This suggests that companies in this sector are actively pursuing strategic acquisitions to meet growing global demand for sustainable energy solutions. Figure 3.4 provides an overall picture of the sector-by-sector deal story.

The Regional Picture

It will come as no surprise to most readers that the Americas, led by the United States, attracted the highest investment flow and deal volume, ahead of EMEA. However, although APAC was behind both regions in terms of deal value and volume, it emerges from our research as the clear winner in terms of sustainable transactions growth driven, as we will discover, by new green technologies.

The Americas Over the 2020 to March 2025 research period, the Americas saw capital flows of £2.8 trillion funding 95,000 deals. The TMT, IaM and Consumer sectors dominated deal flow, with over 20,000 sustainable transactions per sector, highlighting the focus on technological innovation, sustainable mobility and meeting consumer demand for green products and services. Examples from the research period included the Canadian Pension Plan (CPP) and other investors who contributed a total of $2.25 billion in Waymo's first external funding round, a US-based autonomous driving technology company (Crunchbase, 2020).

Overall, the United States dominated the Americas region, accounting for an 86% share of total deal value and an 81% share of deal volume. Its flagship status was further underlined by the US focus on innovative, high-growth areas, including the deployment of clean energy, electrification and carbon management technology.

Given the region's dominance, it is interesting to note that the overall trend is downward. Since 2020, the sustainable transaction volume in the area has declined at a compound annual growth rate (CAGR) of 3.9%, primarily driven by the United States.

EMEA In a region where $1.9 trillion was invested in over 80,000 sustainable transactions during the research period, TMT was the standout sector in terms of volume, notching up more than 19,000 deals. IaM attracted the highest total value, clocking up over $430 billion worth of deals. The United Kingdom, Germany and France collectively accounted for a 48% share of deal value and a 43% share of deal volume. Since 2020, the sustainable transaction volume in the region has declined at a compound annual growth rate (CAGR) of 1.7%, primarily driven by the United Kingdom.

APAC While APAC scored the lowest among the regions in terms of its $1.7 trillion total deal value and 50,000 deal volume, it emerges from our research as the clear winner in another key metric: growth. It is the only region where the volume of sustainable transactions has risen since 2020. APAC posted a sustainable compound annual growth rate (CAGR) of 0.9%, primarily driven by investment growth in countries such as India, South Korea and Japan.

Across the region, the IaM sector attracted the highest investment flow. With over 13,000 sustainable transactions across this sector alone, exceeding $640 billion in total value, it is evident that new, cleaner technologies are very much part of the landscape in APAC. One example is Chinese car maker Changan's further $1.5 billion investment in Avatar, a China-based platform of smart electric vehicles' technology (China Daily News, 2024). Looking across the region as a whole, China accounted for 47% of deal value and 32% of deal volume.

Who Is Buying?

Notably, the most significant players in the sustainable transaction field are corporates, which are responsible for 55% of the total deal volume. This reflects the need for businesses to incorporate sustainability in their strategy, comply with regulations, reduce waste and energy costs and meet the needs of socially and environmentally aware consumers. A typical example of a corporate transaction is provided by British specialty chemicals company Croda International, which operates primarily in the cosmetics and personal care market. In 2021, it acquired French company Alban Muller, which develops and supplies botanical extracts and natural ingredients that meet the demands of consumers and global beauty brands (Global Cosmetics News, 2021). The strategic driver for the $35m deal was to strengthen and expand Croda's portfolio of sustainable ingredients for the personal care market. In a nutshell, this is a deal between two mature and established businesses driven by a strategic approach to sustainability.

Given the opportunities we have seen for value creation, why are sharp-eyed Private Equity and Venture Capital participations playing a smaller part than corporates? One contributory factor is that corporates can take a longer-term view of their sustainability investments. In contrast, Private Equity firms may find it tougher to source opportunities which meet the bar for returns required within the timeframe set by funders. On the other hand, our research shows that Private Equity and Venture Capital funds are more willing to invest in early-stage, higher-risk companies, reflecting their higher risk appetite and greater experience in nurturing and incentivising emerging companies. This is evident in the smaller average deal size of their investments: $27.8 million against $34 million for corporates. Key players in this space include US venture capital specialist Plug and Play, startup accelerator Techstars Central and the EU-funded European Innovation Council Fund. In total, Private Equity/Venture Capital players invested $1 trillion in 36,000 sustainable transactions during the research period. Please note that Figure 3.5 also includes a combined institutional and strategic category where Private Equity/Venture Capital funds and corporates invest together on a deal.

An example transaction from our research period involves an investment in a company that recycles and repurposes valuable

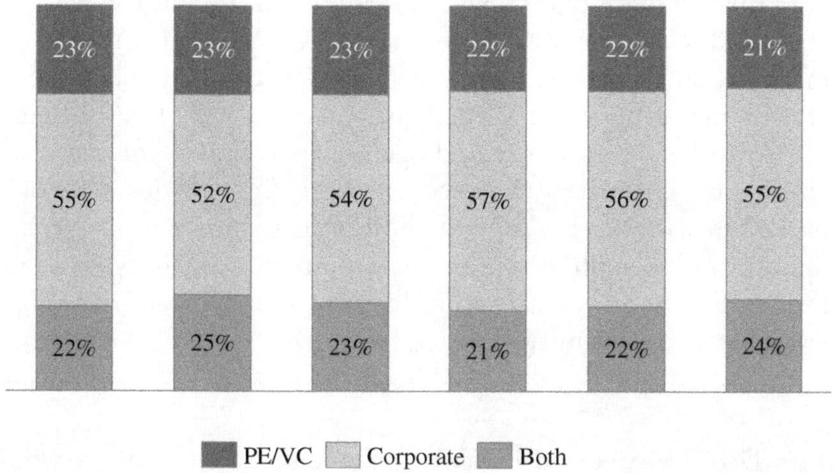

Figure 3.5 Transaction volume by investor type for the period Jan 2020–March 2025.

Source: S&P Capital IQ

metals. In 2022, Ara Partners, a Private Equity firm with a focus on industrial decarbonisation investments, led a $36 million funding round for Continuum, a metal recycling and supply company (ESG Today, 2022). The investment will expand the production of recyclable materials and support research into similar technologies and applications. Cory Steffek, partner at Ara, was quoted in ESG Today explaining that 'Creating a circular metals economy is critical to meeting the world's sustainability goals. Titanium, stainless steel and Inconel alone account for tens of millions of tons of scrap metal each year that will need to be repurposed in the new sustainable economy'.

Corporate Versus Private Equity Buyers in the ESG World

Typically, corporates follow a long-term strategy, carefully considering regulatory trends and the impact of physical and transition risks on their operations and product/service portfolio. This constant scanning for risk and opportunities in order to secure long-term survival/success means corporates have the commercial case, long-time horizon and funding to justify ESG-related M&A.

Private Equity players will typically track investor appetite and trends closely. For example, the post-COVID boost to ESG-related equity stories and business cases moved sustainable transactions higher up the Private Equity agenda, with funds often willing to be opportunistic and open to investing in innovative companies. Ultimately, however, if those ESG stories are not backed by a strong investment thesis that indicates a potential financial value uplift within the typical investment lifecycle, the Private Equity player will typically keep their powder dry and await better opportunities.

Future Deal Drivers and Blockers Three specific trends are worth highlighting, not only because they illustrate the historic relationship between ESG and financial value creation, but also because they may signal the future.

In our research, the oil and gas sector exhibited the highest growth in sustainability investments. At first glance, that may seem poised to reverse, as the current US administration reduces support for renewable energy. However, the quest for cheaper, more efficient and more sustainable energy sources shows little sign of being satisfied, driving investors and entrepreneurs to seek new solutions. ESG is now a crucial criterion when initiating acquisitions, owing to increasing pressure from stakeholders and investors to disclose their sustainability performance and, as we outline in this book, their ability to create financial value. Industry players are therefore actively pursuing acquisitions that strengthen ESG credentials. This makes companies with effective ESG platforms, data and techniques valuable targets. On the other hand, there is a growing realisation that implementing sustainable practices within businesses often leads to higher costs, potentially impacting profits. Our view is that deals to improve ESG credentials are only successful if the product or service portfolio will be strengthened after the deal. If the deal is just to improve ESG credentials, without changing the operational footprint, it is unlikely to create financial value and growth.

This cost factor is a driver for our next trend, leveraging technology and digital transformation for sustainability. Tech companies have gained traction due to the growing integration of green tech solutions with emerging technologies, including GenAI, advanced analytics, IoT, blockchain and big data. Over the past five years, our research has identified nearly ten thousand transactions in AI-oriented companies with sustainability-related objectives. The potential goes beyond driving individual deals, however. The ability of these technologies to analyse ESG data more quickly, accurately and efficiently is much needed. However, the ability to standardise this data and make it more transparent could be the real green game-changer.

How Deals Address the Plastics Problem and Create Value

Now we move on to the second area of focus in this chapter, how one single aspect of sustainability – namely, the demand for greater recycling of plastics – drives deals that create financial value.

Consumer goods companies face mounting pressure from regulators, consumers and other stakeholders over their use of plastic product packaging. The 2024 Big Plastic Count, conducted by Greenpeace UK and Everyday Plastic, with academic support from the Revolution Plastics

Institute at the University of Portsmouth, found that UK households alone discard an estimated 90 billion plastic pieces annually, with only 17% of these pieces being recycled (Big Plastic Count, 2024).

Over the past five years, regulators have intensified their efforts to address the issue. At the beginning of 2021, the EU introduced a plastic tax on waste to boost recycling rates. The United Kingdom followed suit on 1 April 2022 with its tax on plastic packaging containing less than 30% recycled content.

Given the global scale of the problem, multilateral rules are emerging. The UN-led Global Plastics Treaty aims to tackle plastic pollution through a legally binding instrument, but the specific target remains a subject of ongoing negotiations. The treaty also aims to address the entire lifecycle of plastics, from production to disposal, to achieve a circular economy.

In the United States, the approach to reducing plastic waste is more complex and less uniform, as it is governed by changing state laws. At the time of writing, several US states had laws in place to improve recycling rates through various measures that impose costs on businesses related to plastic waste.

In summary, businesses which produce and/or use plastic packaging face increasing regulation and taxation. From 2030, manufacturers must meet minimum recycled content in plastic packaging (e.g., 30% for PET contact-sensitive packs, rising to 65% by 2040). The EU may set binding targets for bio-based plastics. E-commerce packaging may not exceed 50% space, and at least 40% of certain transport packaging must be reusable. They are also exposed to further risks of financial penalties, reputational damage and loss of customers. While the environmental and social drivers tend to dominate the conversation around plastics, it is increasingly evident that there will also be financial value for those who can develop and apply the best solutions.

Consumer Sentiment

A 2024 WWF study found that 85% of Americans believe plastic waste pollution is a serious problem, with over two-thirds supporting either a ban (71%) or a fee (70%) on single-use plastics (WWF, 2024). As a product that we all see and touch, awareness of the problem is high worldwide, with survey after survey suggesting that it is something consumers care deeply about and want to see action taken to address it. For example, the same WWF survey revealed that 82% feel very or somewhat positive about the idea of a new global agreement to stop plastic pollution.

Environmental Harm

One of the reasons consumers are aware of and concerned about plastics is that, whether seen in person or on TV, their impact is all too evident: from overflowing landfill sites and despoiled beauty spots to otherwise pristine seas awash with plastics. One alarming and still much-quoted prediction was that there could be more pieces of plastic than fish in the ocean by 2050. Public concerns have also been raised by the fact that the vast majority of plastics are made from fossil fuels. Plastic production requires chemical and energy-intensive processes that produce substantial greenhouse gas (GHG) emissions and other pollutants (Jambeck & Walker-Franklin, 2023).

Time for Action – A Case Study in Capital Flows

A combination of regulatory and consumer pressure, along with the need to reduce the use of fossil fuels and cut harmful emissions, makes this a pressing problem for all companies, particularly for major producers of consumer goods, who, as we will see, are responsible for a significant proportion of plastic waste.

For the big, established consumer players, this is a problem with the potential to threaten their license to operate. For the innovative and fast-moving, it offers opportunities to differentiate and grow. In other words, fertile ground for those seeking to create financial value through ESG.

Please note that this case study is essentially a snapshot in time, examining how the industry perceived this problem in 2020 and the way the market responded in the years that followed, with transactions being a key element of the story.

Figure 3.6 illustrates the use of plastics and the 2020 recycling rate of just 9%. To meet the aim as set out in the OECD's Global Ambition Policy, this needs to increase to 47% by 2050 and 59% by 2060.

Plastic waste outlook to 2060

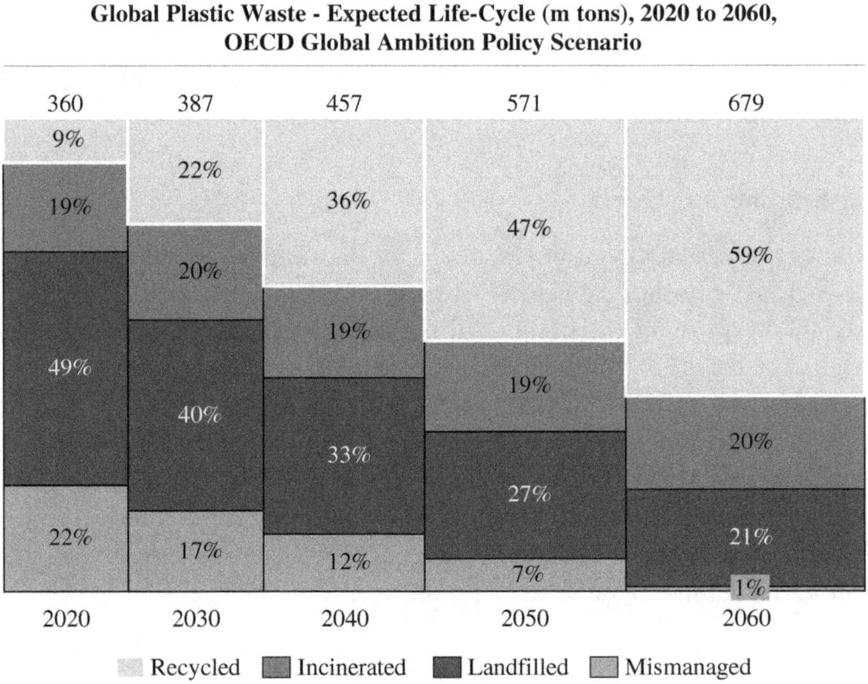

Key Insights

- Per the OECD scenario, reductions in waste would largely be achieved through a tax on plastics that increases to $750/tonne globally by 2030 and to $1,500/tonne by 2060
- Recycling proportion to increase to ~ 60%, as it becomes the most common waste management option, and as more companies adopt recycling initiatives given stringent regulations adopted across regions

"Despite this ambitious circular plastics policy package, the use of plastics globally will still grow beyond 2019 levels...Almost all the increase in demand for plastics can be met by recycled secondary plastics, which grow to 41% of total plastics production."

– OECD Global Plastic Outlook

Figure 3.6 Overview of recycled plastics as a percentage of total plastics used.

Adapted from OECD 2060 Global Plastic Outlook

Figure 3.7 shows the key uses of plastics, revealing that plastic product packaging is responsible for 32% of the total. Just eight major food and beverage companies are responsible for 10 million tonnes of all plastic used.

There are several potential ways in which major food and beverage companies can address the plastic problem. These include replacing plastics with other packaging materials, such as cardboard. However, costs for alternative solutions remain significantly higher, so the focus for consumer producers and the case study below is on plastics recycling as a way to reduce overall plastics production and pollution.

Understanding the Recycling Value Chain

Given the scale of the problem, the pressure for change and the value of the markets involved, the need for change is clear, as is the route: changing consumer behaviour to improve recycling rates, and materials innovation to improve the recyclability of plastics.

To see how capital flows are driving change, let us first look across the value chain, where we can identify three distinct segments, each with its characteristics:

Collectors – those at this stage of the value chain have the relatively straightforward but highly labour-intensive task of picking up refuse from households, commercial sites or other locations. This is a relatively disorganised marketplace, with larger players typically operating at the county or district level under rules and requirements set by local government. There are also commercial operators providing services directly to private companies. Additionally, numerous smaller operators offer specialised services. Typically, those participating in this segment are not involved in any other stages of the value chain.

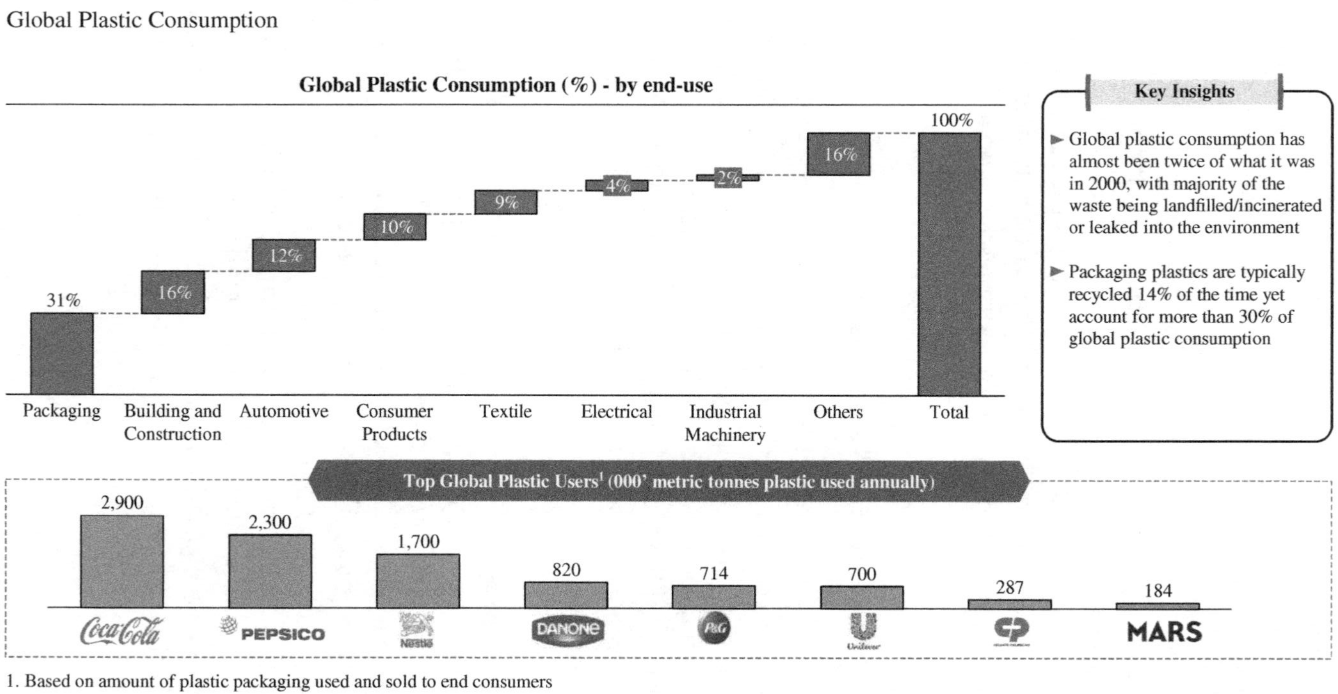

Figure 3.7 Plastic product packaging is responsible for the most extensive use of plastics.

Source: OECD 2060 Global Plastic Outlook

Preparers – play a crucial role in the recycling process by sorting and cleaning materials, making them ready for recycling. This is not as simple a task as it may appear. Certain types of plastic can only be recycled using specific methods; therefore, they must be separated and handled accordingly. Accurately identifying every kind of plastic from millions of waste items can be a challenging process. This segment of the value typically comprises players which offer both preparation and recycling services.

Recyclers – this is where the magic happens, in the sense that worthless and potentially harmful plastics are transformed into usable and saleable raw materials and products. That makes this segment of the market the most exciting in terms of innovation. Please note that we will not go into the science of these methods in any detail, but there is plenty of information online if readers wish to explore further. Methods of recycling can be broken down into two basic categories.

1. **Mechanical Recycling** describes the processing of plastic waste into secondary raw material without changing the chemical structure of the material. Typically, it involves shredding and melting waste plastics to create new products.
2. **Chemical Recycling** is a new and evolving process. It breaks down plastic waste into its basic chemical components, enabling the creation of new plastic products or even feedstock. A further advantage of chemical recycling is that it can be used for plastics that are otherwise difficult or uneconomical to recycle, such as mixed polymers or contaminated plastics.

The Role of Advanced and Innovative Technologies

Another crucial aspect of innovation within the plastics recycling market and value chain is the use of advanced technologies. From robotics to smart plastic labelling, new technologies are making it easier not only to collect, sort and prepare waste but also to identify its source. This has the potential to empower regulators, governments, tax authorities and responsible businesses to monitor waste more effectively and determine who is responsible for it. Crucially, these technology solutions can often operate right across the plastic recycling value chain. As key enablers for the recycling industry's growth, they are also attracting investor interest. One example of these valuable technologies is sorting and collection systems that utilise AI, Blockchain and Robotic solutions to improve efficiency significantly. Another example is tracing technology such as digital markers, barcodes and RFIDs that can track plastics across and beyond the value chain.

Value chain key points to take into account

1. Fragmentation. Each segment of the value chain has multiple companies operating within it, but no single company is active right across the collector, preparer and recycler segments.
2. Disruption. Innovation is bringing new companies and methodologies into the market. Primarily due to new chemical recycling (but also see below).
3. Connection. Although the market remains fragmented, technology firms are providing advanced services that support growth and forge links across the value chain.

Capital Flows

Having established the value chain and the problem it must collectively solve, let us examine how capital flows act to overcome the sustainability challenge in their quest to create financial value.

As Figure 3.8 shows, transactions are evident right across the value chain, but with the majority of investment focused on the recycling segment. Note also the relatively small deal size: an average of $24.75m across the whole value chain.

Given its power to attract investors and deals, let us examine where the money is going within the recycling services segment of the value chain.

Figure 3.9 illustrates how transaction volume and value rise sharply during the research period as new methodologies are supported by investors eager to capitalise on a rapidly evolving market. The most promising and innovative new method, chemical recycling, attracts the majority of funding. This reflects its greater innovative potential and

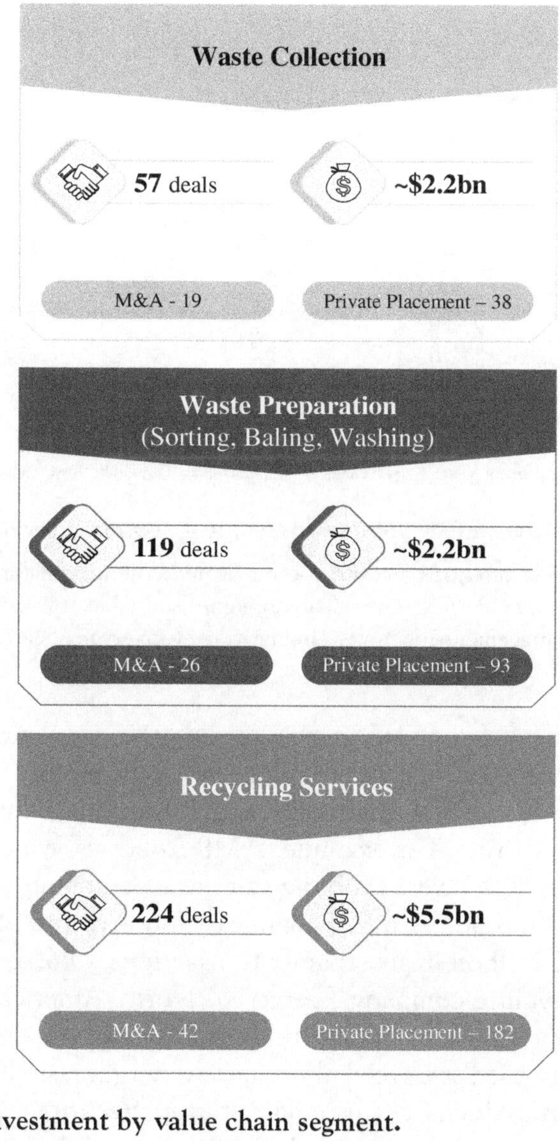

Figure 3.8 Investment by value chain segment.

Adapted from https://www.capstonepartners.com/insights/services/mergers-acquisitions/

inherent advantages over mechanical recycling. Note also how resilient dealmaking within this sector proved during the COVID-19 pandemic, when the broader market typically saw subdued M&A activity.

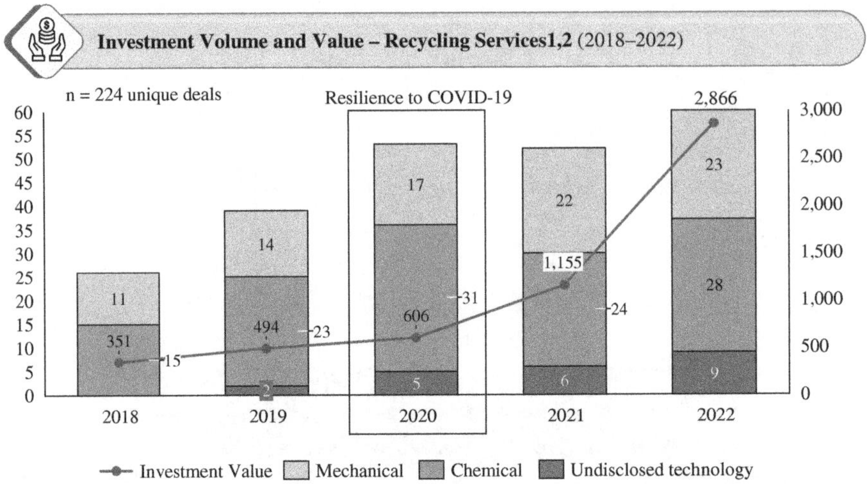

Figure 3.9 Investment volume and value – recycling services.

Source: Adapted from https://www.capstonepartners.com/insights/services/mergers-acquisitions/ and https://blogs.worldbank.org/en/sustainablecities/covid-era-trash-surge-waste-management-ingenuity-circularity-and-investments-are

The other key area of innovation within the sector was the rise in advanced and innovative technologies, which further attracted deal activity. Figure 3.10 highlights investments in innovative technology enabling companies. For example, AMP Robotics, which designs and manufactures AI-powered robotic systems to automate the identification, sorting and processing of complex waste streams, saw investment of over $172 million in six separate transactions. One of the key investors was recycling company Evergreen, North America's largest producer of high-grade recycled polyethene terephthalate (rPET), a recycled resin used as a green alternative to virgin resin. Other innovative companies include Australian startup Security Matters, whose track-and-trace solution marks physical objects with a unique barcode and connects them to a digital twin. The fact that one of Security Matters' key partners is the global giant BASF indicates how the biggest and smallest companies collaborate in this space to find cost-effective, scalable solutions to the recycling challenge.

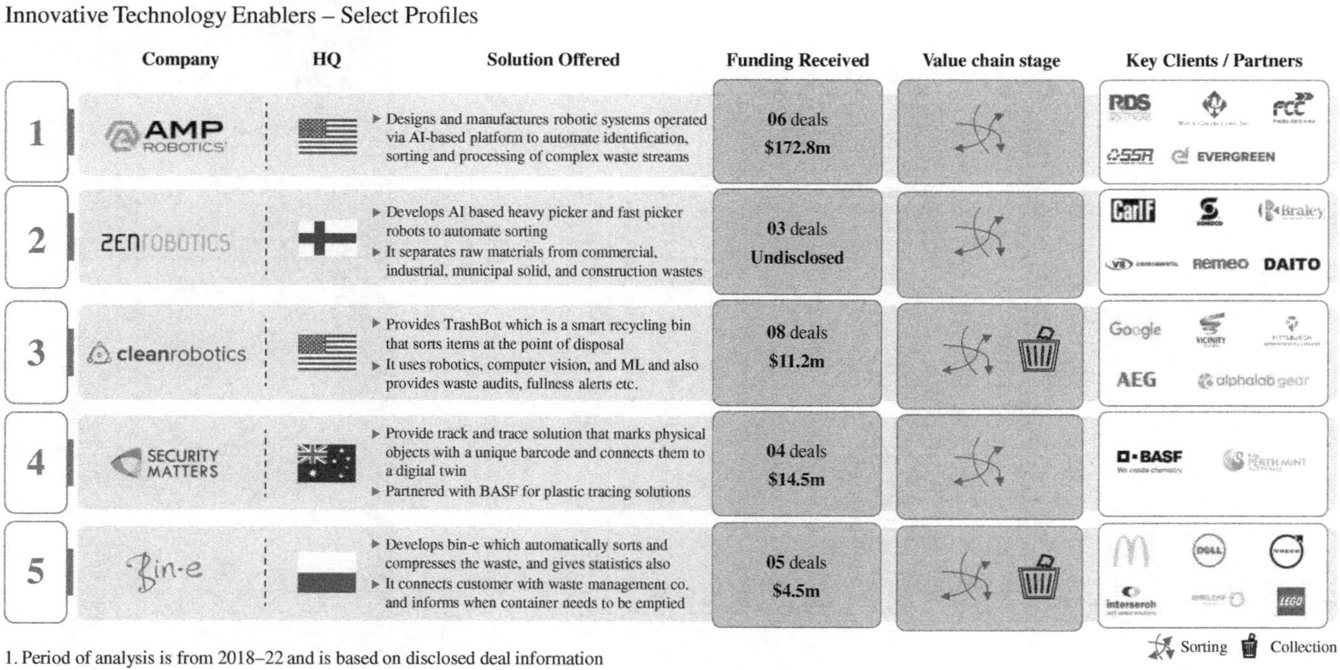

Figure 3.10 Investments in innovative technology enablers.

Source: Pitchbook, News Articles

Startups Dominate the Scene

As readers might expect in such a segmented, disruptive and innovative marketplace, startups dominate the investment scene. As shown in Figure 3.11, just over half (53%) of all target companies were less than 10 years old, and financial investors were the most active, accounting for 60% of all deals.

While strategic investors may make fewer investments in startups compared to financial investors, they often target high-potential, opportunistic companies that can enhance their core products or services through innovation. This approach allows them to gain early-stage exposure to transformative technologies without the complexities and costs associated with full-scale acquisitions and integrations.

Overall, the most prominent investors in green plastics recycling startups are typically the same large consumer products groups, which, to a large extent, are also the source of the problem. An environmentalist might see a paradox in that observation, but from a financial value perspective, it makes perfect sense. Food and beverage companies, including Coca-Cola and Suntory, are seeking new methods and opportunities to enhance recycling, thereby reducing risks and attracting customers. Major manufacturers also have a stake in the game,

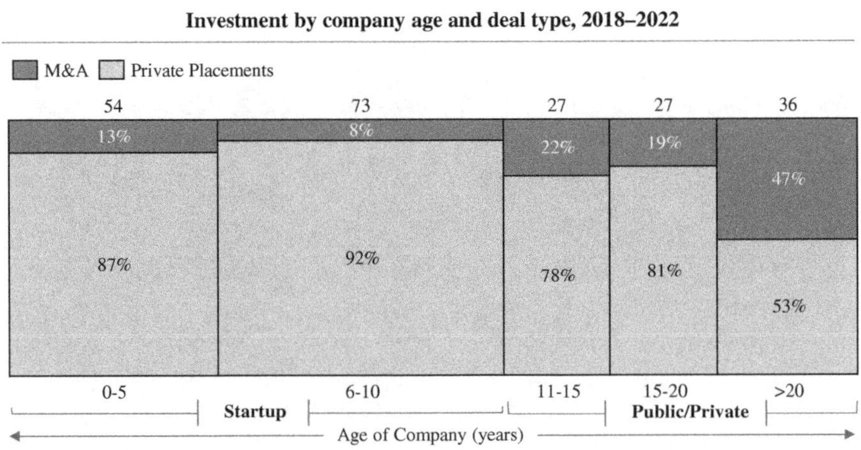

Figure 3.11 Startup analysis.

Source: Pitchbook

as suppliers of equipment vital to the recycling process and users of plastic packaging. Chemical companies also have multiple points of common interest, from the need to recycle their materials to supplying chemical recyclers and even as potential buyers of recycled materials.

Overall, our study of capital flows in plastics recycling highlights how investment spreads across the entire ecosystem as it seeks out promising solutions to the recycling conundrum, and in doing so creates financial value for investors – a clear example of how the pursuit of economic value can generate positive environmental, social and governance (ESG) outcomes. In comparison, regulatory progress for plastics recycling has encountered headwinds. At the time of writing this book, while many countries are making progress individually, global consensus remains elusive. The 2025 Plastics Summit in Geneva sought a landmark treaty to end plastic pollution, but talks collapsed amid sharp divisions between governments.

PureCycle One example of a company that has undergone the process described above is the US-based PureCycle, which began as a startup in 2018 and at the time of writing in 2025 is now listed on the NASDAQ with a market capitalisation of $3.3 billion.

PureCycle's foundation story is built on its innovative recycling solution: a groundbreaking, patented process for recycling polypropylene that separates colour, odour and other contaminants from plastic waste. This waste can then be transformed into an ultra-pure resin that can be used to create new, recyclable products.

Its first funding round in 2018 raised $10.8 million and was supported by Closed Loop Partners (Recycling Today, 2018). This social investment group raises finance for investments in sustainable consumer goods, advanced recycling technologies and the development of the circular economy. Subsequent funding rounds attracted investors, including the sustainable mobility fund BMWi Ventures (BMWi Ventures website, 2025) and the US-based venture capital fund Tri-State Angel. Today, PureCycle has ambitious plans to invest up to $2 billion in new plastics recycling plants in Thailand, Belgium and the United States (Chemical Engineering News, 2025).

Customer Sentiment and the Key to Sustainable Success

In this section, we will explore the impact of customer sentiment on sustainable transactions. Then, we will examine how entrepreneurs and investors can leverage consumer needs to create value during and beyond the transaction process.

Measuring Customer Sentiment Towards Sustainability

There is no shortage of surveys on customer sentiment towards sustainability, so we will guide readers through a selection and pick out the common themes.

Let us begin by examining the sustainability issues that are on customers' minds, starting with climate change. 'What do consumers really want?', a 2024 study by management consultancy Bain of nearly 19,000 consumers in 10 countries found that 60% of consumers said that their concerns about climate change had increased over the past two years (Bain & Co, 2024).

However, climate change is not the only sustainability-related issue on the public agenda. Environmental pollution, harm to wildlife, exploitative labour practices, intensive farming, ethical sourcing and the use of genetically modified crops are just a few examples of the many concerns that impact sentiment towards specific industries. There are also likely to be national and regional differences, as illustrated in Figure 3.12, which shows the views of UK consumers.

Remarkably, according to this survey, in 2024, UK consumers prioritised river and sea pollution over global warming as an environmental concern. While non-UK readers may be baffled, locals will quickly understand the reason. The actions of water companies and their regulators over the previous decade led to mounting public dissatisfaction and extensive media coverage about sewage overflowing into UK rivers and coasts (BBC News, 2025). The bigger point is that any understanding of customer sentiment around ESG must take into account local and regional sensitivities. Making assumptions can be dangerous. For example, few would guess that, as shown in Figure 3.13, consumers in Indonesia and Brazil are nearly five times more likely to be concerned about the environmental impact of product packaging than their counterparts in the Netherlands or Japan.

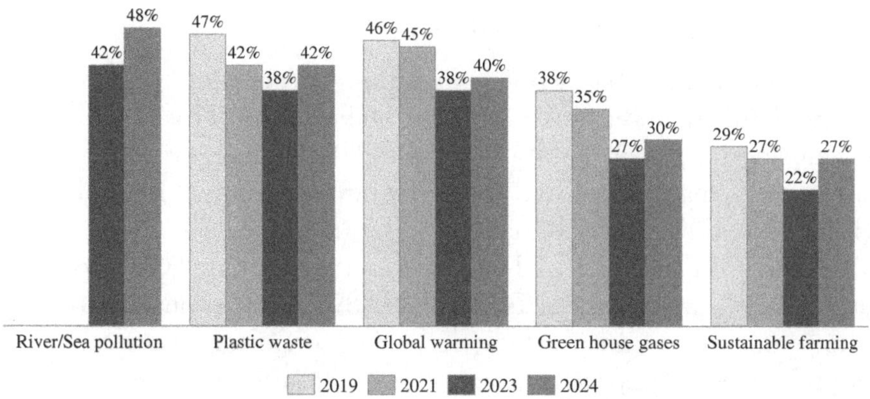

Figure 3.12 UK customer sentiment towards ESG topics.

Adapted from AHDB/Blue Marble Trust Survey 2024

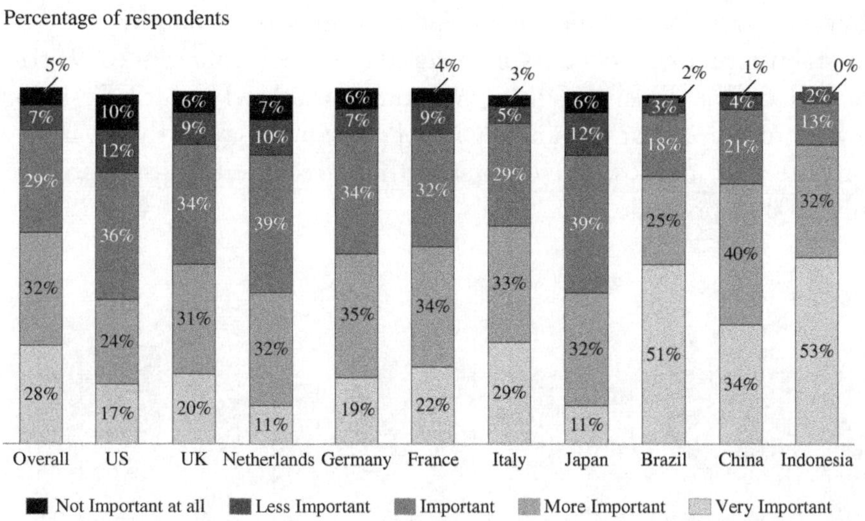

Figure 3.13 Global customer sentiment towards packaging choices.

Source: Bain & Company, Inc / https://www.bain.com/insights/what-do-consumers-really-want-ceo-sustainability-guide-2024

The Connection Between Concerns and Actions

Most will recognise that, while many things may concern us as human beings, there are fewer that inspire us to take action. This is an important distinction because the task of the B2C company is to persuade customers to make a positive choice by buying sustainable goods and services. In other words, to turn feelings into action.

In the Bain study referred to earlier in this section, 'What do consumer want?', as shown in Figure 3.13, 89% of consumers globally believe that a sustainable lifestyle is very important because their actions have an impact. Euromonitor International's Voice of the Customer: Sustainability Survey 2024 found that, as shown in Figure 3.14, that 76% of global consumers reported trying to have a positive impact on the environment through their everyday actions (Euromonitor International, 2024).

So, we can conclude from these findings that the intent is there. However, translating this into specific actions is a complex process which entrepreneurs need to understand to unlock value. A 2019 article called The Elusive Green Consumer in the Harvard Business Review revealed that, although 65% of consumers stated they want to purchase from purpose-driven brands that advocate for sustainability, only 26% go on to do so.

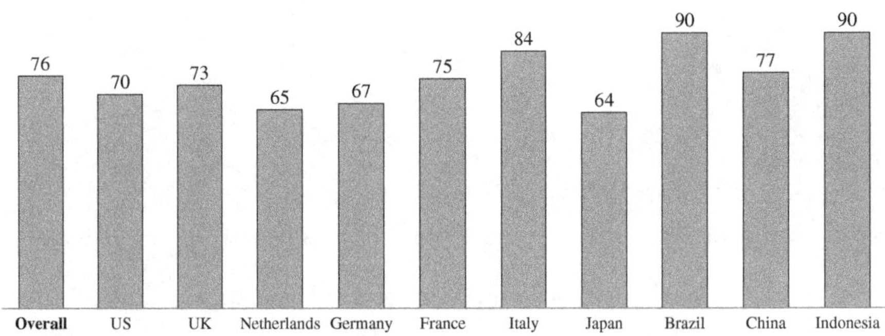

Figure 3.14 Percentage of respondents for whom practising a sustainable lifestyle is important.

Source: Euromonitor International's Voice of the Consumer: Sustainability Survey, fielded January to February 2024 (n=40,236)

The Barriers to Action – Cost and Confusion

So, if consumers are not short of motivation, what is holding them back? Before we outline some of the reasons, it is essential to note that these are based on consumer perceptions, not necessarily the underlying facts. That is a crucial point to understand, particularly for readers with a purely financial background. In the consumer world, perception can be reality.

The first issue is cost. According to the fifth edition of Deloitte's Sustainable Consumer Report, published in 2024, the proportion of consumers stating that they have not acted sustainably because it is too expensive has risen significantly in the last two years, up from 52% in 2022 to 61% in 2024.

Paradoxically, as shown in Figure 3.15, consumers in wealthier nations are more likely to believe that sustainable products are more expensive than those in poorer nations.

The second factor is fatigue. As readers have already discovered, sustainability is a complex and multifaceted term. It is challenging for consumers to determine the sustainability of a product, its impact and whether that would be sufficient to justify the perceived added expense. Little wonder, then, that according to the same 2024 Deloitte survey, 61% of respondents cite a lack of interest in sustainability, and 47% believe that adopting a more sustainable lifestyle makes no difference (Deloitte, 2024).

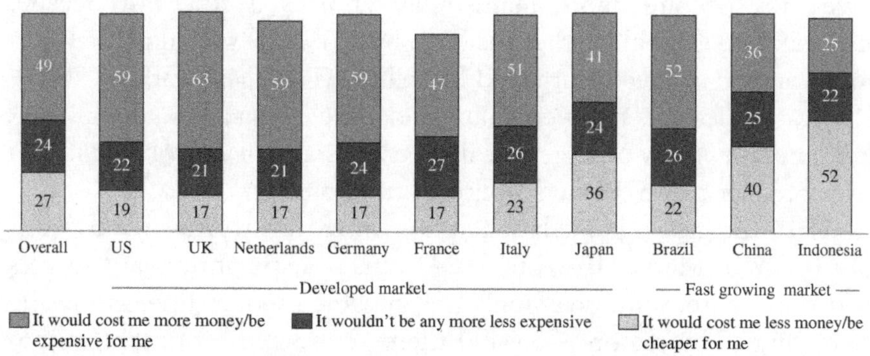

Figure 3.15 Consumer attitudes towards the costs of a sustainable lifestyle.

Source: Euromonitor International's Voice of the Consumer: Sustainability Survey, fielded January to February 2024 (n=40,236)

Overcoming the Barriers – The Green Premium

Given the picture so far, some ESG entrepreneurs may be getting downbeat. However, there is plenty to suggest that cost concerns are overcooked. According to PwC's 2024 Voice of the Consumer Survey, shoppers are willing to spend an average of 9.7% more on sustainably produced or sourced goods, even at a time when cost-of-living and inflationary concerns were weighing heavily on their minds, purses and wallets (PwC, 2024). Regarding motivation to act, the same survey reported that 85% of respondents had experienced the disruptive effects of climate change firsthand in their daily lives. Evidence that consumers are taking action can also be found in the same PwC survey: 73% of UK consumers reported recycling household waste, 68% reduced their food waste and 61% limited the use of single-use plastics.

Unlocking Value

While surveys are helpful, the more you read, the more confusing and contradictory they risk becoming. So, let us look at some real-life examples of how understanding consumer sentiment has created financial value.

We will begin with a quick overview of the non-dairy milk market to illustrate some key points. While plant-based milk alternatives, such as soy and almond milk, have been around for centuries, they have only become more mainstream choices in the last decade. According to Global Market Insights, by 2019, the global plant-based milk market had already surpassed $12 billion (Food Manufacture, 2023). The reasons for this rise were many and varied: veganism, animal welfare, land use, dairy allergies, health benefits and, it is probably fair to say, a broader trend centred around natural products.

With the global plant-based milk market now worth over $31 billion (Custom Market Insights, 2024), this is a straightforward success story. Not quite; some seemingly unstoppable product lines are losing their shine. The reason is our old friend, consumer sentiment, turbo-charged by ESG concerns. Issues include the amount of water used in the production of plant-based milks, intensive farming methods and associated nature degradation, as well as health concerns about some of the added ingredients used (Times of India, 2025). In other words, the healthy and sustainable alternative is now being questioned regarding its healthiness and sustainability. As a result, new options are emerging and grabbing market share, including hemp-based and pistachio-based alternatives. The same issue can be seen in packaging alternatives like bamboo, which is commonly regarded as more sustainable than plastic, but can still pose environmental challenges. That is because, while bamboo is biodegradable and renewable, its cultivation, processing and transportation can carry significant ecological footprints, making it not entirely eco-friendly. Both the plant-based milk and bamboo examples illustrate the bigger point: no investor can sit back when it comes to sustainability products, particularly in the fast-moving consumer goods world. Without the proper insight, marketing and execution skills, today's green solution may become tomorrow's problem.

Summarising the Investment Opportunities and Value Traps

To some readers, the ever-changing and highly subjective world of customer sentiment is frustratingly elusive. Just when we think we have a handle on it, it changes. Consumers can overlook companies that behave responsibly with great sustainable products and practices, while those with superficial but easily grasped credentials can seemingly capture market share in minutes. However, difficult though it may be, harnessing the power of customer sentiment is crucial in creating financial value from ESG investments.

These five approaches towards customer sentiment have all proved effective ways to create financial value:

Close the consumer's 'say-do gap' – consumers want to buy sustainably, but do not always do so. Companies with a clear message that resonates with customer aspirations, and a product at the right price point, can tap into pent-up demand to drive sales. In a complex sustainability world, making the offer clear and straightforward will cut through.

Improve customer sentiment towards existing products and services – customers do not necessarily need to buy from a sustainability-centred company. However, they do expect their purchases to meet minimum requirements at the right price.

Innovate new products and services – creating new lines that better match customer sustainability aspirations and price points can be a highly effective way to target and capture new customers. A high demand for new products might open the way to increasing pricing and margin.

Rebrand – a brand perceived as green may add value to all its products and services, but be aware of the danger that one product with a poor ESG record can damage the entire brand.

Leverage startups – emerging companies respond and act quickly. Buying a great idea that is already gaining traction and then investing to scale it up can be a very effective strategy. However, it comes with costs and risks – is the product scalable at a price point that consumers will tolerate?

Let us look at three real-life strategies:

Existing Product Revamp

On the face of it, the manufacturers of billions of plastic toys that are opened, used for a few months and then thrown away are always going to find it tough not only to adopt sustainability but also to convince their customers that they are doing so. However, in 2019, global giant Mattel began a new range of ESG initiatives. These included promoting sustainability, reducing waste, lowering the company's carbon footprint and enhancing practices throughout the supply chain. To achieve 100% recycled, recyclable or bio-based plastic materials in products and packaging by 2030, Mattel has incorporated more sustainable raw materials and integrated principles of product stewardship and circular design. While credible data on any boost to sales, pricing or costs is not currently available, we believe it still stands as an example of how existing players can adjust their existing business model to ensure they stay on the right side of consumers, and by doing so, preserve value and ensure their license to operate.

Our following example is another well-established company, Unilever, which has a long-standing commitment to sustainability deeply embedded in its business. In 2018, Unilever launched a new brand and product range, Love Beauty and Planet. Significantly, this was neither an acquisition nor a makeover of an existing Unilever product line, but was developed by a small, dedicated in-house team. The brand achieved rapid success, reaching $100 million in sales within its first year of trading (EMARKETER, 2020) and continuing to grow at a fast pace since. Backed by the scale and infrastructure of Unilever, but without the cost of acquisition and subsequent scale-up investment, Love Beauty and Planet was able to retail at similar price points to other comparative Unilever brands. So, consumers received the sort of market-leading sustainability credential that even Gen-Z consumers demand, but at a standard high street price, making this a textbook example of how even the biggest consumer giants can get it right for profit, the planet and punters.

Our final example also concerns Unilever, but involves its 2024 acquisition of 'sustainability native' startup, Wild (The Guardian, 2025). Started by childhood friends in 2019, Wild reinvented the 'stick' deodorant, eschewing aerosol sprays with a refillable container that houses an all-natural, plant-based, solid, biodegradable deodorant. Wild's lip balms, body washes and hand washes also feature plant-based ingredients and are available in refillable packaging. The deal rationale is straightforward: Unilever acquires exciting new products that complement existing lines and appeal to environmentally conscious consumers. Wild gets added investment and access to Unilever's extensive distribution networks, global markets and research and development capabilities. This provides an interesting contrast to the previous example. Wild's key product, the stick deodorant, not only retails at a challenging price point, but it also asks consumers to make a significant behavioural change: from spray-on to stick. Only time will tell which strategy proves most effective. However, perhaps the lesson for now is that, for companies as large and financially strong as Unilever, multiple approaches can be taken. In the race to bag the big green prize, maybe it is not a bad idea to spread your bets by having more than one horse in the race.

Our Research on Customer Sentiment

We hope to have made the case to readers that customer sentiment is a powerful force in creating value from an ESG approach. However, as we have made clear throughout this section, customers' sentiment can sometimes be elusive and even contradictory. In the final part of this section on customer sentiment, we conducted our research to examine its relationship to financial value. We took publicly available historical data on customer sentiment and financial performance to explore the relationship between the two.

Our first example tracks the customer sentiment score of an honest, but anonymised, global beverage company. The top line in Figure 3.16 represents negative customer sentiment, and the lower line represents positive customer sentiment. If we focus on the period from 2021 onwards, we can observe a sharp rise in negative customer sentiment. Further research reveals that the driver of this negative spike is a series of ESG-related controversies that made headlines between 2021 and 2023. These range from product recalls due to mislabelling of ingredients, labour disputes and societal concerns about junk food and plastic pollution.

When we examine their rate of revenue growth over the same period, as shown in Figure 3.16, there is a strong correlation. Note also that peers did not exhibit the same trend, suggesting that specific factors related to the specific global beverage company's customer sentiment, rather than industry-wide trends, drove revenue growth rates lower over this period.

Let us now examine the company's ESG score during the same period. We can observe a connection between ESG performance, customer sentiment (as reflected in the ESG controversies score, which encompasses the negative news stories mentioned earlier) and revenue growth (or the lack thereof). Figure 3.16 also illustrates how ESG controversies lower the company's overall ESG rating.

Based on our findings, which rely solely on publicly available data, we can observe a strong connection between ESG-related controversies, customer sentiment and financial performance (specifically EBITDA). This indicates that robust ESG performance, especially when effectively communicated, can improve customer sentiment and consequently boost revenue and profit.

Years	ESG Combined Score	ESG Score	ESG Controversies Score
2019	72.26	87.85	56.67
2020	89.48	89.48	91.18
2021	83.47	87.77	79.17
2022	57.30	85.43	29.17
2023	41.45	80.90	2.00

Global Beverage Company – Revenue Growth

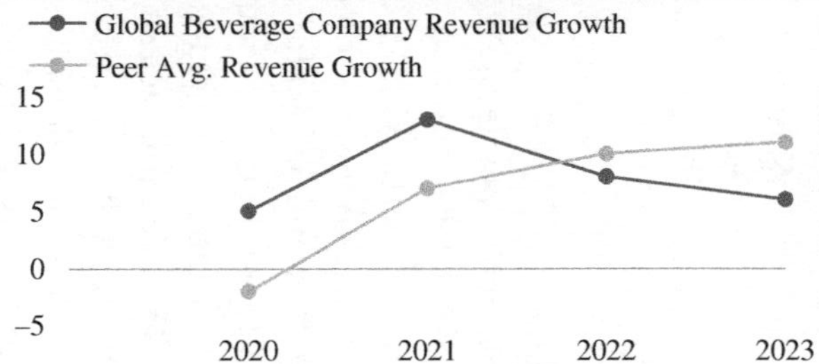

Global Beverage Company - Consumer Sentiment

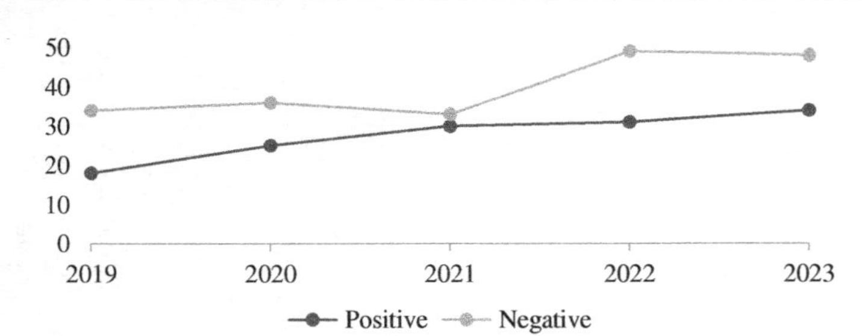

ESG Performance –
Consistently good ESG performance. However, controversies play a significant role and are significantly impacting Global Beverage Company overall ESG performance in 2022, and 2023

Consumer Sentiment –
1. Negative consumer sentiment rose sharply in 2022 and 2023
2. This brought the Net sentiment down for Global Beverage Company significantly

Effect of the ESG controversies driven consumer sentiment is partially reflected in Revenue growth of Global Beverage Company Inc declining sharply in 2022 and 2023 and these are also the years when ESG controversies were high

Figure 3.16 Customer sentiment toward a global beverage company.

Source: LSEG, Global Beverage Company Sustainability Report

Chapter Summary

- Sustainability drives deals and creates value. It was key to the rationale behind 226,000 deals that generated $6.4 trillion in deal value between 2020 and Q1 2025, with notable sector and regional variations.
- The pursuit of financial value drives solutions to some of the world's key sustainability challenges. We explored how regulatory and customer demands on major consumer groups to enhance plastic recycling rates fostered an ecosystem of innovation and transaction-focused investment.
- Customer sentiment is a key driver for ESG-related value creation. Despite being hard to track and ever-changing, customer behaviour is one of the most potent drivers of ESG value and deals.

References

Bain & Co. (2024). The Sustainability Puzzle: What Do Consumers Really Want? https://www.bain.com/insights/what-do-consumers-really-want-ceo-sustainability-guide-2024 (accessed 11 August 2025).

BBC News (2025). Serious Water Pollution Incidents up 60% in England, Environment Agency Says. https://www.bbc.co.uk/news/articles/cg5zl75dmm0o (accessed 11 August 2025).

Big Plastic Count (2024). Results. https://thebigplasticcount.com/results (accessed 11 August 2025).

BMWi Ventures (2025). Portfolio. https://www.bmwiventures.com/portfolio (accessed 11 August 2025).

Bus News (2024). Siemens Completes Acquisition of Heliox. https://bus-news.com/siemens-completes-acquisition-of-heliox/ (accessed 11 August 2025).

Chemical Engineering News (2025). PureCycle to go on $2 Billion Building Spree. https://cen.acs.org/environment/recycling/PureCycle-2-billion-building-spree/103/web/2025/06 (accessed 11 August 2025).

China Daily News (2024). Investors Ploughing Billions into China's Electric Vehicle Sector. https://epaper.chinadaily.com.cn/a/202412/23/WS6768afb4a3105c25b38eea9c.html (accessed 11 August 2025).

Crunchbase (2020). Alphabet's Autonomous Vehicle Bet Waymo Raises $2.25 Billion In First Outside Funding Round. https://news.crunchbase.com/venture/alphabets-autonomous-vehicle-bet-waymo-raises-2-25-billion-in-first-outside-funding-round/ (accessed 11 August 2025).

Custom Market Insights (2024). Global Plant-based Milk Market 2024–2033. https://www.custommarketinsights.com/report/plant-based-milk-market/ (accessed 11 August 2025).

Deloitte (2024). Cost and Sustainability Fatigue Stifle Consumers' Efforts to Adopt More Sustainable Lifestyles. https://www.deloitte.com/uk/en/about/press-room/cost-and-sustainability-fatigue-stifle-consumers-efforts-to-adopt-more-sustainable-lifestyles.html (accessed 11 August 2025).

Emarketer (2020). Industry Voices: Marketing in Uncertain Times with Love Beauty and Planet. https://www.emarketer.com/content/love-beauty-planet-industry-voices-marketing-uncertain-times (accessed 11 August 2025).

ESG Today (2022). Circular Metals Provider Continuum Raises $36 Million to Meet Demand for Sustainable Materials. https://www.esgtoday.com/circular-metals-provider-contiuum-raises-36-million-to-meet-demand-for-sustainable-materials/ (accessed 11 August 2025).

Euromonitor International (2024). Voice of the Consumer: Sustainability 2024 Key Insights. https://www.euromonitor.com/article/voice-of-the-consumer-sustainability-2024-key-insights (accessed 11 August 2025).

Food Manufacture (2023). Plant Milk Market Projected to Exceed £17bn by 2026. https://www.foodmanufacture.co.uk/Article/2023/10/16/Health-and-environmental-consciousness-fuelling-plant-milk/ (accessed 11 August 2025).

Forbes (2020). Amazon Buys Zoox: Why Self-Driving Technology Is Existential. https://www.forbes.com/sites/tomtaulli/2020/06/27/amazon-buys-zoox-why-self-driving-technology-is-existential/ (accessed 11 August 2025).

Global Cosmetic News (2021). Croda Acquires French Beauty Ingredient Supplier Alban Muller in €25m Deal. https://www.globalcosmeticsnews.com/croda-acquires-french-beauty-ingredient-supplier-alban-muller-in-e25m-deal/ (accessed 11 August 2025).

The Guardian (2025). Wild Co-founders 'land £100m' from Sale of Natural Deodorant Maker. https://www.theguardian.com/business/2025/apr/01/wild-co-founders-sale-of-natural-deodorant-maker-unilever (accessed 11 August 2025).

Jambeck, J., and Walker-Franklin, I. (2023). The impacts of plastics' life cycle. One Earth 6 (6): 600–606.

PwC (2024). Consumers willing to pay 9.7% sustainability premium, even as cost-of-living and inflationary concerns weigh: PwC 2024 Voice of the Consumer Survey. https://www.pwc.com/gx/en/news-room/press-releases/2024/pwc-2024-voice-of-consumer-survey.html (accessed 11 August 2025).

Recycling Today (2018). Closed Loop Fund Invests in PureCycle Technologies. https://www.recyclingtoday.com/news/closed-loop-fund-invests-purcycle-technologies/ (accessed 11 August 2025).

Reuters (2021a). France's Waste and Water Groups Veolia and Suez Approve Merger Deal. https://www.reuters.com/article/business/frances-waste-and-water-groups-veolia-and-suez-approve-merger-deal-idUSL8N2N158J/ (accessed 11 August 2025).

Reuters (2021b). SoftBank to Take 40% Stake in Warehouse Robotics Firm AutoStore for $2.8 bln. https://www.reuters.com/business/media-telecom/softbank-take-40-stake-autostore-28-bln-2021-04-05/ (accessed 11 August 2025).

Tech.eu (2024). Atlas Metrics Bags €12.2M to Simplify ESG Reporting and Compliance. https://tech.eu/2024/09/30/atlas-metrics-bags-eur122m-to-simplify-esg-reporting-and-compliance/ (accessed 11 August 2025).

Times of India (2025). Unknown Risks of Drinking Plant-based Milk you Should Know. https://timesofindia.indiatimes.com/life-style/health-fitness/health-news/unknown-risks-of-drinking-plant-based-milk-you-should-know/articleshow/117031686.cms (accessed 11 August 2025).

UK Government (2020). The Ten Point Plan for a Green Industrial Revolution (HTML version). https://www.gov.uk/government/publications/the-ten-point-plan-for-a-green-industrial-revolution/title (accessed 11 August 2025).

UK Tech News (2022). ESG Book Raises £29m for Corporate Sustainability Data Platform. https://www.uktech.news/big-data/esg-book-corporate-governance-data-platform-20220623 (accessed 11 August 2025).

WWF (2024). 85% of People Want Global Ban on Single-Use Plastics. Press Release (April 11).

4

Establishing the Link Between ESG Performance and Financial Value

In this chapter, we will further examine the link between ESG and financial value, using both existing and original research. To achieve this, we will closely analyse three areas where we believe there is a strong connection between ESG-related activity and financial performance.

The first area we put under the microscope is the cost of capital, explaining how and why it relates to ESG performance.

We then focus on the relationship between price multiples and ESG performance, investigating how some sectors correlate more strongly than others.

Finally, after assessing the strengths and weaknesses of the previous two methods, we present a third. This adopts a more detailed view, analysing how corporate investments in ESG can enhance performance and generate financial value. We call this the ESG Value Bridge.

The Cost of Capital – What's ESG Got to Do with It?

In this part of the chapter, we thoroughly examine the theory and evidence showing that firms with strong ESG performance can access both debt and equity capital at lower costs. We will illustrate the different types of capital and the factors linking the cost of capital to ESG.

In simple terms, the cost of capital is the rate of return a company must offer investors to attract their funding. It is essentially the minimum return investors expect in exchange for taking on the risk of investing in that company. The riskier a company, the higher the cost of capital will be, as investors or lenders will require a greater return to offset the increased risk. The cost of capital is also commonly used by international investors, appraisers and banks to determine the enterprise values of unleveraged companies.

Calculating the Cost of Capital – Debt and Equity

The Cost of Debt (Kd) refers to the interest rate a company pays on its outstanding debt. However, since interest expenses are generally tax-deductible, the cost is typically calculated on an after-tax basis. Therefore, if the company's interest rate was 10% and its tax rate was 20%, the cost of capital would be 8%.

$$\text{After-tax cost of debt} = \text{Interest Rate} \times (1 - \text{Tax Rate})$$

Not all companies have observable interest rates. They may be relatively new and therefore not yet assessed for a loan or issued bonds. The complexity of their debt profile might make assessment more difficult. In such cases, the approach to calculating the cost of capital involves examining the credit rating of the firm and/or its peers, as assigned by credit rating agencies such as S&P, Moody's and Fitch. A yield spread over sovereign bonds of the country in which the company is operating can be determined based on the given rating. This yield spread can then be added to the risk-free rate of the country to ascertain the company's cost of debt. This approach is beneficial for private companies that lack a directly observable cost of debt in the market.

It is essential to note a caveat that we will revisit later: the interest rates offered to borrowers are determined by a process that typically considers numerous factors. Therefore, while it may be possible to observe that a leading ESG performer benefits from lower rates than its peers, it is challenging to demonstrate precisely which aspect of that reduced rate is attributable to its ESG performance and which to other factors.

The cost of equity (Ke) is generally more complex to calculate, as the rate of return expected by equity investors is not as clearly defined as that demanded by lenders. The cost of equity is approximated by the capital asset pricing model as follows:

$$ERi = Rf + \beta i(ERm - Rf)$$

where:

ERi = expected return on investment

Rf = risk-free rate

βi = beta of the investment

(ERm – Rf) = market risk premium

For those less familiar with such equations, the key point to grasp here is the significance of risk in calculating the cost of equity. In this context, risk is represented by beta, a measure that reflects how strongly a stock's price moves in relation to the broader market. This helps investors estimate how much a stock might amplify or dampen the market's fluctuations when added to a portfolio. It is employed in finance to signify the volatility or systematic risk of a security or portfolio compared to its peers or the broader market. Stocks with betas higher than 1.0 are considered more volatile than their peers or a relevant market index. For public companies, beta can be calculated using the company's share price or based on listed peer companies facing comparable risks and operating in comparable markets. For private companies, beta is based on the average among a group of similar public companies.

The Weighted Average Cost of Capital (WACC) The weighted average cost of capital (WACC) represents the average cost of capital for a company and is widely used among international investors, appraisers and banks to determine enterprise values. It is calculated by multiplying the price of each type of capital by the debt/equity ratio, considering the market value of the company's capital.

Many companies have both debt and equity capital, so it is necessary to consider both when measuring the overall cost of capital.

Cost of Debt + Cost of Equity = Overall Cost of Capital

The firm's overall cost of capital is based on the weighted average of these costs. For instance, consider an enterprise with a capital structure comprising 80% equity and 20% debt, where its cost of equity is 10% and the after-tax cost of debt is 8%. Therefore, its WACC would be: (0.8 × 10%) + (0.2 × 8%) = 9.6%

Key Drivers in the Relationship Between ESG and the Cost of Capital

Having considered the calculations, let us step back and think more generally about why and how a company's ESG performance might influence its cost of capital.

The first point to highlight is risk management. In the first two chapters of the book, we emphasised several areas where ESG has a strong risk management component. Considering E, S and G in order, a manufacturing company may face environmental risks if it does not properly consider the impact of rising temperatures, water scarcity, pollution and extreme weather events on its operations. Social risks could result from neglecting to assess the impact on communities near its factory sites. Weak governance might harm the company's ability to identify and manage these and other risks effectively. In summary, better ESG performance can give lenders and investors greater confidence that risks have been carefully evaluated and incorporated into decision-making and operations, making them more willing to provide funds at lower rates.

As we discussed in Chapter 1, there is a growing shift towards considering not only the risk-preventative aspects of ESG but also its potential for value creation and growth. Examples where ESG can offer opportunities for companies to boost returns and, consequently, make investors more willing to supply funds include its positive impact on energy and resource efficiency. Another area might be a company's enhanced ability to meet customer expectations, which, as shown in

Chapter 4, are often influenced by the ESG performance of some companies. While we will not explore these areas in detail here, it is generally understandable how all three components – E, S and G – could lead to better investment returns and, if proven, encourage lenders and investors to allocate their capital at preferential rates.

Let us return to a more scientific approach to the cost of capital. MSCI (formerly Morgan Stanley Capital International, spun off from Morgan Stanley in 2007) is a global provider of investment decision-support tools. It is best known for creating MSCI indices, which are widely used benchmarks in the financial industry. MSCI is also a major player in ESG analysis, where it rates companies on their ESG risks and performance, ranging from CCC (worst) to AAA (best). Its status and reputation in the ESG world is high, with its ratings and other analyses utilised by many primary market participants, including lenders, asset owners and investors. The MSCI schematic reproduced in Figure 4.1 brings together some of the factors, or what MSCI terms 'transmission channels', by which a company's sustainability profile may affect its financial and market performance.

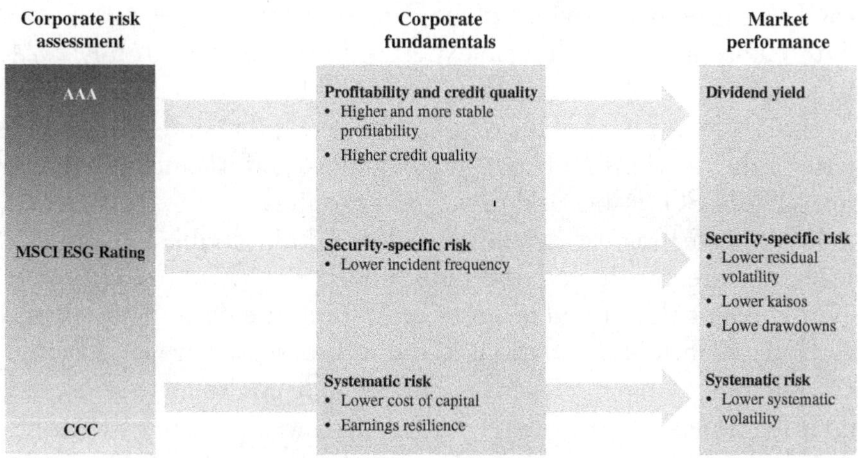

Figure 4.1 Transmission channels for how the sustainability profile may affect financial performance.

Source: MSCI ESG Research

While this schematic does not solely focus on the relationship between ESG and the cost of capital, instead taking a broader view of financial performance, it is easy to identify the relevant areas. Improvements in credit quality and cash flow, accompanied by lower risk, all indicate a reduction in the cost of capital. Put simply, banks and other capital providers (for example, private capital and pension funds) are more likely to lend at lower interest rates to a better-managed, more stable and higher-performing company. It is also important to note how volatility/beta is likely to decrease in such a company, directly impacting the cost of debt capital. We will provide evidence for this later in the chapter.

Linking ESG Performance to Financial Value We hope readers have accepted the thesis that there is a link between the cost of capital and ESG performance, and that, on this basis, a company with strong ESG performance can access both debt and equity capital at a lower cost. However, we suspect you may be seeking something more substantial in terms of evidence.

The first piece of such evidence we put to the jury is also from MSCI. As a global provider of ESG-related products, it possesses a robust dataset and considerable expertise in the market. In July 2024, the company published a report titled 'MSCI ESG Ratings and Cost of Capital' (MSCI, 2024). This report aims to explore and provide evidence of the relationship between companies' performance relative to their MSCI ESG ratings and their cost of capital.

Before revealing the headline results of their findings, it is worthwhile to share the basic hypothesis underlying their research. The report explains that 'In addition to examining the costs of equity and debt and to control for variations in these costs caused by macro factors (e.g., differences in the relevant risk-free rate or equity-market risk premium for issuers based in different regions), we examined the issuer-specific, market-determined components (or proxies) of each. In the equity market, we use stock beta (β), which measures systematic risk exposure and translates the equity risk premium into the required rate of return for a company. In the bond market, we use the credit spread of an issuer's outstanding bonds, which, on aggregate, reflects the

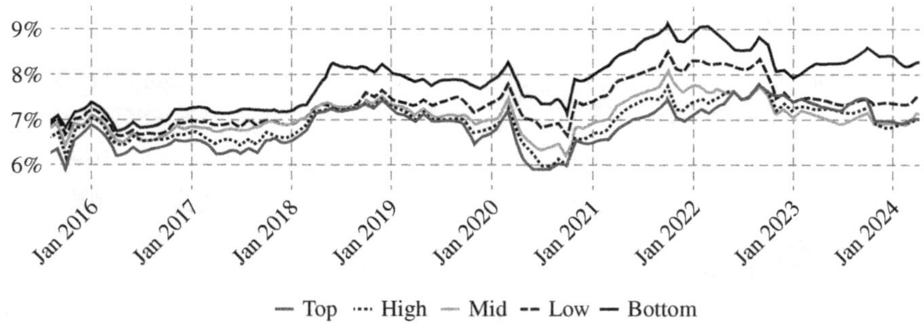

Figure 4.2 Cost of capital across MSCI ESG rating quintiles.

Source: MSCI ESG Research

issuer-specific credit risk add-on to the benchmark rate (usually a duration-matched government bond or swap rate)'.

So, let us cut to the chase, as shown in Figure 4.2, MSCI found a direct and distinct correlation between ESG ratings and cost of capital.

Figure 4.2 shows that the lowest-rated companies had the highest financing costs (7.9% on average over the study period), while the top-rated companies financed themselves at the lowest rate (6.8%). While Figure 4.2 displays the overall cost of capital, the same MSCI study also examines the cost of capital and the cost of debt separately. It finds that either singly or in combination, these factors correlate strongly with ESG performance. For more detailed information, please read their July 2024 report.

Our Research into the Cost of Capital While we regard the MSCI research as thorough and robust, we also believe it is prudent to examine additional sources, or, better still, to conduct and share our research.

We mentioned earlier in the chapter that beta, as a measure of risk and volatility, has a direct relationship with the cost of capital. Figure 4.3 illustrates how our research, utilising publicly available information, reveals a strong correlation between ESG performance and beta. The term unlevered beta, as presented in Figure 4.3, is adjusted to exclude any financing-related risk factors, enabling comparison of the operational risks of companies against the overall market.

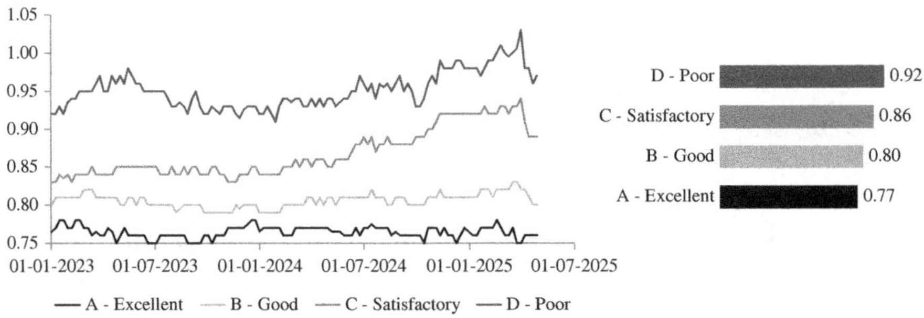

Figure 4.3 Relationship between ESG performance and market risk (beta).

Source: LSEG and S&P Capital IQ

Note also in Figure 4.3 how large the gap is between the highest and lowest ESG performance quartiles. Given the central role of beta in the formula for calculating the cost of capital, the impact on borrowing and financing costs is significant. While in the first few months of 2025, the gap between the highest and lowest ESG performers has narrowed, possibly in response to a more sceptical view of ESG in general and ESG ratings in particular, the gap remains significant.

ESG-Flavoured Funding Is a Factor Because it is impossible to see inside the rooms of credit committees of financial institutions or the formulas they apply to agree on loan and interest rates, it is, as discussed earlier in the chapter, difficult to ascertain with certainty how strong ESG performance, as distinct from other factors, directly contributes to lower capital costs. What we can say, however, is that several visible factors shape the lending market and drive down costs for strong ESG performers.

Sustainable funds had $3.56 trillion in assets under management at the end of 2024 (Morgan Stanley, 2025b). Typically, such funds only invest in companies or other entities that meet specific ESG criteria.

According to the Morgan Stanley Institute for Sustainable Investing's 2025 Sustainable Signals: Individual Investors report, 88% of global investors showed interest in sustainable investing, with levels of interest in the US and Europe remaining largely stable since late 2023. This was backed up by the European Investor Intentions Survey

2025, which found that less than 5% of respondents said that they do not consider sustainability in their investments.

Since 2019, the Bank of England ('BoE') has set supervisory expectations for banks on the management of climate-related financial risks, encompassing governance, risk management, scenario analysis and disclosure. Partially as a result, banks have been increasingly incorporating ESG factors into their risk assessment models. The EU's 2021 SFDR sets out mandatory ESG disclosure requirements for asset managers. Restriction screening has significantly increased since the implementation of SFDR. Similarly, the European Central Bank's (ECB) position on the Omnibus amendments to CSRD and CSDDD is supportive of simplification but highly critical of scope reductions and weakening of requirements to ensure the ability to integrate climate and ESG risks into monetary policy operations.

It is reasonable to assume that the substantial volume of funding and positive investor sentiment directed towards ESG-friendly companies will influence the cost of capital. This is because companies that meet the lender/investor ESG criteria will not only have greater access to capital but, by simple supply and demand rules alone, a greater chance of securing it at lower cost.

So, even though we cannot see behind the closed doors of credit committees, read confidential lending criteria and download loan portfolio allocation models, we can reasonably conclude that there is strong empirical evidence to suggest that higher ESG performers can access capital at lower cost.

Another intriguing view on how ESG lowers the cost of capital comes from our interview with Henri Servaes, a Professor of Finance at London Business School. He believes that some investors benefit not only from a purely financial perspective but also from what he calls the 'warm glow' of investing in a company that does the 'right thing'. 'Therefore, investors may sometimes be prepared to accept lower returns as long as there is that "warm glow"', Henri says. We think that, although the term 'warm glow' may seem unscientific for seekers of financial value, it has relevance. What better way to describe the feeling that drives customers to purchase a premium-priced jacket from the leading sustainable clothing company Patagonia? For more on customer sentiment towards sustainable products and services, you may wish to revisit Chapter 3.

Our Research into the Cost of Capital by Sector Here we share some of the authors' research exploring the relationship between WACC and ESG performance across and within sectors. In Chapter 1, we discussed how specific sectors are more likely to benefit from what we described as 'sustainability tailwinds' in terms of financial performance. We also described how others have faced what we described as sustainability headwinds. Now, let us adopt a more scientific approach to examining sector differences.

In this research, we refer to an analysis showing the simple average of the WACC for ESG leaders and laggards within each sector based on capital market information using standardised KPIs. And ESG ratings. Sustainability leaders are those rated in the top quartile, focusing on Environmental Scores, while laggards are those in the bottom quartile of the same measure. The scope of the research is restricted to European companies.

The dotted line across the middle of the chart in Figure 4.4 represents the average rate reduction that sustainability leaders enjoy in securing capital, namely 169 basis points.

What does Figure 4.4 tell us? Firstly, it demonstrates that the cost of capital can vary significantly between ESG leaders and laggards. In the case of Automotive, ESG leaders can secure capital at rates as much as 470 bps below the average score.

Secondly, it highlights the greater sensitivity some sectors exhibit regarding ESG and the cost of capital. Take the industry with the least divergence between the leaders and the laggards in terms of cost of capital – Chemicals. Here, while ESG is an important aspect of operations in this highly regulated industry, it is unlikely to serve as a key differentiator unless there is an adverse event that highlights any ESG failings. The situation is markedly different for the automotive industry, which encompasses everything from zero-tailpipe emissions and sustainable mobility pioneers to traditional auto parts manufacturers. Customer sentiment and expectations vary significantly across various segments. An eco-conscious customer may be willing to pay considerably more for green transport. In contrast, the buyer of a replacement part for their used diesel vehicle is unlikely to do so. This variation is reflected in the substantial difference in the cost of capital between ESG leaders and laggards within the sector. Understanding these

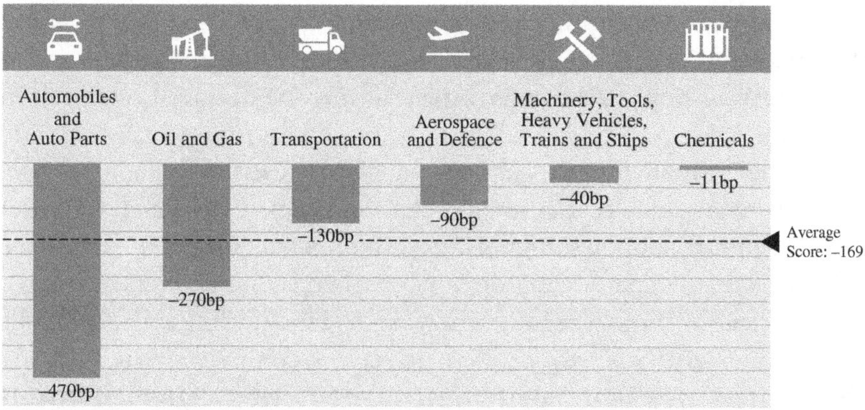

Figure 4.4 Average cost of capital (WACC) of European sustainability leaders versus laggards (2022)

Source: LSEG

sector differences and the role that customer sentiment plays within them is crucial not only for readers interested in a specific industry, but also because of what it reveals about how ESG generates financial value, and how it supports the thesis that a detailed analysis of the business model increases transparency over individual ESG factors and how they are linked to financial performance. We will return to this sector perspective later in the chapter. It is worth noting, however, that B2C businesses are likely to be more ESG-sensitive than their B2B counterparts, although this is shifting as supply chains are becoming increasingly subject to scrutiny through an ESG lens. In other words, even if a company does not supply the consumer directly, it is likely to be part of a supply chain that eventually does, so its ESG performance will become a factor, with transparency and accountability required by regulation or for brand or reputational reasons.

Establishing the Link Between ESG Ratings and Price Multiples

Before going on to scientifically examine this using our research, let us begin by exploring some of the general factors or drivers that we might reasonably expect to explain a link between ESG and price multiples.

First up is the area we have just covered. Because the cost of capital effectively represents the minimum return that investors require on an investment, it impacts price multiples, as it is the discount rate used in valuation models. A higher cost of capital means future cash flows are discounted more heavily, resulting in a lower present value and, consequently, lower price-to-earnings (P/E) multiples. Conversely, a lower cost of capital supports higher valuations and multiples. Thus, we already have an apparent reason why strong ESG performers may have higher price multiples: because they can access funding more cheaply. Continuing with investor-related drivers, a company with a strong ESG rating may be more appealing to investors who align their investments with specific values or minimum ESG requirements. Therefore, these investors may be willing to pay a higher price (and thus a higher price multiple) to acquire a stake in such a company, particularly if demand for such companies is high and supply is low. Even those investors without such strict requirements may believe that a company with a higher ESG rating could, by being more sustainable, generate greater long-term returns or, as it is commonly referred to, long-term value. Just as a car buyer may be willing to pay a premium for a car that is built to last longer, an investor might pay more for a company that is perceived to have greater resilience and therefore long-term value. More specifically, the investor rationale may be that companies with strong ESG performance are judged as better able to address the risks and opportunities ahead of them. In contrast, low performers are discounted for investment because they are judged as less able to do so.

Similarly, investors may be inclined to pay a higher price for companies that have thoughtfully considered and mitigated risks. By this logic, companies with a robust ESG strategy and performance will have a better understanding of crucial environmental, social and governance risks. Reduced risk translates to less potential downside, leading to greater upside and, consequently, a higher valuation. This further justifies higher price multiples. If ESG high performers are both more resilient and consistent, they are also likely to enjoy more stable and longer-lasting positive cash flows. Another potential driver is how ESG initiatives can lead to cost savings through waste reduction, energy efficiency and improved supply chain management. By reducing costs through such efficiencies, profits rise, and so too do valuations.

Moving on to the least clear but potentially most valuable drivers, we first consider what is often referred to as moral value. This could also be referred to as reputational power or customer credit. It is based on the idea that companies with strong ESG performance can build stronger trust with stakeholders, leading to 'moral capital' that serves as a buffer during times of crisis. Although this may sound somewhat fanciful, it is becoming increasingly important in a world of social media shaming, greenwashing and cyberattacks. For example, when a major retailer suffered a crippling cyber-attack that shut down online sales and forced in-store customers to pay for items in cash, many commentators believe that the company's long-standing reputation for trust and fair play mitigated the damage to its bottom line.

Innovation is another often-cited but difficult-to-prove benefit of ESG performance, which could drive higher valuations. The angle here is that ESG requires new approaches to everything from product development to packaging, pushing proponents into new and exciting avenues. While we agree it can and often does so, with many examples provided throughout the book of the financial value created in doing so, it is essential to note that this is not always the case. One such example is BP, which embarked on a much-heralded transition away from fossil fuels to green energies, but arguably at substantial expense to shareholders. The Guardian commented in February 2025 that 'BP has lost almost a quarter of its market value in the past two years while the market value of its rivals Shell and ExxonMobil has increased as they pursued greater oil and gas production' (The Guardian, 2025). Our final growth driver is customer sentiment and behaviour, as explored in Chapter 3. The crucial point is that for many (but not all) customers, sustainability is a key factor in the buying decision. Throughout the book, we have shared examples of new, ESG-focused companies growing rapidly, new products being adopted quickly with little advertising and old ideas being repackaged for the green economy to significant effect. Better still for the companies involved, such products and services often command a higher price, creating the potential to increase revenue and profits. One refinement, which we will explore later in greater detail, is that sensitivity to each driver will depend on the sector, region and likely other specificities. For example, while ESG performance would likely be a key driver for the price multiples of a Swedish building firm operating in a highly regulated country, serving progressive, environmentally aware households, it would be less likely to influence the price multiple of its counterpart in a less regulated country with a more cash-strapped customer base.

Figure 4.5 supports our general comments on the link between ESG performance and financial value by listing the types of practical ESG steps that a company might take to create financial value.

Revenue gains	**Cost reduction**	**Capital and tax impact**	**People**	**Digital**
Sustainable products/ innovations	Eco efficiency gains from reduced energy, water and material use.	Green subsidies and tax incentives.	Higher productivity and level of retention.	Automation of recurring processes to achieve compliance and address customer needs.
New markets/ customers		Green financing and Real Estate consolidation	Remote working opportunities to reduce OpEx.	
Sustainable product pricing adjustments	Supply chain and/procurement optimisation			
Marketing/ awareness of ESG practices to boost sales				

Figure 4.5 ESG performance and financial value.

Source: Industry Research

Establishing the Link – Our Research

To test our theory, does research and complex data support the argument that there is a connection between ESG performance and company valuations as reflected in their price-to-earnings multiples? By utilising publicly available data from providers and platforms, such as Refinitiv and Cap IQ, the results of the analysis are illustrated in Figure 4.6.

These demonstrate a clear correlation: the higher the ESG rating, the higher the valuation in terms of price multiples. Note how, in 2025, the gap in price multiples between excellent and poor ESG performers narrows slightly. This likely reflects the passing of 'peak

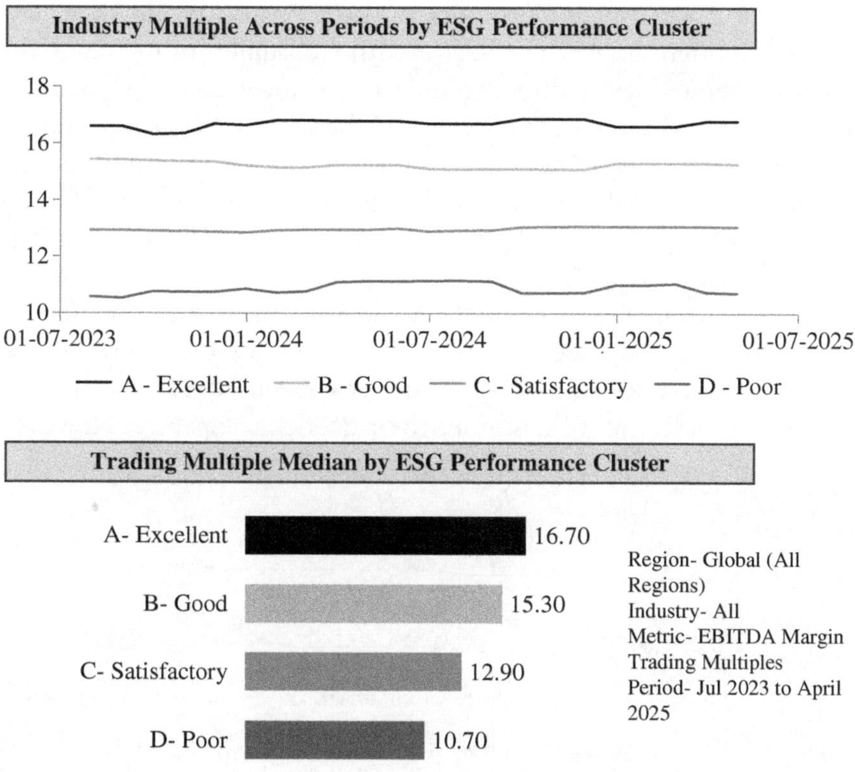

Figure 4.6 Price multiples by ESG performance cluster (all regions/ industries).

Source: LSEG and S&P Capital IQ

ESG' and a reset by investors, who are less willing to pay a very high premium for top sustainability performers. However, it is worth noting that the price multiples gap between poor and excellent ESG performers remains significant, demonstrating a strong link between ESG performance and valuations/price multiples.

The Sector Story As described earlier in the chapter, different sectors are likely to have varying sensitivities regarding the link between ESG performance and valuations, influenced by factors such as customer sensitivity and regulatory environment. To explore this further, we present our research into two contrasting sectors and examine how each one's price multiples correlate differently with ESG performance. In Figure 4.7, we display the results for the consumer products sector.

As one might expect of a sector with 'consumer' in its name, the ability of companies within the industry to meet customer needs is vital to their revenues and margins, and therefore to their price multiples. Put simply, the sector is in a stronger position to enjoy superior pricing and profitability by meeting customers' demands, expectations and desires around sustainability. In contrast, Figure 4.8 shows a very different sector: Mining.

Here, customers are unlikely to be influenced by ESG factors when making buying decisions. Yes, miners do operate in an increasingly regulated world and will consider environmental and social factors in their activities to maintain their licence to operate. However,

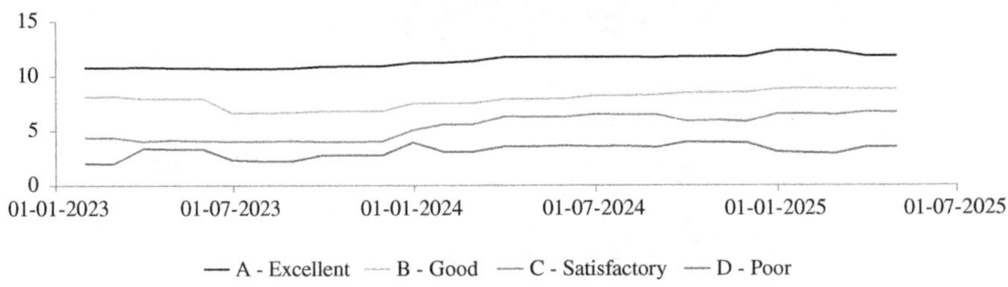

Figure 4.7 Correlation between ESG performance and price multiples in the consumer products sector.

Source: LSEG and S&P Capital IQ

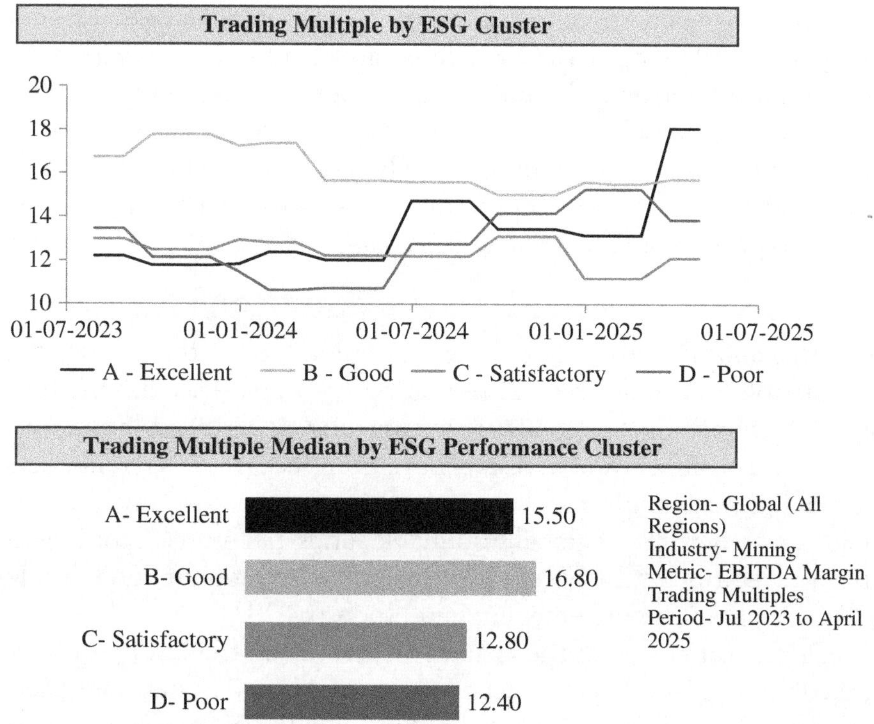

Figure 4.8 Price multiples by ESG performance cluster (mining sector).
Source: LSEG and S&P Capital IQ

this is not, in most cases, a value-additive or differentiating factor. Figure 4.8 supports this view. In comparison to Figure 4.7, the price multiples difference between Excellent and Poor ESG performers is smaller. Also, note the overall shape of the graph, where the lines representing each quartile of ESG performance regularly intersect with one another. In contrast, Figure 4.6 shows a more regular pattern, with each quartile separated and primarily in parallel. We conclude that the mining sector has a less precise and more complex relationship with ESG value creation. Another reason for this disparity is that companies in consumer-facing sectors are likely to have built up, over the last decade, strong ESG data points, and by reporting on them, improved their robustness and accountability. Industries like mining are following that track but still have a way to go before the dataset is good enough to close the gap. In addition, sectors and companies following a B2C business model must typically provide more relevant and granular ESG performance data to comply with the behaviour and customer needs. The mining industry does not have this strong link to end consumers. Therefore, companies have not been under the same regulatory pressure as Consumer Products businesses to provide such extensive ESG data.

The Regional Picture The European Union has historically taken a leading role in promoting and regulating ESG practices, driving substantial change in corporate reporting and investment strategies. European consumers and investors have been recognised as trailblazers in making sustainable purchasing and investment decisions. Europe holds a massive 85% of global sustainable funds' net assets according to the latest edition of the European Sustainable Investment Funds Study (Association of the Luxembourg Fund Industry, 2024).

On the other side of the Atlantic, even before the ESG pushback linked to President Trump's second term, the United States was generally viewed as a laggard in terms of ESG regulation, investment and consumer awareness. The Asia-Pacific region (APAC) has been more challenging to categorise regarding attitudes towards ESG. On one hand, state subsidies have helped China to take a leading role in solar power and electric vehicles. On the other hand, China is the clear global leader in CO_2 emissions. Figure 4.9 illustrates the variation in the relationship between ESG performance and price multiples across these regions. So, how do those regional stereotypes compare when we examine the ESG price multiples premium across Europe, the United States and APAC?

It may come as a surprise to discover that, according to our research (based on Refinitiv data for over 10,000 companies globally for which ESG ratings were issued), the gap in price multiples between a Poor and Excellent ESG performer is far higher in the United States than in Europe. As we highlighted in Chapter 3, this may be driven by the high-tech focus of many US sustainability-focused companies in a market with deep capital and a high appetite for risk. Although APAC posts the highest price multiple globally for Excellent ESG performers,

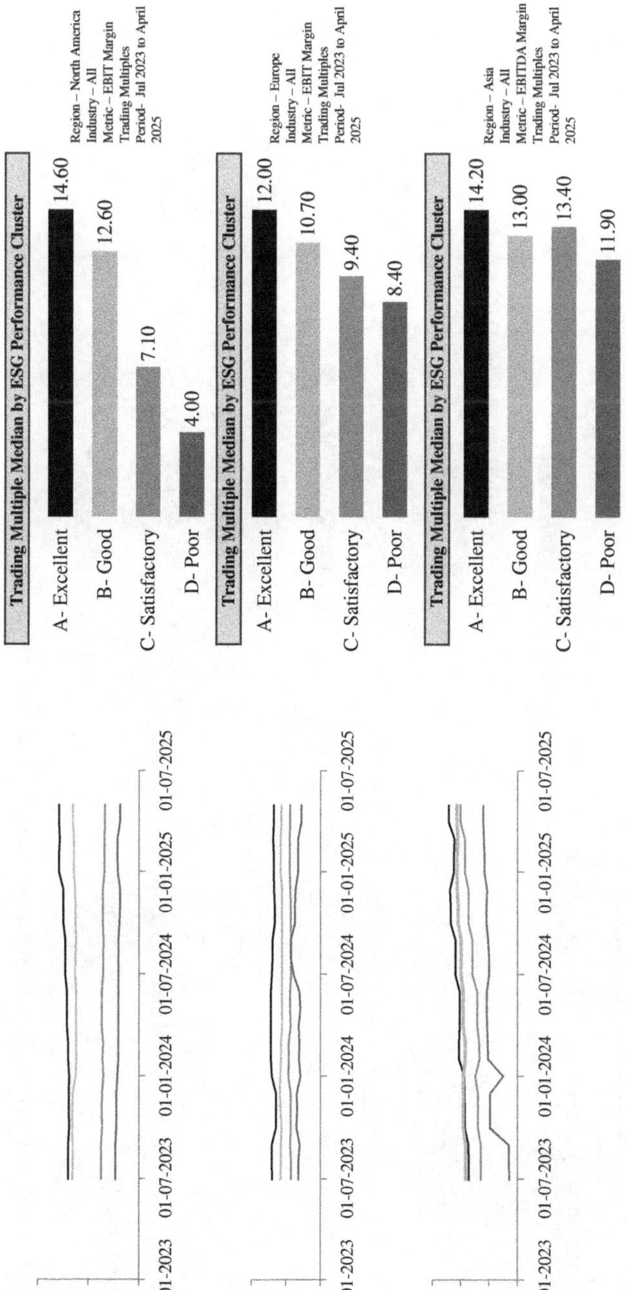

Figure 4.9 **Relationship between ESG performance and price multiples per region.**

Source: LSEG and S&P Capital IQ

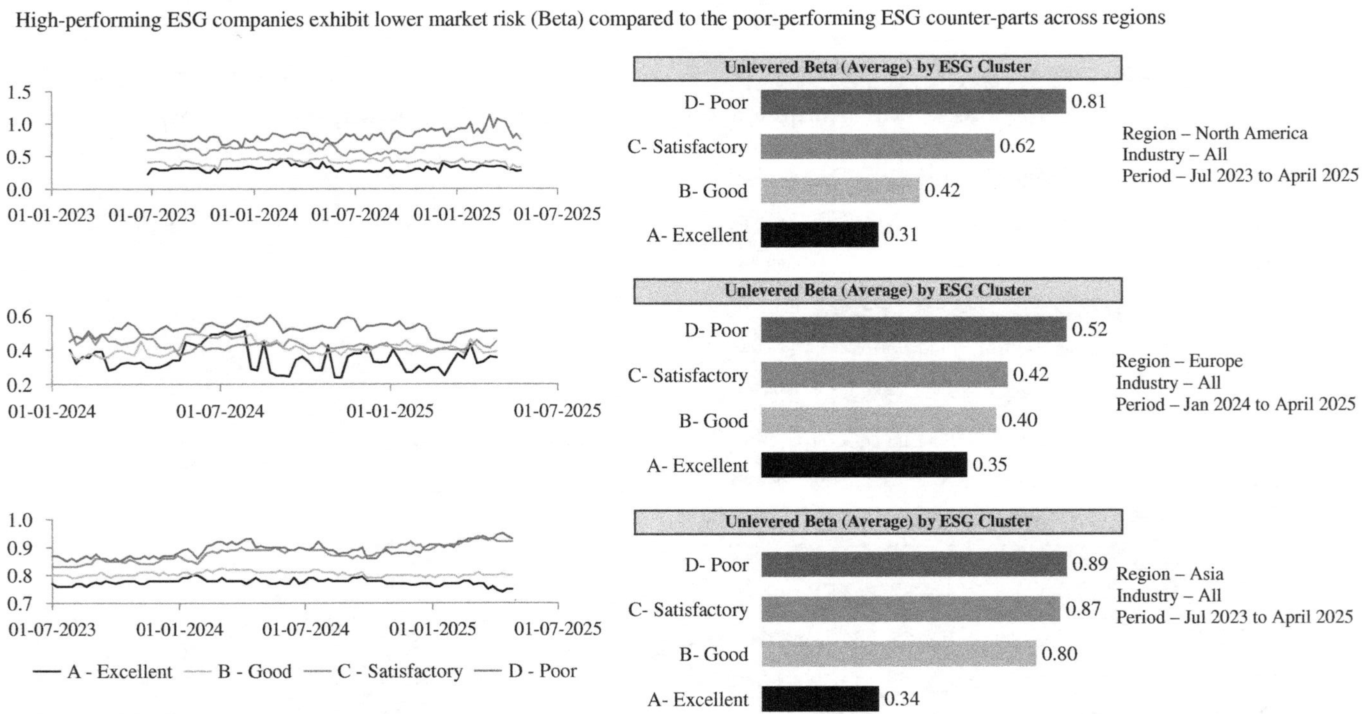

Figure 4.10 Relationship between market risk (beta) and price multiples per region.

Source: LSEG and S&P Capital IQ

it is notable how small the price multiple difference is for Poor ESG performers. This could suggest a region where ESG performance is less finely calibrated than in other regions, perhaps reflecting a combination of factors including a lack of standardised ESG frameworks, inconsistent data availability and differing regulatory landscapes. However, the sharp rise in price multiples for top ESG performers (based on Refinitiv data for over 10,000 companies globally for which ESG ratings were issued regularly) at the beginning of 2025 does imply that change may be on its way. Remember beta, which is a key driver for the cost of capital? Figure 4.10 measures beta against ESG rating. Note the similarity to the pattern for price multiples.

The Greenium Let us refer to the increase in price multiples attributed to stronger ESG performance as the green premium, or to shorten it further, the greenium. How has this changed over time? Figure 4.11 examines the size of the greenium between 2020 and 2024.

Between 2022 and 2025, we see that the gap between weak European ESG performers (Poor and Satisfactory) and strong European

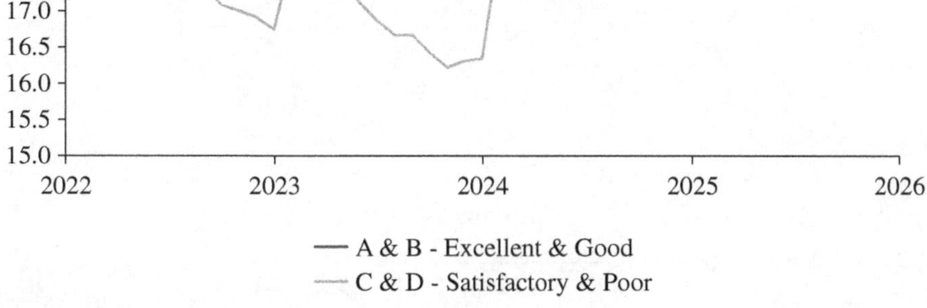

Figure 4.11 Price multiples versus ESG performance over time – the greenium.

Source: LSEG and S&P Capital IQ

ESG performers (Good and Excellent) has widened. One explanation is that, during and in the immediate aftermath of the COVID-19 pandemic, companies focused solely on overcoming the crisis and returning to normal operations. Subsequently, as ESG regulation strengthened and positive customer sentiment towards sustainability deepened, both the risks associated with poor ESG performance and the rewards of strong ESG performance increased. Note that although Q1 2025 saw price multiples fall, the price multiples gap between higher and lower ESG performers remained constant.

A *Single Case* Let us conclude this section of the chapter by examining, using publicly available information, a single company and its relationship between financial and ESG performance. Oersted is a publicly listed renewable energy company headquartered in Denmark, with assets and operations in both Denmark and the UK, and a recognised pioneer in sustainability reporting. As shown in Figure 4.12, we begin by examining Oersted's ESG performance in relation to its peers in the electric utilities sector.

Note that Oersted's ESG score is not only higher than its peers but also more stable. Now, as shown in Figure 4.13, we examine how Oersted and its peers' EBITDA margins vary over the same period. Although this differs from the price multiples measure, which we have previously tracked in relation to ESG, EBITDA still stands as a significant measure of financial performance and value creation and is a

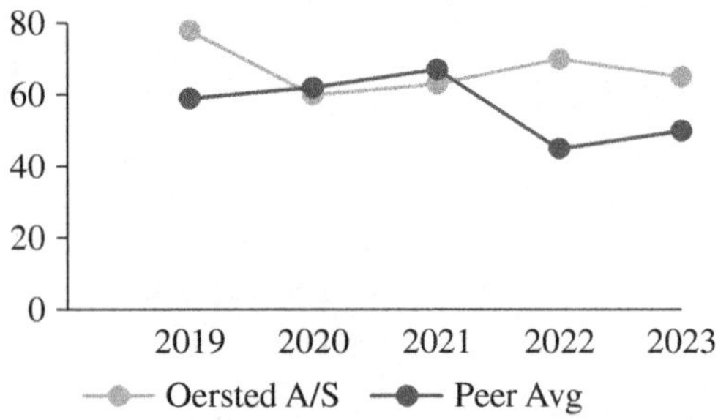

Figure 4.12 ESG score for Oersted and industry peers.

Source: LSEG, S&P Capital IQ, Industry Research

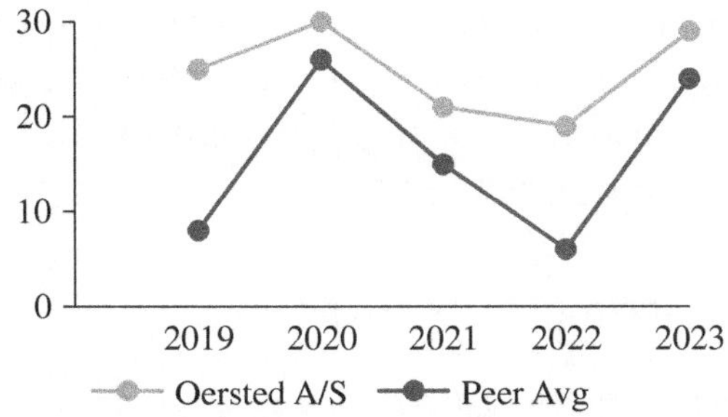

Figure 4.13 Oersted EBITDA margin in comparison to peers.
Source: LSEG, S&P Capital IQ, Industry Research

strong correlate with price multiples. Here, we see that, just as with its ESG score, Oersted consistently outperforms its peers.

So, what underpins Oersted's outperformance? One factor that correlates strongly with Oersted's performance is its controversy score. This score tracks the number of adverse ESG-related events that are publicly reported. As illustrated in Figure 4.14, not only did Oersted consistently perform better than its peers over the period, but it also averted the significant drop experienced by its peers from 2022 to 2023.

One reason that Oersted outperformed its peers in this respect was its ability to avoid some of the substantial ESG-related issues that impacted its peers, causing significant damage to people and property. We examine the relationship between ESG controversies and their impact on customer sentiment and financial performance

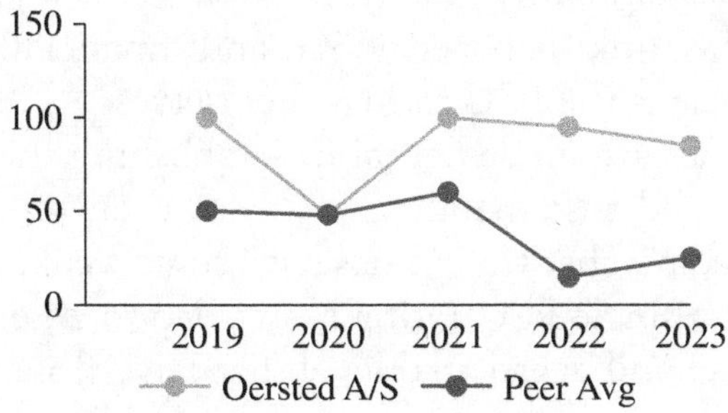

Figure 4.14 Oersted and peers' controversy score (the higher the better).
Source: LSEG, S&P Capital IQ, Industry Research

in Chapter 3. For now, we cite it as an example of how Oersted's high ESG performance seemed to reflect an underlying reality that, in comparison to its peers, it excelled at identifying, mitigating and managing sustainability-related risks.

Weak Links and Refining the Model

While the evidence is mounting in our quest to establish the link between financial value and ESG performance, it is only fair to acknowledge that there are weaknesses. Taking the cost of capital as an example, although we can safely assume that better ESG performers pay less for capital, how do we know their ESG performance directly causes this reduction? Yes, banks or other capital providers may offer lower rates to ESG high performers. Still, we cannot see the inner workings of their credit committee and loan writing processes to determine exactly how much of this lower cost of debt can be attributed to ESG performance, and how much to other factors such as the bank's asset allocation ratio. In terms of equity capital, we can see that the cost of capital is related to the company's beta but again, attributing exactly how much of that is due to ESG performance and how much to market position, strength of management, product portfolio and so on is hard, if not impossible, to calculate without having the credit rating scoring model in front of us. With price multiples, we can observe a clear correlation with ESG performance; however, beyond the generic drivers described earlier in the chapter, we cannot directly tie this improved performance to specific ESG investments.

This lack of granularity and clear causation is a key problem in determining the link between ESG and financial performance. Another key issue is the ESG ratings themselves. As discussed previously, ESG ratings are fundamental in establishing the link between financial value and sustainability, yet even their greatest advocate would have to admit that the ratings have some weaknesses. One key problem is that a single ESG rating is awarded to an entire company at a consolidated and aggregated level. For large firms with multiple divisions, this can render ratings somewhat of a blunt instrument. For instance, back in 2018, German chemical giant Bayer acquired the prominent American agrochemical and agricultural biotechnology corporation Monsanto. This severely impacted Bayer's ESG rating because one of Monsanto's flagship products, the weed killer Roundup, was linked to cancer cases. To this day, although most of Bayer's divisions, including pharmaceuticals and consumer health, display exemplary ESG performance, Bayer's overall ESG rating remains negatively affected.

This example illustrates a broader point: the factors we use to connect ESG and financial performance are inherently 'outside-in'. The ESG ratings are evaluated by third parties that assess companies based on the data points they set and then aggregate using often opaque processes. Likewise, the credit scores used to determine the cost of capital are generally based not on a company's own cost of capital, but on calculations derived from credit spreads, bond prices and peer companies.

As seekers of financial value, our ultimate objective is to determine whether applying an ESG lens can directly contribute to financial performance and value. While establishing a generalised correlation between ESG and financial performance is beneficial to the broader investment rationale and thesis, it does not provide much support for discussing more specific actions. We will see this reflected in Chapter 5 in the behaviour of Private Equity players who are cautious about investing in any generalised assumption about ESG boosting performance. Instead, they tend to approach ESG predominantly from a risk and compliance perspective. If, during that process, they see an ESG-linked opportunity, they will do their research. Rather than rely on external ratings, they will get up close and personal to identify the best ESG levers to pull to maximise value.

The ESG 'Value Bridge' – Taking a More Granular Approach

Weaknesses in the existing methodologies linking ESG to financial performance have prompted the authors to develop a new model, which we outline in this section. To begin with, this methodology identifies ESG areas within individual companies' or business units' operations that can be improved by adopting a specific course of action. It then aims to plot both the costs associated with such a

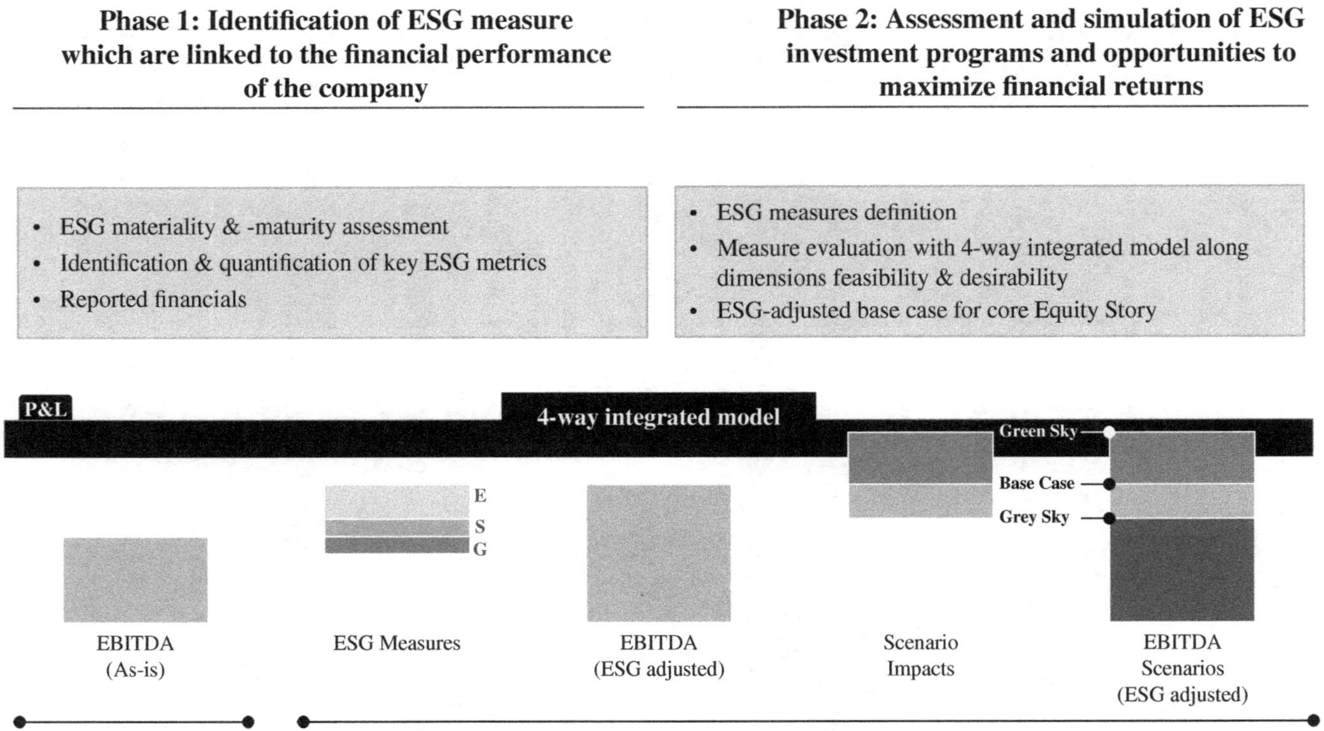

Figure 4.15 The four-way integrated model that supports ESG analysis.

Source: Industry Research

programme and the cumulative financial returns that will emerge within a particular timeframe. We refer to this as the four-way integrated model, as illustrated in Figure 4.15.

In terms of practical steps, the methodology can be broken down into three stages of business modelling, as shown in Figure 4.16.

In the first stage, titled Status Quo, the business's current financial state and ESG metrics/activities (internal and specific to the company, not from external ESG providers) are established. Current investment programmes and measures are evaluated based on their net present value. The second stage, referred to as Risk/Opportunities, identifies potential ESG-related initiatives that could positively impact financial performance. With these potential projects and initiatives identified, the next stage of the process, Measures and Strategies, involves impact modelling and scenario analysis to project the net financial outcome of any proposed initiative. These initiatives are selected by management based on the company's risk appetite, available funds and the ability of individual measures or programmes to impact the business's financial performance positively.

Example Case Study, BorgWarner

So much for the theory, how does the model work in practice? Based on public information, we illustrate how our methodology is applied to an individual company in order to link ESG risks and opportunities to financial value creation. BorgWarner Inc. is an American manufacturer of components and parts for the automotive industry. Based in Michigan, its 2024 revenues exceeded $14 billion, and the company maintains production facilities and sites at 92 locations across 24 countries, employing nearly 40,000 people. BorgWarner's primary purpose is 'to deliver innovative and sustainable mobility solutions to the global transportation industry. This includes designing and manufacturing systems for various applications, with a strong focus on reducing emissions, improving fuel economy and enhancing performance for combustion, hybrid and electric vehicles'. It is clear from these published statements that the company regards sustainability as integral to its business. It is also relatively easy to grasp how this might translate into financial value, as the company aims to grow revenues and

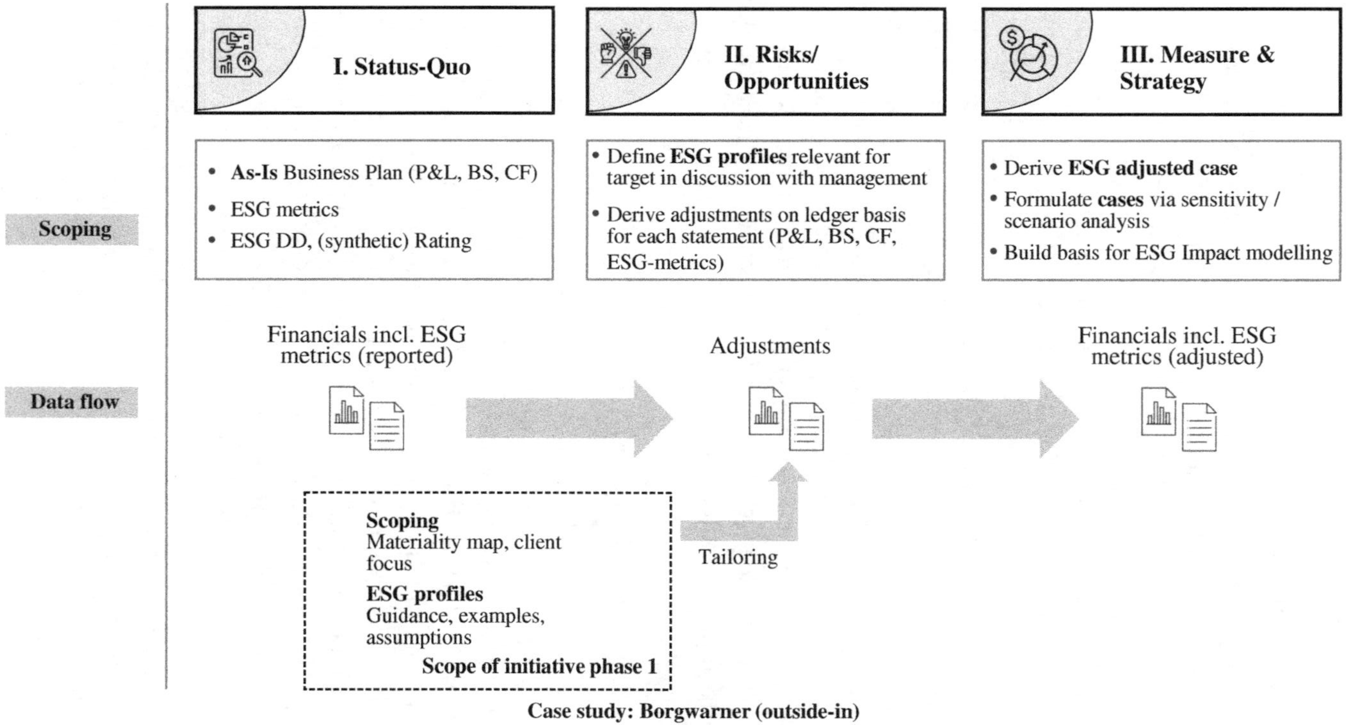

Figure 4.16 The three stages of ESG business modelling.

Source: Industry Research

margins by innovating and manufacturing products that meet customer and regulatory requirements for clean transportation. However, such a general relationship between sustainability and value is unlikely to satisfy readers of this book. We could delve further, applying the methods we have explored so far in this chapter. These might involve comparing BorgWarner's cost of capital, beta and price multiples or EBITDA to the company's ESG performance to demonstrate the link between its sustainable purpose and financial value. While all of these approaches are valid, they have two main flaws. Firstly, as just outlined, all these methodologies have individual weaknesses, typically centred on their inability to single out and separate the ESG contributor from other factors. Secondly, and more broadly, they show correlation rather than cause and effect. Put bluntly, what we want to know is: if you invest a dollar in sustainability initiatives, what return can be expected? Therefore, let us apply the three-stage process that has just been highlighted. Please note that this study is hypothetical and based on historical data.

I. Status Quo BorgWarner's financial and non-financial KPIs were compiled and analysed based on the company's published financial and sustainability reports, as shown in Figure 4.17. Of significance in this regard was BorgWarner's annual sustainability report, which underscores the group's governance, oversight, policies, programmes and performance on issues pertinent to sustainability. The report adheres to the standards issued by SASB, TCFD and GRI, providing not only enhanced visibility into ESG activities but also assurance that they are grounded in established methodologies that facilitate peer review and comparison.

Although external ESG ratings are not a core part of the Value Bridge methodology, they can provide valuable data and insights into areas of underperformance and effective peer comparison. According to Refinitiv information, more than 630 ESG measures are captured, of which 186 drive the overall scoring process. Subsequently, these measures are aggregated into 10 categories and three pillars, ultimately resulting in the ESG score. The ranking is based on Boolean, numeric and industry group data points.

Financial KPIs

Currency: $ m	FY19 A	FY20 A	FY21 A	FY22 A	FY23 A	FY24 B	FY25F	FY26F
Revenues	10,168	10,165	11,803	12,635	14,198	14,086	13,938	14,579
EBITDA	1,742	1,186	1,468	1,561	1,757	1,231	1,978	2,075
EBITDA-margin	17.1%	11.7%	12.4%	12.4%	12.4%	8.7%	14.2%	14.2%
Total assets	9,702	16,029	16,575	16,994	14,453	13,993	15,328	16,385
Trade Working Capital	1,363	1,869	2,173	1,556	1,894	2,099	1,620	1,694
TWC as % of revenues	13.4%	18.4%	18.4%	12.3%	13.3%	14.9%	11.6%	11.6%
Capex	n/a	(445)	(508)	(602)	(802)	(649)	(642)	(774)
Free cash flow	–	(2,420)	(396)	(53)	2,988	952	1,641	795

Source: Annual report, analyst consensus forecast, simplified assumptions

Segments

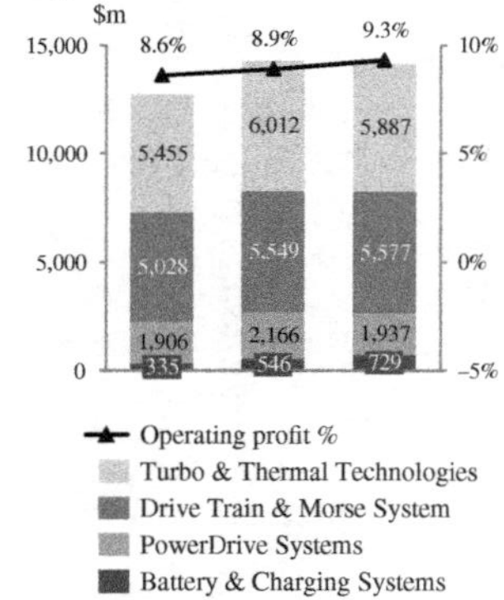

Regions

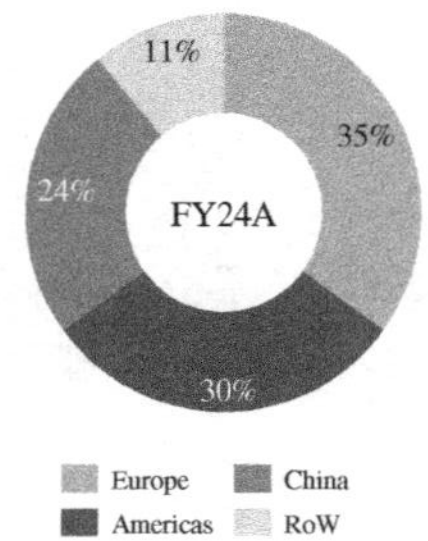

ESG metrics - Environmental

		FY21A	FY22A	FY23B
CO2 emissions	kt	538.6	407.4	379.4
Energy use	kGJ	5,602	5,184	3,913
Renewable energy purchased	kGJ	144	846	765

ESG metrics - Social

		FY21A	FY22A	FY23B
Employees	#	>29,000	>50,000	>49,300
Turnover employees	%	21.9	22.8	18.0
Women employees	%	30.1	30.8	30.1

ESG metrics - Governance

		FY21A	FY22A	FY23B
Audit committee independence	%	100	100	100
Board gender diversity	%	30	37.5	37.5
Sustainability reporting	y/n	Y	Y	Y

Figure 4.17 BorgWarner KPIs at a glance.

Source: Annual Report, Analyst Consensus Forecast, Simplified Assumptions

II. Risk and Opportunities The next stage is to identify the ESG risks and opportunities within BorgWarner's operations that could potentially weaken or enhance the company's financial performance. This was achieved by following up on the 'leads' identified during the scoping/status quo process. For example, as shown in Figure 4.18, it was evident from examining the financials that energy use and costs were rising sharply. Reducing these could result in a 'triple win' by cutting costs, reducing emissions and improving environmental ratings. Social risks and opportunities included enhancing product safety and quality to boost customer satisfaction. Other social opportunities involved improving staff retention and turnover by, for instance, offering child-care solutions. Additionally, better incentivisation of staff through a combination of performance tracking tools and rewards for achieving set goals was recognised as a social opportunity that could drive financial performance (higher retention, higher engagement, less sick leave, etc.). In the Governance pillar of ESG, key risks and opportunities were identified concerning board skills, accountability for key targets and enhancements to the quality and cost of company audits. Rather than presenting a list of 'nice to haves', each element was assessed against a set of requirements, identifying any need for further work.

III. Measure, Monitor and Strategies – Building the Value Bridge Having identified areas for potential improvement, the means to achieve them, and the likely outcomes in terms of both financial enhancement and ESG performance, the next step is to model any proposed investment and/or initiative. As we outlined at the beginning of this book, ESG investments may provide environmental or social value, either within the company or beyond it; however, our focus is on demonstrating financial value to the company and its investors. The aim of our Value Bridge methodology, then, is to project the financial value (less costs) of specific ESG investments in the form of enhanced EBITDA and/or free cash flow. Figure 4.19 summarises the costs and revenue enhancements of specific projects and their contribution to overall value.

A note on methodology: The level of EBITDA improvement may vary according to several factors, including investor profile, regional

ID	• ESG category: ENVIRONMENTAL – CO_2 Emissions • Primary transmission channel: Manufacturing demand, Secondary transmission channels: Transportation / Distribution Supply	
Risk vs. Opp.	Risk	
Description	Increase in CO_2 emissions from manufacturing processes and transportation	
Methodology	I. Assess **current emissions for Scope 1, Scope 2 and Scope 3** II. Improvise methods of reduction of CO_2 emissions from each individual process.	
Required metrics & data source	**Inside-out** • Details on manufacturing process • Energy consumption in processes • Benchmarking with peer groups • Electricity & other fuel consumption • Business travels & transportation details	**Outside-in/ Peer Group** • Discussion with Sustainability department • Electricity & energy consumption within industry • Annual / Sustainability reports • Current methods & processes • Average business travel within locations
Impacted ESG-metrics	• CO_2 Emission KPI's according to the environmental pillar	
Literature, sources	• GHG Protocol, TCFD, SASB, UN SDG(s), GRI	

Figure 4.18 Key environmental risks and opportunities.

Source: GHG Protocol, TCFD, SASB, UN SDG(s), GRI

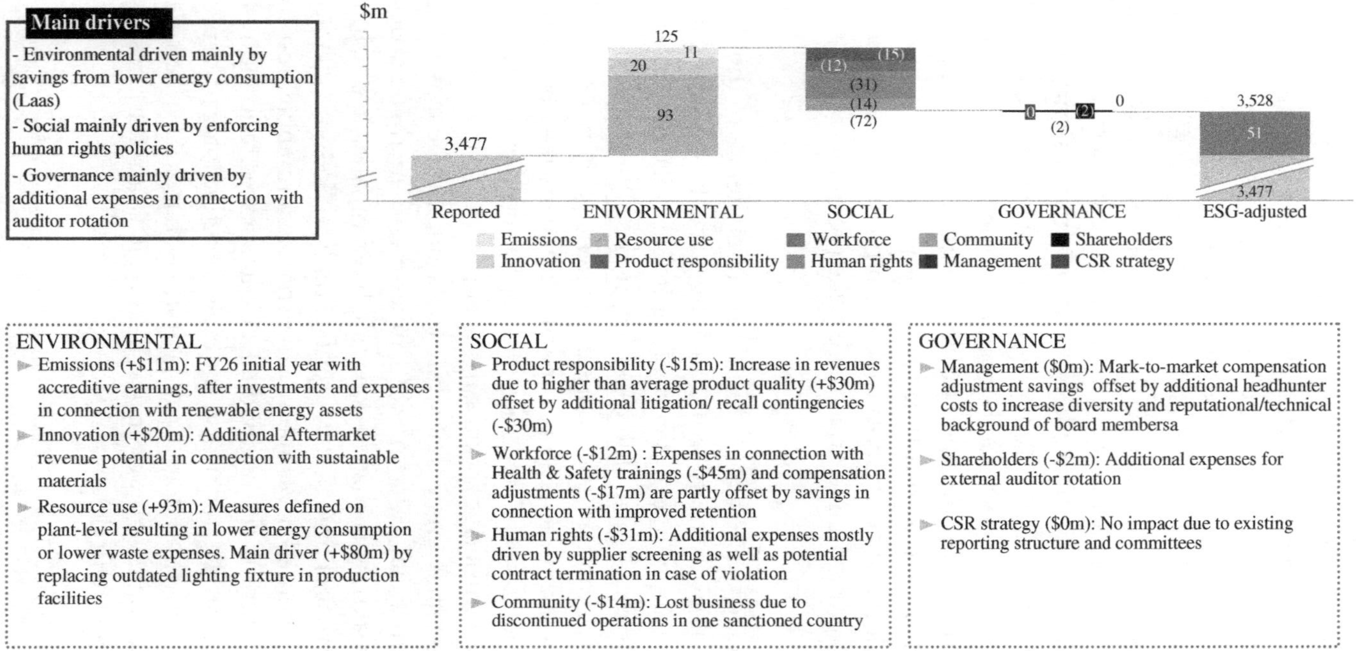

Figure 4.19 The Value Bridge – from ESG investment to projected financial return.

Source: Industry Research

perception and the influence of ESG factors, as well as the potential to generate synergies out of different asset portfolios.

It is essential to remember that, although this is a practical and highly focused tool, it remains a theoretical one. It is designed to provide the foundation upon which strategic ESG investments can be identified and decided. The effectiveness of their execution, along with any unexpected events along the way, will ultimately determine their success. However, what we can say with some certainty is that this more granular approach is likely to offer better insight into how improved ESG performance can positively impact financial value. This concept or model could also be applied to support discussions and decisions regarding a company's product portfolio. This approach could forecast the success or otherwise of product lines, taking into account any necessary investments to stay compliant, and even address the potential to grow volume or achieve price premiums.

Stepping Back to Consider The counterargument to the Value Bridge methodology is that, while avoiding the broad correlations between ESG performance and cost of capital or price multiples that previous models rely on, it shifts too far in the other direction. By becoming overly granular, the counterargument goes, it loses value. Hundreds of hours of research on a specific company may be required to evaluate all its ESG-related risks and opportunities to model the financial value of initiatives addressing them.

So, detractors may argue that while the Value Bridge may reveal a lot about the financial value of ESG investments in that particular company, its weakness is that it does not have broader applicability. We can answer that charge on two fronts. Firstly, there is no guarantee that any ESG-flavoured investment will generate a financial return; it will always depend on the individual circumstances. Secondly, this may be a one-off study, but it also outlines a methodology. Applying the Value Bridge methodology is no guarantee that ESG investments deliver financial value. However, we believe it is a robust means to assess whether they will do so or not.

Chapter Summary

- There is a strong correlation between a higher ESG performance and a lower cost of capital, primarily driven by a combination of lower beta, improved risk management and the ESG appetite of banks and other investors.
- There is also a strong correlation between high ESG performance and higher price multiples. This results from lower costs of capital, enhanced risk management and more substantial margins achieved from meeting customer expectations. We found that EBITDA and free cash flow also correlate positively with higher ESG performance.
- Although these correlations may imply that investing in high ESG performers is sufficient on its own to create value, this is not the case. The correlation is based on aggregated data and largely external factors, such as ESG ratings, and cannot be reliably applied to specific investment decisions regarding individual companies.
- Our Value Bridge methodology seeks to determine, on a case-by-case basis, whether investments are likely to deliver financial value by carefully examining the company's current status, identifying ESG risks and opportunities and modelling the financial benefits over time.

References

Association of the Luxembourg Fund Industry (2024). European Sustainable Investment Funds Study 2024. https://www.alfi.lu/en-gb/pages/setting-up-in-luxembourg/responsible-investing/european-sustainable-investment-funds-study-2024 (accessed 12 August 2025).

The Guardian (2025). BP Blames 'Misplaced' Faith in Green Transition for its Renewed Focus on Fossil Fuels. https://www.theguardian.com/business/2025/feb/26/bp-oil-and-gas-spending-green-energy-scale-back (accessed 12 August 2025).

Morgan Stanley (2025). Sustainable Fund Returns Lag Peers' in Second Half of 2024. https://www.morganstanley.com/insights/articles/sustainable-funds-performance-second-half-2024 (accessed 12 August 2025).

MSCI (2024). MSCI ESG Ratings and Cost of Capital. https://www.msci.com/research-and-insights/paper/msci-esg-ratings-and-cost-of-capital (accessed 22 July 2024).

5

ESG Due Diligence and the Private Equity Playbook

In Chapter 4, we examined the link between ESG performance and financial value. Now, we move on to consider the vital role of ESG due diligence in realising that value, by identifying and quantifying ESG risks and value creation opportunities during the transaction process. We then explore how, during the due diligence process, Private Equity firms use ESG insights to support the investment thesis and develop a business case that can deliver financial value within the required timeline. Finally, we examine the framework and playbook that Private Equity players use to unlock this value.

What Is ESG Due Diligence? An Overview

During ESG due diligence, value identification and creation stem from assessing the current ESG situation (what has already been done in terms of ESG, to what extent and how it compares to its peers and the industry) and identifying the risks, opportunities and sustainability strategies (including planned initiatives, investments, impact and their progress to date) that enhance a portfolio company's financial performance. These may include improvements that reduce costs, increase revenues, enable access to green capital and tax incentives, align/adjust the business model or mitigate risks associated with business disruptions and value erosion.

In broad terms, the ESG due diligence process should be regarded as an integral part of the standard diligence process and can be broken down into the following three main steps:

1. Scoping
   - Define the ESG materiality for the sector and transaction, including:
     - o Identify material ESG topics based on industry and business model
     - o Incorporate client and target ESG priorities into material topics
     - o Tailor the evaluation criteria and metrics to assess current ESG performance.
     - o Perform a value chain assessment to consider additional ESG factors.
2. Analyse the ESG maturity and align with relevant ESG frameworks (e.g., SASB, GRI, TCFD):
   - Evaluate Target's ESG profile, focusing on current initiatives and investments related to significant ESG topics/issues.
   - Examine trends and market influencers relevant to ESG.
   - Identify areas of ESG non-compliance, focusing on industry and business model-specific aspects; evaluate the impact of ESG actions and risks; and conduct benchmarking analysis.

Both of these first two steps will include review of ESG policies, audits, certifications, historical ESG performance data and legal and compliance records (for more detail see Appendix 1).

3. Undertake an Impact Assessment
   - Recognise the risks and opportunities (ESG red flags) associated with the current ESG landscape, including possible corrective actions and potential deal-breakers.
   - Assess the impact of ESG on the business model, market/customer connections, competitive dynamics and significant effects on the business plan.

- Understand how ESG can be utilised as a value driver in the future and create a value roadmap.
- Provide a comprehensive assessment of potential performance improvement opportunities and value actions (size, timing, complexity, effort) required to realise and link the financial implications to the business case or investment thesis.

The outcomes of the three main steps will form part of and will be integrated into the valuation, adjusting financial models and cash flows for ESG (including capex for remediation, carbon pricing) as necessary. Furthermore, the cost of capital should reflect the risk exposure and mitigation strategies as well. At the same time, a Post-Deal Action Plan will be developed, focusing on key areas and priorities, implementation and the capabilities to track and monitor progress, intervening or correcting as needed. The Post-Deal Action Plan will be further discussed in the Private Equity Playbook section.

Today, most companies conduct ESG diligence and analysis to satisfy compliance requirements for the investors and avoid (unnecessary) liabilities and unforeseen risks, which could be described as a 'hygiene' or 'tick the box' approach. However, as we will examine, advanced investors are increasingly applying ESG diligence and analysis to evaluate the impact of ESG factors on the business models and to identify value drivers that are and can be linked to financial benefits (including cost savings, revenue opportunities, capital access or tax incentives). As mentioned before, another driver for detailed ESG due diligence is that the scores from the ratings agencies are not always sufficient to satisfy the requirements of the investor or investment committee of a Private Equity when assessing a thesis/proposal, especially when it relates to the acquisition of a division or business unit of a larger company.

ESG Due Diligence and the Shift to Value

In Chapter 1, we examined how, as ESG has evolved, the focus has been shifting from risk identification and mitigation to value identification and creation.

In other words, companies that traditionally utilised ESG primarily to mitigate regulatory, financial or reputational risks have begun to view it as well as a potential opportunity for differentiation and new

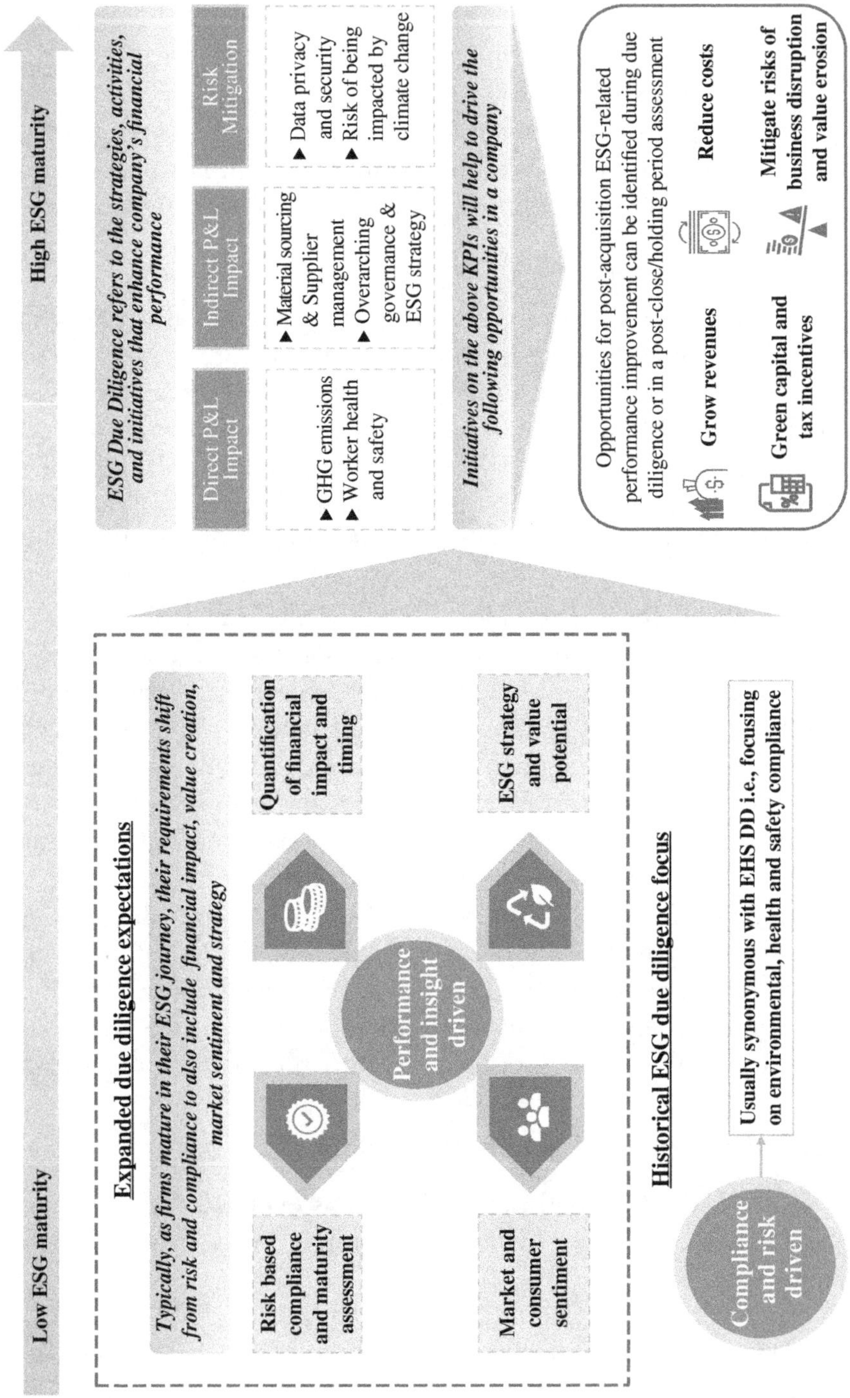

Figure 5.1 Shift in focus from risk mitigation to value creation.

Source: Industry Research

products/markets, ultimately leading to a potentially higher valuation and lower cost of capital, as explored in Chapter 4. This change in focus and mindset is also reflected in evolving attitudes towards ESG due diligence. Figure 5.1 illustrates how, historically, ESG due diligence has concentrated on risk and compliance, but the scope is now gradually broadening. Of course, this depends on the type of asset and industry sector. Still, in general terms, as firms progress in their ESG journey, their requirements evolve from risk and compliance to value creation.

Supporting Evidence of the Shift to Value

The Global ESG Due Diligence+ study 2024 (KPMG, 2024) supports our view that ESG due diligence is increasingly important and value-additive to transactions. It found that four out of five dealmakers had ESG considerations firmly on their radar during M&A. This is a growing trend, with 71% of respondents reporting an increase in the importance of ESG in transactions in the last 12 to 18 months. It also looks like the role of ESG due diligence is set to rise further, with 57% of global respondents saying they expect to perform ESG due diligence on most of their transactions over the next two years (up from 44% in 2022). On the opposite side of the fence, only 6% say they will continue not to conduct any ESG due diligence over the same period (down from 19% in 2022).

What is behind this trend? The study found that 58% of global respondents were motivated by the belief that ESG due diligence increases financial value. One reason, perhaps, is that 59% of global respondents are willing to pay a premium for a target that demonstrated a high level of ESG maturity.

Figure 5.1 maps this evolution of ESG due diligence from a compliance and risk driven focus (focused on regulatory exposure, management systems and recordable incidents) to a more performance and insight-driven focus (focused on ESG-related risks and their impact on business operations and business models, consumer sentiment and market perception of ESG performance, and quantified financial impacts and valuation of target).

Three Approaches Towards ESG Due Diligence in Transactions

Overall, we can identify three approaches towards ESG diligence in transactions and their application levels.

The first approach is focused on ensuring ESG compliance with a primary focus on identifying any areas of non-compliance that may facilitate price reduction. This non-compliance can adversely affect investment returns and be a deal-breaker, primarily due to increased regulatory pressure from the SFRD, CSRD and EU Taxonomy. This approach/focus is considered and applied in almost all transactions.

The second approach is focused on considering the impact ESG may have on the fundamentals of the business model, market dynamics, customer behaviour and competitive dynamics. The primary focus is on identifying risks and opportunities beyond compliance to ensure the long-term attractiveness of the business model. This approach/focus is increasingly considered and applied in transactions.

The third approach focuses on leveraging or optimising ESG drivers and initiatives crucial for realising growth potential. This means a detailed understanding of the ESG-related value drivers on revenues, profits, enterprise value and fundraising conditions so that EBITDA, Capex and Opex can be managed strategically to maximise overall investment returns. This approach/focus is now also increasingly considered and applied in transactions.

As a result of all the above, ESG due diligence is evolving and becoming more an integral part of the core investment decision. It is probably fair to say that Private Equity firms have been at the vanguard of this shift, so let us look at how they do it.

The Private Equity Approach to ESG Due Diligence

Why are we focusing on Private Equity? Because the Private Equity sector is home to some of the most experienced and detail-oriented investors and operators, if they recognise the financial value of sustainability, you can be sure it is real and that their tools and techniques are likely to interest any reader seeking practical insights. Therefore, let us explore how Private Equity operators identify, nurture and operationalise financial value.

We will focus on how Private Equity identifies, assesses, values and addresses ESG considerations. We will demonstrate how the investment thesis (and business case) is central and core to the entire Private Equity transaction process, as well as the level of detail of due diligence conducted on the target company. The results of the due diligence process will, in turn, influence and shape the content, the focus areas and the financial implications of the investment thesis. Next, we will uncover the ESG-related levers that value-driven Private Equity firms utilise to achieve strong returns in their portfolio companies. Along the way, readers will find that there is nothing new under the sun, in the sense that many aspects of ESG diligence have always been integral to traditional due diligence processes, such as operational and commercial due diligence but with a specific focus on ESG, particularly in identifying the key risks as well as cost and revenue levers that will have a financial, commercial, operational and tax impact.

First, to better understand their unique approach, let us take a moment to explain what Private Equity is and how it operates.

What Is Private Equity, and What Can It Tell Us About ESG-driven Value?

In its simplest form, Private Equity raises funds from investors. It uses the proceeds, along with borrowed money, to acquire private companies, increasing their value and realising that value through a sales process. It approaches these investments with an expected/anticipated specific return and timeline in mind, typically five to seven years, depending on the type of asset and industry sector.

In terms of the focus of our book, two critical areas emerge from this high-level introduction. Essentially, Private Equity has a relentless focus on both time and value. As we discussed in Chapter 1, the ‘payoffs’ for sustainability tend towards the longer term, potentially creating challenges for Private Equity timescales. As for value, we have already explored in detail that measuring the relationship between ESG and financial value is complex and at times elusive. Private Equity has the potential to shed light on both areas, providing valuable insights into how value can be created from ESG within a short- to medium-term perspective.

The role of ESG-related due diligence is critical in this respect. By examining how Private Equity utilises due diligence to identify and execute ESG initiatives, we can gain valuable insights into the relationship between sustainability and financial value.

Private Equity – Types and Variants, Including Venture Capital and Impact Funds

It is worth briefly noting that there are different types of Private Equity transactions, ranging from single versus club deals to majority versus minority holdings. The nature and size of the individual transaction, as well as the type of Private Equity firm involved, will influence this.

A club deal is a Private Equity buyout in which several Private Equity firms pool their assets to acquire a company. By collaborating on these deals, Private Equity firms can purchase more expensive companies and distribute the risk among the participating firms.

A minority investment involves a Private Equity firm acquiring a non-controlling stake in a company. In contrast, majority investments give the Private Equity firm control, allowing it to influence board composition and management decisions.

In addition to Private Equity, it may be helpful to identify and distinguish between venture capital (VC) and impact funds.

Venture capital refers to a type of Private Equity financing that investors provide to early-stage, high-potential startups and small businesses that are believed to have long-term growth potential. In general, venture capitalists provide companies with seed funding in these cases in exchange for a share of the business. Typically, venture capitalists do not require a majority share (over 50%), an arrangement which can appeal to founders who prefer to maintain control of their startup. Typically, VCs target companies that have not reached a level of maturity that allows them to pass the credit and investment committees of other financing institutions.

Impact Funds – The Exception That Proves the Private Equity Rule?

Impact funds are typically investment vehicles designed to generate both financial returns and measurable positive social or environmental outcomes. These funds are part of the broader impact investing movement, but with the scale, discipline and capital associated with Private Equity.

In other words, their objective is to create measurable nonfinancial benefits alongside making a financial return. Typically, these funds are thematic, investing in areas including energy transition, sustainable agriculture, education and healthcare.

At first sight, impact funds may seem to counter the argument we have made so far in this chapter, that PE has a relentless focus on financial value alone. However, some Private Equity firms also feel a broader responsibility and Impact Funds can provide a way to attract pools of capital with a focus on sustainable investing and/or theme(s) of the individual fund. Impact funds can also enhance reputational value, establish differentiation in a crowded marketplace and help Private Equity funds attract talent.

According to Phenix Capital's 2024 Impact Report, the number of Private Equity impact funds increased by 219% over the previous decade to a total of 1,459 funds by early 2025, raising a combined €214 billion in capital (Phenix Capital, 2024). So, perhaps this is the exception that proves the rule. While social or environmental impact may be the goal of these funds, in almost all cases, it is their financial value to Private Equity players that drives their creation.

In Appendix 2 we have compared three global Private Equity firms, on an illustrative basis, on how they approach ESG in their own firms.

The Private Equity Process from Start to Finish

Figure 5.2 provides an overview of the Private Equity transaction process and investment lifecycle from Opportunity Identification and Evaluation to Exit/Sale of the portfolio company. Although it is not necessary to describe every stage here, several key points are worth highlighting, as we will later connect them directly to ESG-related aspects of value creation.

The first point to note is how early the assessment of the potential target and value creation process begins. This means in practice that in the early stage of the transaction, when developing the investment thesis or investment strategy, ESG will play a substantial role in the pre-screening of the target (any big issues or risks to be aware of), the sustainable business model valuation and the deal team education on ESG. In the Opportunity Evaluation phase, Private Equity firms comprehensively analyse the target company and the broader market to identify the foundation and key components of the investment thesis, value opportunities (both top and bottom lines) and develop a strategy. At this stage, key ESG issues and a high-level estimate of their potential financial impact will already be identified and evaluated. Senior advisers and subject matter experts will often be appointed to inform and develop the investment thesis in more detail, including the challenges and issues to consider and overcome. Any bid for the target company will be based on a specific, well-thought-out plan for value creation and exit. As illustrated with examples later in the chapter, this thesis will have already identified the potential risks/ challenges as well as the key opportunities to create financial value through ESG strategies, primarily if the target company operates in an industry where ESG components are prominent and have a significant impact on the purchase price. A key question in this phase is which ESG metrics matter and the target's performance against these metrics. This key question can be broken down into the materiality and maturity assessment, followed by the identification and quantification of the ESG metrics and how these compare against the peer group and industry in which they operate.

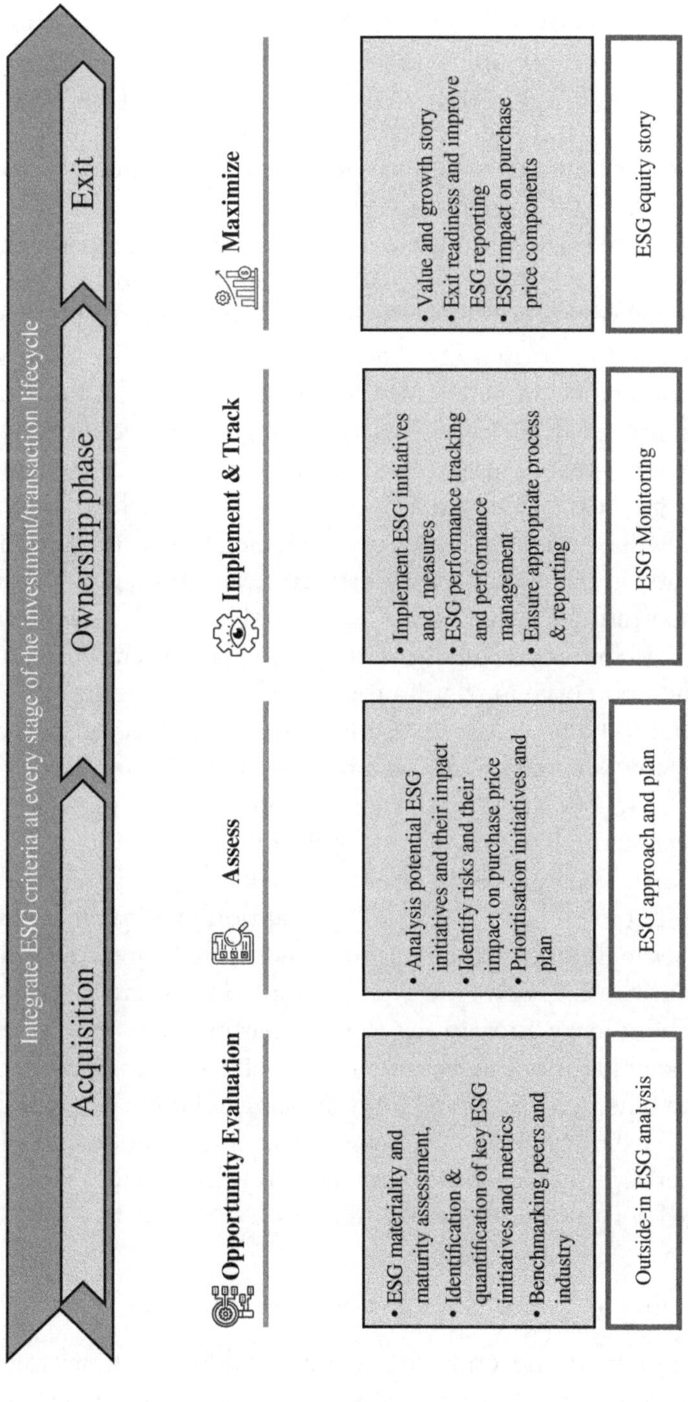

Figure 5.2 ESG along the investment lifecycle of a transaction.

Source: Company Website, Annual Report, Mergermarket

This phase is typically followed by the Assessment phase, which aims to identify what financial returns could be realised from implementing ESG measures in what timeframe and with how much effort/investment. This involves a detailed analysis of the potential measures and their impact, as well as identification of the risks and their potential impact on the purchase price.

Once the Private Equity firm is close to acquiring the company, the focus will be on developing an ESG roadmap, identifying and prioritising the key ESG metrics and implementing and monitoring the progress of the identified and prioritised ESG measures and metrics. Key here is the identification and prioritising of the key ESG metrics, the tracking and reporting of the key ESG initiatives, their progress and performance and link to the identified potential financial benefits (such as cost savings or revenue growth). When the Private Equity firm reaches the exit stage, the focus will be on the equity story, including the position of the portfolio company in the market, its cost structure/cost base, growth trajectory and opportunities. From an ESG perspective, it will include an update on the ESG initiatives and measures put in place, their status and progress and their potential impact on the value/ purchase price.

It is essential to have a clear investment thesis and a 100-day plan once the company is acquired. These are typically achieved through examining the current business model and exploring ways to improve it, whether by incremental improvement (efficiencies) or more radical steps (innovation). The latter is an often-overlooked aspect when referring to Private Equity, as, in the public's perception at least, its value creation revolves mainly around cost savings such as reducing overhead costs and optimising processes. However, substantial value creation may be unlikely without innovation in the form of new products or services, improved customer insights and reconfigured or refined business models. As illustrated in Chapter 1, sustainability can serve as both a catalyst for efficiency, by, for example, reducing energy consumption and waste, and as a transformer, opening up new markets, innovating new products and services and designing new business models.

The Time Challenge – Short-Term Versus Long-Term

Chapter 1 highlighted the enduring commercial trade-off between short-term priorities and long-term benefits, particularly regarding

ESG. This dynamic exists because many positive impacts, such as strong environmental stewardship, may not become evident for several years. However, the associated costs will show up on the balance sheet much sooner. A Private Equity investor is likely even more aware of this conundrum, as the typical holding period for a portfolio company is, in general, five to seven years. The risk is that by the end of this holding period, some of the ESG investments made during their holding time may not yet be fully realised. There are several ways to look at this challenge. Strong ESG initiatives which have not yet fulfilled their full value creation promise by the point of sale but are clearly on track to do so may have this future promise reflected in the price achieved, enabling the investor to benefit from a more profitable exit (depending on how close to realisation they are and therefore whether they will be accepted in the buyer's valuation assessment). Secondly, as we explore in this chapter, many astute ESG investments and approaches can generate financial value within the Private Equity life cycle. Thirdly, as highlighted in our section on impact funds, there may be specific occasions where funds designed primarily to create longer-term social or environmental value for investors may be more willing to operate within different parameters in terms of both holding period and value expectations.

Dealing with the Time Challenge – The Private Equity Mindset

Private Equity firms often adopt a specific mindset during the transaction process, and particularly from the moment the company has been acquired. This can be broken down into six key areas.

- Cash is king – Private Equity acquisitions are highly leveraged, which instils focus and a sense of urgency into the portfolio company to identify and generate cash as expeditiously as possible.
- Right team in place – Assessment of management often begins even before diligence and intensifies after closing the transaction. Once conclusions made, decisions will be quickly executed.
- Skin in the game – Management often has a substantial stake in the performance of the business, both upside and downside.
- Select stretch points – Private Equity firms quickly identify the few key metrics critical to driving value capture and then track them rigorously.

- Use a long-term lens – While Private Equity firms act with speed, they do not forsake rigorous analysis and thoughtful debate, but without allowing it to become a delay tactic.
- Time is money – There is a bias for action most visibly demonstrated in the 100-day programme that Private Equity firms invariably impose on portfolio companies during the first few months of ownership.

Not much in the six key areas of the Private Equity mindset appears to connect with ESG, except perhaps the long-term lens. Instead, speed, cash and incentives stand out and might appear to have little to do with sustainability. However, there is a central point that underpins all six areas covered and is central to both Private Equity and our book: it is all about (financial) value. To attract investment, Private Equity firms must be laser-focused on value creation, not just through financial engineering but also through substantive operational improvements. This means that ESG often becomes a key value driver and realiser of value, especially in industries where consumer sentiment can play a prominent role. When realising that value, Private Equity focuses on the trinity of cash, revenue and costs. Figure 5.3 illustrates that this combined top and bottom-line approach is constructed from a set of individually achievable initiatives that significantly enhance EBITDA and cash flow. It is important to note that, as in the BorgWarner example in Chapter 4, each of these factors is embedded in the business case and can be tracked in financial terms, thus making a strong link between financial value and ESG. In preparation for an exit, the journey starts with the equity story for the target company, even in scenarios where PEs favour an IPO.

Private Equity ESG Due Diligence in Practice – Asking the Right Questions

In this section, we will describe in more detail the key components of ESG due diligence, which are:

- Materiality Assessment – focus on the areas of ESG that most impact performance

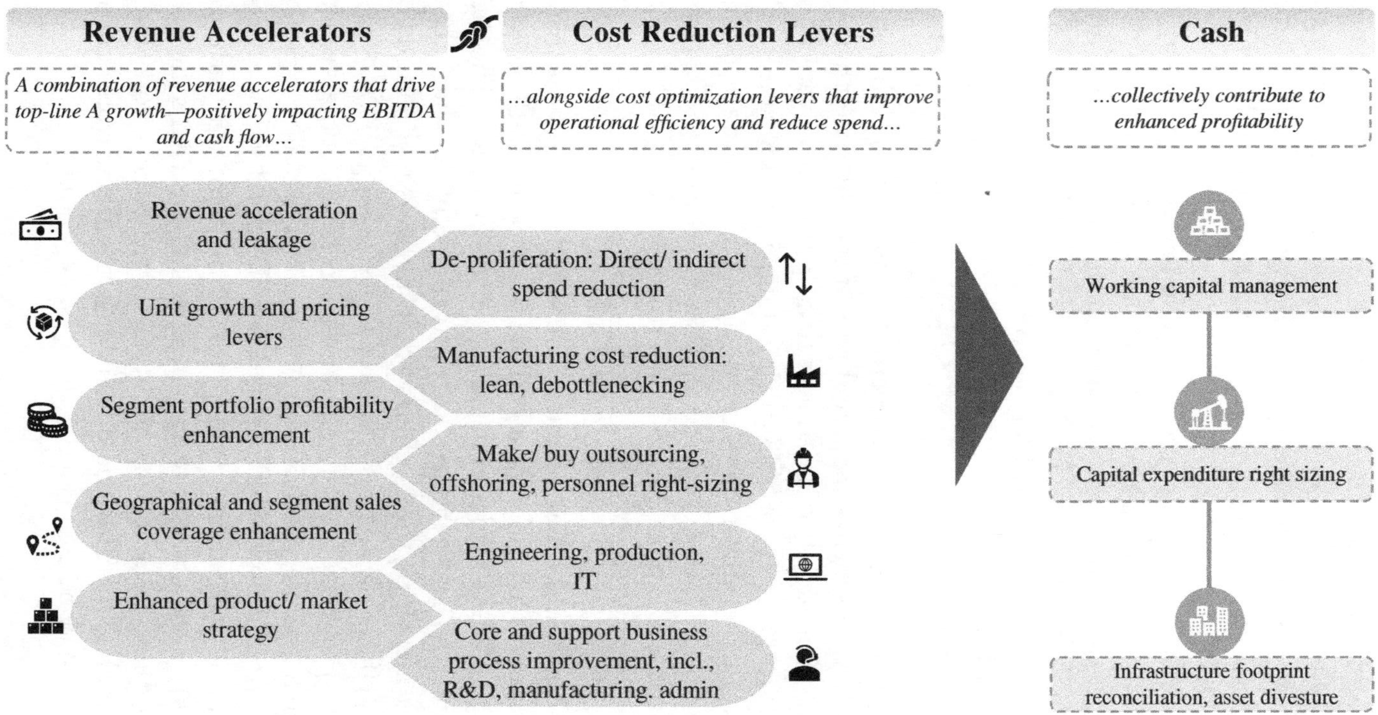

Figure 5.3 The Private Equity focus on Topline, Cost and Cash.

Source: Industry Research

- Maturity Assessment – ensure focus on the ESG aspects most relevant to the target's business model and impact on performance.
- Impact Assessment – focus on identifying key areas post-deal, assessing its potential impact on financial value and evaluating its ability to execute.
- Valuation – focus on and ensure financial implications are included in the valuation and purchase price.
- Post-Deal Action Plan – ensure identified initiatives are implemented, and that progress is monitored, tracked and embedded in the organisation (which is covered in the Private Equity Playbook section of the book).

Materiality and Maturity Assessment As mentioned earlier in the chapter, these assessments are a vital part of the diligence phase of a transaction. A materiality assessment helps potential Private Equity buyers focus on the areas of ESG that most impact performance, either in terms of risk prevention or value creation. The maturity assessment focuses on how well equipped and experienced the target company is to implement and exploit the ESG opportunities identified.

The ESG Materiality Assessment The key objective of the materiality assessment is to ensure focus on the ESG aspects most relevant to the target's business model and impact on performance. This helps allocate financial and other resources to the activities that add the most value, increasing the likelihood that investors will reward companies that effectively address these key issues.

The first problem that a materiality assessment encounters is determining where to start, as there are numerous sustainability topics and subtopics within each of the E, S and G pillars, and various ways of listing or prioritising them. A helpful starting point is to utilise an existing framework. One of the most popular and effective is the SASB Materiality Map, a leading materiality assessment framework and an essential baseline for ESG due diligence. (Other frameworks are also available and may be more suitable for specific sectors.)

The three key steps:

- Identify the ESG topics that are most important to the target sector by using a recognised framework, and supplement or cross-check with other frameworks if necessary.
- Get specific. Frameworks like SASB should be used only as a baseline for materiality assessments. Most companies have unique business models that involve different risk exposures than those suggested by SASB, and these should be identified and assessed.
- Prioritise. After identifying the most critical considerations, evaluate and prioritise the key impacts for due diligence, considering factors such as value impact, company size, sector, deal structure and timeline.

The ESG Maturity Assessment

Essentially, maturity assessments evaluate a business's ability to manage and respond effectively to ESG risks and opportunities. This is crucial because if the target lacks the necessary infrastructure to address any identified ESG-related risks or opportunities during due diligence, its ability to benefit will be significantly hindered.

A maturity assessment examines the infrastructure, governance structures, data collection processes and systems, capabilities, ambitions, procedures and protocols that the target has in place. It helps organisations understand their current ESG status, identify gaps and develop strategies for continuous improvement.

Key steps:

- Assessing the Current State: The assessment begins by evaluating the company's current ESG practices, encompassing strategy, objectives, reporting measures and stakeholder engagement.

(continued)

- Benchmarking: Compare the company's ESG performance to industry and peer benchmarks and best practices to identify its strengths and areas for improvement.
- Gap Analysis: The assessment highlights the gaps between the current state and the desired level of ESG maturity, pinpointing areas where resources and efforts should be directed.
- Action Planning: Based on the assessment, the company can create action plans and strategies to address identified gaps and enhance its ESG performance.
- Continuous Improvement: ESG maturity assessments are typically conducted periodically to monitor progress and ensure the company remains aligned with its ESG goals.

The ESG Impact Assessment

The ESG Impact Assessment focuses on identifying areas of focus post-deal, assessing its potential impact on financial value and evaluating its ability to execute. The outcome of this assessment will inform the prioritisation of areas post-deal, focusing on growth, profit and exit price realisation.

The Impact Assessment focuses on Compliance, Financial Protection, Customer Requirements and Value Creation/Growth, which we will cover in more detail in the following pages.

Compliance The compliance rationale involves evaluating whether the target company has established the necessary components to meet the minimum ESG standards required for compliance and can therefore operate.

This involves verifying that the company meets its disclosure requirements and mandatory certifications. In other words, is it positioned to comply with all current and forthcoming sustainability reporting legislation? Additionally, examining the broader regulatory landscape, is the target abiding by mandatory legal guidelines for all its operations across relevant jurisdictions?

The compliance aspect of ESG encompasses not only assessing the target against external frameworks but also ensuring that internal controls are vital. Does it have the capabilities and resources – whether skills, infrastructure or systems – in place to mitigate key risks in its operations and value chain? This consideration goes beyond regulation. For example, although current legislation may not require the target to apply an ESG screening process to its suppliers, failing to do so could expose it to financially harmful risks. It is essential to recognise that, while all these aspects of ESG due diligence focus on risk prevention, they are also key value drivers. Simply put, a company that is well-compliant and controlled is inherently more valuable, just as a bank that safeguards its depositors' money is likely to be more highly regarded than one that leaves its safe doors open.

Key question: Can the target company comply with existing and upcoming regulations and regulatory requirements?

Supporting questions:

- Is the company compliant with current regulations and legislation, and the buyers' policies and codes of conduct?
- Is the company prepared for the upcoming changes to regulations and legislative requirements?
- What gaps exist in the company's ability to comply, and what investments are necessary to address these gaps (and how they will impact the business case)?
- Are there any incidents in the past that have resulted in liabilities or indicated key risk areas that may impact the business case?

Financial Protection

The Financial Protection rationale reflects the crucial role that ESG plays in the efficient and optimal operation of an organisation through internal enablers, most notably in the effective use of resources. By reducing waste and minimising energy consumption, ESG contributes to optimising the use of energy and materials. Research indicates that adopting sustainable practices can lower long-term operating expenses. For instance, switching to solar energy can decrease utility bills, and most businesses recoup the cost of panels within three to five years. Recycling, enhancing waste management and streamlining energy use can further reduce costs.

Human resources also play a role in the margin, as investing in initiatives to attract and retain talent can enhance revenue and reduce costs.

The next area to consider is access to capital. Does the target company meet the necessary ESG requirements to access the optimum debt or credit-related products and services, many of which have sustainable lending criteria? For example, many banks and lenders consider ESG criteria in their loan approval and pricing decisions.

In a similar vein, has the target made full use of any ESG-related financial incentives? These often take the form of tax breaks (and occasionally hikes) based on the target's ESG performance. As we discovered during Chapter 4, ESG factors can lower the cost of capital, particularly when such factors facilitate access to specific green finance initiatives. In summary, this margin protection and value driver element arises from tax incentives and ESG-linked credit facilities, offering appealing monetisation opportunities.

Key question: Is the target capitalising on the growth and improvement opportunities provided by the increased focus on ESG?

Supporting questions:

- What ESG-related initiatives or investments are planned, and are they appropriately reflected in the Company's business plans?
- What potential opportunities related to ESG exist and are available in the company to improve the cost base/structure and operational efficiency; what would be required to achieve them?
- What is or has been put in place to track and measure progress on the value improvement initiatives? How much will it cost to align the company's non-financial reporting with the buyer's?
- What is the position of the Company's ESG performance and ambition in comparison with those of its peers and competitors in the industry? What is required to become a leader?

Customer Requirements

Meeting customer requirements is central to the company's ability to protect revenue. This involves first understanding current customer needs from an ESG perspective and assessing these against the company's existing practices. For instance, if the target company produces cosmetics tested on animals while customers are increasingly avoiding such products, this would be identified as a threat to revenue. More broadly, are the customer procurement frameworks meeting the minimum standards required by both current and prospective customers? This protective element is not solely focused on meeting minimum standards. For instance, while using plastic packaging may be perfectly legal, failing to transition to recyclable cardboard could result in lost customers and revenue. Meeting customer requirements and protecting revenue involves proactively understanding and somewhat anticipating customer ESG expectations. This is especially true for premium and discretionary consumer products, where tastes and expectations can change quickly, potentially jeopardising value for those who fail to adapt. However, it is essential to recognise that significant investment in revenue protection should be avoided in most cases. Many larger organisations have made the mistake of investing heavily in expensive mergers and acquisitions or extensive operational overhauls that, although they might be described as transformational, are protective.

Key question: With the changing and evolving customer and societal requirements, is the target company able to maintain its current competitive advantage, market position and market share?

Supporting questions:

- To what degree will movements in customer and societal requirements have an impact on the target company's competitive advantage, market position and future revenue stream?
- Which existing and potential new critical ESG risks and challenges is the company facing, what can be done to mitigate these and at what cost?

(continued)

- What is the target company's ESG reputation, and what are the key issues? Will the acquisition have an impact on the buyer's own ESG reputation? What needs to be put in place to protect or improve reputation, and how much will that cost?
- Will the company be able to meet the buyer's ESG targets and ambitions upon acquisition? If not, how much will it cost to bring the company to the required level?

Value Creation and Growth

Now, we transition from compliance and protection to value creation and growth. This involves two distinct components, and we will start with the first: facilitating customer ESG targets and ambitions.

This shift from compliance to value creation and growth means examining ESG aspects that do more than sustain business as usual; instead, they have the potential to influence financial performance positively. This entails a careful trade-off between fulfilling customers' ESG aspirations and growing revenues and managing costs. As discussed in Chapter 1, even a minor improvement, such as altering product packaging, can be highly costly, but unless it is effectively communicated, it may have a minimal impact. Conversely, for instance, replacing one negatively perceived ingredient with another that is more ESG-friendly may incur little expense but can significantly boost sales.

What does this mean in practice? Above all, Private Equity buyers will focus on the direct impact of ESG initiatives on the company's cost base and potential improvements in profit and revenue.

Secondly, how can an initiative assist existing and new customers in reaching their ESG targets or ambitions in the short term? In 2017, UK supermarket chain Asda announced the phase-out of single-use plastic bags, becoming the first supermarket to do so. This aligned with growing customer concerns about their proliferation and the resulting environmental damage.

Can the investment thesis and business case create a long-term competitive advantage, such as being a first mover or capturing market share? Examples in Chapter 1 included an analysis of the breakthrough deodorant, Wild. By reinventing the 'dry stick' deodorant, which had long fallen out of favour with consumers who preferred aerosol options, as a green product, Wild prominently showcased its ESG credentials, securing shelf space and attracting customers.

The second element of value creation is to realise the identified financial value. Let us break this down into three parts:

The first and most important way to realise value is through the customer-facing brand, reputation and market position. This means delivering products that possess the ESG credentials customers desire, supported by appealing products and a strong brand (see Chapter 3 for analysis of customer sentiment towards sustainable products). It is essential to note that business-to-business customers are also increasingly influenced by ESG concerns in their purchasing decisions. The primary drivers for this are the need for corporate buyers of B2B services to have supply chains that meet the corporation's own ESG standards. The second component is employer brand and talent attraction and retention. This recognises that a company's ability to attract, engage and retain employees is crucial to its success, and strong ESG factors can play a significant role in this. It does so in two ways. Firstly, through the environmental and social aspects of ESG. Companies with a positive environmental and societal impact tend to be more attractive and motivating to younger individuals. Secondly, the governance aspect of ESG encompasses human capital governance, now recognised as a core element of the enterprise risk management framework, following the post-pandemic surge in skills shortages. Numerous research findings demonstrate that investing in initiatives to attract and retain talent can lead to enhanced revenue and reduced costs.

The third and final element of realising value is often overlooked and almost always undervalued: communicating the ESG benefits to customers. From a financial perspective, there is little point in having a strong ESG story if you do not convey it to customers convincingly. First movers on sustainability can be the worst offenders in this regard. Such organisations spend years and millions establishing fair practices with suppliers and reducing emissions, setting high standards for disclosures and regularly topping industry benchmarks; yet, little of this may resonate with customers. The second movers often identify what customers want to see and tailor their products and services accordingly, effectively realising the financial rewards. An example here could be a laundry detergent manufacturer with a decade of carefully built sustainability credentials, which then loses out in the marketplace to a newcomer whose brand is built around a simpler sustainability message that resonates with customers and makes them feel good about choosing it. Therefore, a savvy Private Equity player will always pay careful attention to the clarity and impact of their target or acquired company's ESG actions.

Key question: Is the business and operating model of the target company set up to succeed in an impact-focused economy?

Supporting questions:

- Which ESG topics have the highest degree of materiality for the company, and to what degree are they connected to realisation of financial value? What does the company need to do to create this link and alignment?
- To what degree are the target company's existing and new products or services set up to meet the requirements of impact-focused customers?
- Are the target company's infrastructure and operations set up to reduce and create minimal negative impact and optimise and maximise value for stakeholders efficiently?
- Does the target company have R&D plans and programmes in place that can deal with the scale of the company's ESG ambition, and are these costs incorporated into their business plans?

A Bias Towards Compliance

It is noteworthy that three of the four aspects – compliance, financial protection and customer requirements – are defensive, while only one, revenue growth, is directly focused on creating value. Given that Private Equity revolves around value creation, this might come as a surprise. However, it serves as a valuable reminder that in a world where sustainability can often seem somewhat 'fluffy', its greatest strength lies in its ability to protect value.

The Three Foundational Elements

Delivery of Compliance, Financial Protection, Customer Requirements and Value Creation/Growth must be underpinned by the three platform supports of strategy and governance structure, innovation and digital infrastructure (given the impact of AI).

ESG Strategy and Governance Structure Having an articulated ESG strategy which is aligned with the financials and supported/endorsed by senior leadership is critical. This establishes the framework for senior leadership to drive integrated ESG value, ensuring that each member of senior management is directly involved in delivering the ESG strategy from their specific function or responsibility. As mentioned earlier in the book, a successful execution of the ESG strategy goes across the functions of the organisation. Proper governance clarifies the roles of senior executives and managers, holds them accountable and establishes rewards. It also ensures that the developed strategy will be executed effectively across all processes, systems and divisions.

Innovation As we have seen throughout the book, new products and services often best crystallise the changing relationship between customer requirements and sustainability. Therefore, the ability to develop new products and solutions that support ESG-related requirements is essential. This entails having access to top minds and laboratories to transform ideas into new products rapidly. More generally, it involves fostering an agile, innovative and sometimes even a disruptive organisational culture committed to continuous ideation and improvement, but with clear financial metrics and objectives.

Digital Infrastructure This component plays a vital role in supporting everything from facilitating data-driven ESG insights to promoting agile product innovation and protecting against cybercrime.

AI further enhances the capabilities of digital infrastructure by identifying and delivering value. Research indicates that companies successful in digital transformation are nearly twice as likely to prioritise ESG goals within their digital initiatives.

Valuation As addressed in our detailed assessment of individual cost and revenue driver analysis in Chapter 4, the due diligence procedures are tailored to translate the individual ESG-related risks and opportunities into the spreadsheets of M&A managers and financial analysts, resulting in business plans and cash flow forecasts which serve as a fundamental basis for benchmarking against peers and markets. Those scenarios support internal decision-making processes by acting as an instrument to assess the potential transaction, but also to prepare the bid and set a purchase price or offer to the seller and investors. The ability to quantify the impact of ESG factors on company performance throughout the mid-term plan, as well as customer trends and behaviour, regulatory guidance and product innovation and technology shifts, is a key component in setting long-term margin assumptions and maximising valuation.

The Private Equity Professionals' View

Let us now turn instead to the 'expert panel' of leading professionals we spoke to during the writing of this book. What are their attitudes to ESG due diligence, and how do they put it into practice?

During our conversation with Dave Stangis, Chief Sustainability Officer at the leading asset management firm Apollo, we learned that their team has a formal process in place for assessing the risk and impact of ESG factors and understanding how these can be best managed on the journey towards the projected exit. However, Paul Davison, Partner at Softbank, acknowledges that 'it can be challenging to quantify the financial link between ESG factors in due diligence and the impact on the exit price'. Nevertheless, he believes that ESG has an important role to play as an integrated part of not only diligence but also running the business and the decision-making process. Key to this, Paul believes, is looking at the maturity and materiality curve of the target company.

What about the shift from seeing ESG as a risk to viewing it as an opportunity? James Astor, Portfolio Chair in Private Equity, agrees that risk protection remains the key factor: 'As an investor, I want to buy a compliant company, so in that respect, ESG due diligence is a hygiene factor and a tick-the-box exercise. Beyond that, if there is no direct link between ESG and profitability, its appeal drops away quickly'. However, where that link between ESG and financial value exists, the rewards can be high. As an example, James cites TowerBrook Impact Fund's acquisition of Axil, a waste management, recycling and resources company, whose ability to deliver against its clients' cost and ESG goals also drives growth (MergerLinks, 2025).

Dave Stangis is also focused on finding ESG-related opportunities but acknowledges that 'articulating and identifying an opportunity is more difficult than a risk – you need to understand the market, regulators and customer responses'. David Petrie, Head of Corporate Finance at the Institute of Chartered Accountants in England and Wales (ICAEW), believes that ESG due diligence has an important role to play in supporting transactions, 'Despite the current geopolitical climate in North America and more widely, ESG due diligence and strategy remain an important element, and in some cases are the main driver, of investment activity', he says.

Venture Capital funds typically invest in early-stage companies. Here, our inside sources report that target companies are typically too young and too small to focus on sustainability, and potential funders therefore tend to have limited data available to work with. However, our source explains that risks related to areas such as climate change, forced labour and governance will be scored before investment. Regulatory risks are also carefully considered pre- and post-deal. In summary, the Venture Capital focus is very much on ESG risk rather than opportunity. However, as we saw in Chapter 4, many Venture Capital funds do play a vital role in funding high-risk, high-reward innovators in key sustainability areas such as the development of 'clean' plastics.

In terms of time horizons, Paul Davison addresses the elephant in the room by acknowledging that, in comparison to corporates, 'Private Equity has in general a lower degree of interest in ESG because of its clearer focus on profitability and the short term, whereas corporates normally have a longer time horizon'.

The last word goes to Amy Clarke, Co-Founder and Chief Impact Officer, and Rhodri Mason, Chief Executive Officer, at Tribe Capital, the UK's first dedicated Impact Wealth Manager. They believe that a tipping point in finance has already been reached, supported by a growing understanding of ESG as a risk metric; 'that understanding is still playing out – as the industry and approach further mature, we expect the value-add of both to be much better appreciated'.

ESG Due Diligence Examples

The following real but anonymised cases do not necessarily attract headlines or clicks in financial, much less mainstream, media. Yet they demonstrate how ESG due diligence mitigates risk, eliminates deal blockers, enhances bargaining power and lays the groundwork for value creation. Crucially, they usually achieve this while saving the buyer money, rather than incurring costs.

Compliance Considerations During the ESG due diligence of a renewable energy asset operator with annual revenues of £200 million, several issues were identified. These included the need for contingencies related to environmental regulations and potential costs associated with community commitments and climate adaptation plans. Additional funds were necessary to comply with reporting and disclosure requirements. These issues were communicated to the deal team and included in the net debt considerations, with an estimated financial impact of £4 million.

During ESG due diligence on a target in the IT managed services sector, it became clear that the organisation was unprepared for upcoming corporate sustainability disclosure requirements (CSRD). The need for an estimated £1 million annual investment in compliance was factored into the deal price.

Social and Ethical Considerations The potential buyer of a business that produced plasma-derived treatments had ethical concerns about the way the target company collected blood plasma from donors in exchange for monetary compensation. The data-driven sentiment index used during due diligence indicated that the community viewed the target positively and regarded it as a trusted organisation. This enabled the sale to proceed.

Health and Safety The target company operated data centres. ESG due diligence revealed issues regarding the presence of asbestos at specific sites. This potential deal blocker was addressed by:

Including additional capex in the investment thesis and price calculations to reflect the costs necessary for modifying the assets post-acquisition.

Amending the sale and purchase agreement (SPA) wording to shield the client from litigation and compensation costs related to previous asbestos exposure by current or former employees.

Adding SPA wording to safeguard the client against the costs of remedial work, operational disruptions or cessation of activity should undisclosed or unidentified asbestos be found in additional assets after acquisition.

Applying the Private Equity Playbook

Anyone acquainted with Private Equity professionals understands their affinity for a playbook, and with good reason. Many Private Equity funds (not firms) manage multiple portfolio companies, which entails numerous deals and a host of initiatives focused on everything from cost optimisation to growth generation. Implementing a standardised playbook, albeit one that allows for some flexibility, can save significant time, apply best practices and ensure consistency. Thus, in this spirit, we will share the six post-completion stages that Private Equity follow from an ESG perspective to create value in an acquired company.

The Six Stages of Value Creation (Post-Acquisition)

Please note that the core of these stages will be the investment thesis aligned with the value creation plan, which is developed in the due diligence phase:

1. Confirm the ESG, industry, sector and competitive landscape in which the business operates and adjust, if required, the impact on the business model of the acquired portfolio company.

2. Re-assess the acquired portfolio company's most important ESG opportunities and risks (materiality assessment) and their impact on the financial business case.
3. Cross-check how well equipped the company is to manage its most material ESG opportunities and risks (maturity assessment).
4. Refresh the due diligence assumptions which were made during the diligence phase and mapping of the ESG value drivers, followed by the identification of the ESG value channels and metrics that will influence and impact financial performance and company value.

This marks the point where theory transitions into practice, utilising learnings and insights from due diligence, materiality, maturity and impact assessments to inform the post-deal value creation plan, its execution and monitoring. Or, to put it another way, having confirmed in stages 1 to 3 and refreshed if required in stage 4, the focus will now be on implementation and execution and tracking the progress of the plans.

5. Quantify the ESG value and develop plans to realise it.
6. Execute the plan and measure/report against it.

In other words, having identified and quantified the ESG value opportunity, it is time to develop and deliver the plan. Then, after executing that plan, it is time to measure and report on its success (or otherwise).

This illustrates how DD and ESG play a crucial role in every stage of the transaction. It is also worth noting the similarities between the Private Equity playbook and the Value Bridge methodology described at the end of Chapter 4. In essence, both are identifying the current state, uncovering ESG-related opportunities and then taking action to create financial value from them.

In summary, ESG due diligence starts in the deal generation phase, helps to power the investment thesis and informs execution and sets expectations for value realisation at the exit/sale stage.

An Electric Example

This fictional case study tracks a single ESG-related aspect of the target company through each stage of the playbook. The authors assume that the reader is managing the process and will, therefore, address you in the second person. During your preliminary assessment of the target business, you notice that it operates a fleet of ageing vans that use diesel fuel. You are considering the merits of replacing the fleet with electric vehicles. You then recall the six stages you have just read about in this chapter and begin to apply them. At stage one, the business model and context, you confirm the analysis of the current market situation. How many peer companies are already utilising electric fleets and how successful are they? What trends are emerging? Is the industry moving towards greater electrification? Is the availability of charging infrastructure supporting the business model? You then carry out the materiality assessment (Stage 2). Are the regulatory requirements material to your target? Could the company face fines or additional taxes if it maintains its current fleet? Additionally, you may want to explore customer expectations. If your delivery vans service customer homes rather than delivering to commercial premises, the significance of this factor may be heightened. Stage 3, the maturity assessment, will help determine how well the company can manage the process. Does it have an effective buying process to procure an electric fleet? Which suppliers are they collaborating with? Additionally, does it possess the physical infrastructure needed to maintain and charge the new fleet, and will the residual used vehicle values support the future replacement of the fleet?

You will also assess the fleet from a compliance and financial protection perspective. Further restrictions on vehicle emissions could prevent your fleet from operating in clean air zones or expose it to fines for doing so. The increased costs associated with servicing and additional vehicle excise duties for diesel vehicles could threaten profit margins. More frequent breakdowns and failure to meet minimum customer standards could hinder revenue protection.

Having conducted your due diligence, material assessment and maturity analysis and refreshed these using everything you have learnt so far (Stage 4), it is time to incorporate them into ESG value quantification, Stage 5. What are the costs, working capital requirements and other considerations of the identified initiatives and plans? How do they compare against the opportunities, such as lower energy use, improved efficiency in terms of greater deliveries per driver and enhanced customer sentiment scores (we saw in Chapter 3 how this can strongly correlate with financial performance)? Now, based on the identified value of these plans and the prioritisation of these plans you will develop a programme of plans aimed at achieving the identified financial value of these plans.

As a Private Equity professional, you will initiate your 100-day plan straight away. You organise the procurement and delivery of a new fleet and monitor its performance year by year against the financial value targets and measurement methods you have established. This addresses the sixth and final stage.

Now, let us rewind and review according to the four areas of focus referred to earlier in the chapter: compliance, financial protection, customer requirements and value creation/ growth. First, by electrifying the fleet, you maintain your license to operate by complying with regulatory requirements and industry standards. Second, you protect your financial margins by controlling costs and meeting minimum customer requirements of sustainability. Third, having electrified the fleet, you can now access new opportunities and, fourth, create and exploit growth opportunities. For example, your new fleet may enable your company to enter new market segments that demand higher ESG standards.

What Happens If ESG Is Ignored?

So far, we have examined ESG due diligence, rationale, value levers and strategic enablers. Finally, let us consider the other side. What if we ignored them all?

The white boxes illustrate what may occur if no investment is made in, or attention paid to, ESG. The first white box highlights lost revenue due to the erosion of brand value, as the brand does not align with customer ESG expectations. The adjoining black box illustrates the costs associated with addressing this issue, specifically the investment in product development to create new lines that meet customer expectations.

The following white box focuses on unsustainable operations, which may be characterised by high emissions or excessive energy and water use. The cost here typically involves higher operating expenses resulting from inefficient equipment and manufacturing processes. The adjoining black box demonstrates how ESG-inspired investments in cleaner operating methods can help reduce these inefficiencies.

The next white box addresses value chain disruptions, which may stem from various issues, including raw material shortages, resource scarcity, changing weather patterns and geopolitical conflicts. The adjoining black box illustrates how investing in value chain resiliency can help mitigate this value leakage. Related to this is the subsequent white box, which examines non-compliant fines and penalties resulting from insufficient regulatory awareness and inadequate control over the company's activities concerning ESG rules and frameworks. The associated costs manifest as fines and penalties resulting from environmental and human rights violations, which may arise from supplier actions, underscoring the need for implementing proper ESG screening. Supply chain non-compliance can result in substantial financial and reputational damages, including fines, operational disruptions, revenue losses and damage to a company's reputation and market share. International companies that fail to comply with the EU Corporate Sustainability Due Diligence Directive by 2027 may face fines of up to 5% of their global turnover. The adjoining black box illustrates how these losses are countered by investing in governance improvement costs.

Overall, observing Figure 5.4, it is clear that a lack of ESG-related investment contributes to value leakage, causing EBITDA to decline from left to right. The ESG investments shown in the black boxes mitigate that value loss, keeping EBITDA stable. This further emphasises the robust protective nature of ESG initiatives; however, a savvy Private Equity firm would likely look beyond merely maintaining EBITDA to generate additional value through some of the strategies discussed earlier in the chapter.

This diagram is purely illustrative. The cost of implementing ESG initiatives will, of course, vary significantly based on objectives, investment levels and timelines. However, we believe it is reasonable to assume that in most cases, the costs associated with poor ESG performance will exceed expenditures.

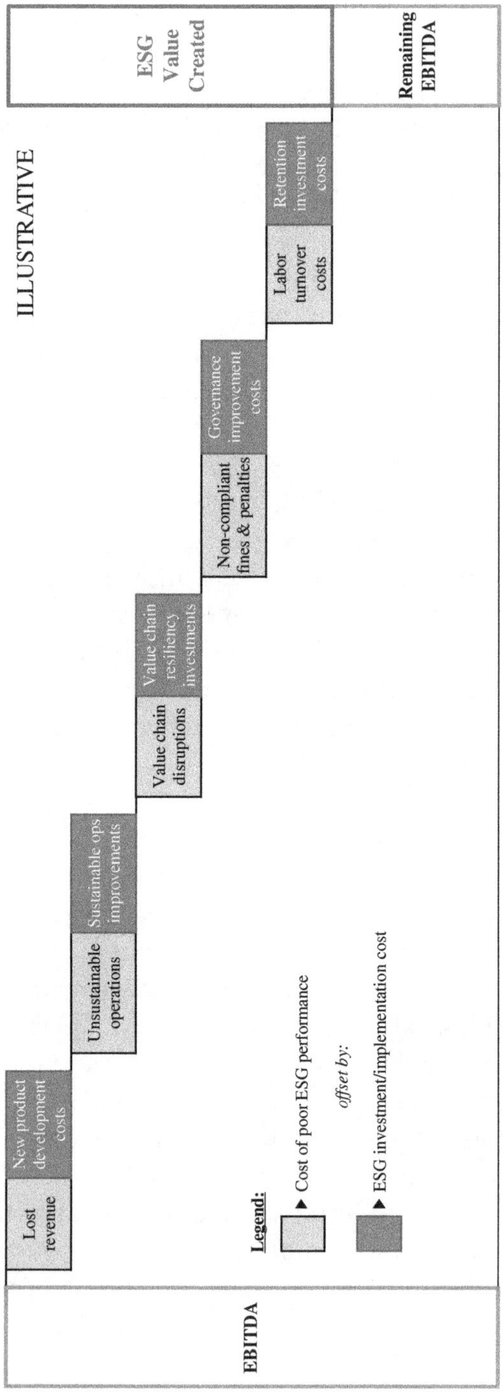

Figure 5.4 The impact of ignoring ESG.

Source: Industry Research

The key point is that, to evaluate potential value creation, it is important to quantify not only the implementation cost but also the impact of neglecting ESG-related improvements. In simpler terms, if you do not incorporate ESG into your investment thesis, it will ultimately affect your bottom line.

Chapter Summary

- Traditionally, the ESG element of due diligence was a tick-box activity primarily focused on addressing regulatory requirements.
- The market increasingly recognises that ESG can, in some instances, have a material impact on the purchase and exit price, and has therefore started to move the focus from risk to value.
- In response, more Private Equity firms embed ESG diligence into their transaction diligence process to uncover critical risks and revenue and cost improvement opportunities that will affect the value that can be realised.
- ESG due diligence can play a crucial role across every stage of the transaction process, from selecting targets and identifying hidden ESG value to deciding whether to acquire them and then realising the value that can be created.
- Private Equity funds have a clearly defined process that, as described in this chapter, can be used during due diligence and beyond to realise the financial value of ESG.
- By understanding and emulating the Private Equity ESG playbook and toolkit, all market participants can learn to identify better and unlock the financial value of ESG.

References

KPMG (2024). The Global ESG Due Diligence+ study 2024. https://kpmg.com/xx/en/our-insights/esg/global-esg-due-diligence-study-2024.html (accessed 13 August 2025).

MergerLinks (2025). TowerBrook Completed the Acquisition of a Majority Stake in Axil. https://app.mergerlinks.com/transactions/2025-04-02-axil-integrated-services/dealmakers (accessed 13 August 2025).

Phenix Capital (2024). Impact Report. https://phenixcapitalgroup.com/impact-report (accessed 13 August 2025).

6

When ESG Goes Wrong (And How to Put It Right)

In this chapter, we examine real, high-profile cases in which sustainability-related events have had a significant impact on financial value. While we have tried to make these case studies an engaging read, the real purpose of sharing them is not to criticise or praise the individual companies involved, but to draw from these examples lessons that can be applied more widely.

The Rise and Fall of Boohoo

The first half of 2020 was nearly perfect for online-only fashion retailer Boohoo, as its annual revenues and profits soared. However, a severe ESG scandal was soon to affect the company. On 5 July 2020, The Sunday Times published the findings of an undercover investigation that uncovered workers at a Leicester factory supplying Boohoo clothing were being paid well below the minimum wage. The response was substantial. As reported in The Guardian on Monday, 6 July, 'Shares in Boohoo slumped by 23% to 297p on Monday, the first day since allegations about its supply chain came to light, as investors digested the potential impact of the revelations. The share slump knocked £1.1bn off Boohoo's value on the AIM market in London' (The Guardian, 2020a). Shortly after, Aberdeen Standard Investments, a major shareholder, sold 27 million shares, representing two-thirds of its stake (The Guardian, 2020b). Days later, major retailers including Next, ASOS and Zalando removed Boohoo clothing from their websites (BBC, 2020).

Why It Hurt Boohoo So Much

In 2023, Clarity AI, a provider of sustainability data and solutions powered by AI, conducted research into the impact of ESG controversies on market value. Their study encompassed over 10,000 controversial incidents involving more than 1,500 corporations over four years. Clarity AI's analysis revealed that controversial actions linked to ESG can significantly negatively affect a company's value compared to its peers, resulting in an average fall in valuation ranging from −2% for less severe controversies to −5% for the most severe ones (Clarity AI, 2023).

In Boohoo's case, the reaction of investors appears to outstrip those parameters by far. Why is that? The first issue was the nature of the ESG breach. Not only did it reveal that COVID-19 regulations at the factory supplying Boohoo clothes were breached at a time when public health concerns were high, but it also exposed the exploitation of workers, not in a far-flung place on the other side of the world, but in the UK city of Leicester. The second reason the scandal hit Boohoo so hard was the gap it revealed between the company's stated commitment to ESG and the reality exposed by the investigation. Boohoo had established a reputation for strong ESG performance. Its 2020 annual report (for the year ending February 2019) contained an Environmental, Social and Governance Report declaring that, 'A central theme of our programme is that of transparency and compliance across our ever-expanding supply chain, to have a positive social impact and reduce our environmental impact throughout'. The company also benefited from strong ESG ratings from external agencies, which now came under increasing scrutiny.

Why Did Boohoo Have a Good ESG Rating?

According to data from CSR Hub, an aggregator of ESG ratings, Boohoo had an ESG rating in the top 29th percentile of over 19,000 companies worldwide before the scandal (CSR Hub, 2020), due in part to its impressive set of targets concerning a range of social and environmental issues.

The challenge of gathering accurate ESG ratings data, a substantial amount of which originates from the companies themselves, has been discussed in earlier chapters.

What Boohoo Did to Put Things Right

Boohoo asked senior barrister Alison Levitt KC to carry out an independent review of its supply chain. The Boohoo board immediately declared an Agenda for Change programme and took several steps, including:

Reduced Supplier Base: Boohoo severed ties with numerous suppliers, particularly those unable to demonstrate transparency and adherence to their standards.

Increased Transparency: Boohoo published a list of its approved manufacturers, enhancing the visibility of its supply chain.

Consolidated Supply Chain: Boohoo aimed to collaborate with suppliers who could demonstrate robust management processes and alignment with its standards, leading to a more controlled and transparent supply chain.

Strengthened Auditing: Boohoo enhanced its auditing programme, employing third-party experts to assess supplier performance against its standards.

New Corporate Governance: Boohoo appointed new non-executive directors, including one specialising in environmental, social and governance (ESG) matters.

Mandatory Training: Boohoo implemented mandatory training for its buying teams to ensure they understand and apply new purchasing principles.

Fair Payment Practices: Boohoo pledged to pay suppliers a fair price for garments within realistic timescales.

Supply Chain Compliance: Boohoo made supply chain compliance a mandatory item on the board meeting agenda.

To provide oversight for Boohoo's Agenda For Change programme, Boohoo appointed former High Court judge Sir Brian Leveson. In his fifth and final report, published in March 2023, Leveson commended the group's progress in addressing ethical concerns within the Boohoo supply chain.

Ongoing Scrutiny – Back in the Headlines

Yet, having received such high levels of public exposure due to its perceived ESG failings, scrutiny remained high. This meant that even standard industry practices, such as discounting, were now viewed by the public through an ESG lens. For example, on Black Friday 2022, a demonstration consisting of environmental protestors, trade unionists and workers' rights groups took place outside the headquarters of Boohoo in Manchester to highlight the impact of making such heavily discounted clothes available for sale (Manchester News, 2022). Note how, although all Boohoo's competitors would almost certainly have been offering Black Friday discounts, Boohoo was singled out due to its previous transgressions.

More damaging was the 2023 BBC Panorama documentary, Boohoo's Broken Promises, which claimed that the company was exerting undue pressure on suppliers to reduce costs. The undercover investigation also claimed, 'that Boohoo's flagship Leicester factory, set up to showcase ethical end-to-end garment production in the UK, had sent orders to other factories – including seven in Morocco'.

Investors Seek Legal Recourse

More trouble was brewing. As mentioned earlier, ESG investors had been disappointed to discover that the company they had chosen to invest in did not meet the sustainability standards that guided their funds. Worse still, the subsequent fall in share price had left them nursing heavy losses. Only too aware of the connection between poor ESG performance and the decline in the value of their investment, some of these investors launched legal claims to retrieve their losses.

Given our focus on financial value, this warrants some exploration because if companies can be held liable for any losses arising from poor ESG practices, then upholding high ESG standards becomes even more of a financial imperative.

The claimants include the California State Teachers' Retirement Fund (with total assets of over £330 billion), and together they are pursuing over £100 million in damages (plus interest and costs) from Boohoo. This is based on the assertion that investors who bought shares in the years before the initial report in The Sunday Times experienced losses due to a drop in share price, as well as additional losses from subsequent reports.

Boohoo is accused of issuing false or misleading information in its published materials, as well as failing to disclose or delaying the release of information regarding the wages of its workers at the Leicester factory. It is claimed that once this information became public, it led to a substantial drop in Boohoo's share price, resulting in investor losses.

The claimants argue based on the statutory liability outlined in Section 90a of the Financial Services and Markets Act 2000. This section stipulates the liability of securities issuers to compensate individuals who incur losses due to: (1) misleading statements or dishonest omissions in specific published information about the securities, or (2) dishonest delays in publishing that information. It states that anyone responsible for listing particulars, supplementary listing particulars, prospectuses or supplementary prospectuses – including the issuer of securities and all directors at the time these particulars were submitted to the FCA – will be liable to compensate a person who has: (1) acquired the relevant securities (in this case, shares in

Boohoo); and (2) suffered losses from any untrue or misleading statement in the particulars, or from any information that was required but not included.

The claim is unlikely to be straightforward, and, at the time of writing, it is yet to be fully resolved. It provides another example of how ESG mishaps can have potentially serious consequences for companies and their investors, even many years after the event.

A More Nuanced View

Although media stories often present a simplistic 'heroes and villains' narrative about companies like Boohoo concerning their ESG performance, the reality is usually more complex. Rapid expansion in the competitive fast fashion industry left Boohoo struggling to balance its sustainability efforts with its business growth. So, was the actual villain here the fast fashion business model? Was it simply impossible to operate successfully and sustainably in that sector? There is certainly plenty of evidence to support this view.

Fast Fashion – Flaws in the Business Model?

The fast fashion model derives its name from the rapid design, production, distribution and marketing of apparel. This approach enables retailers to offer a broader range of products, providing consumers with greater access to fashionable options at more affordable prices.

Well before the Boohoo ESG scandal, sustainability consulting firm Quantis International had run the slide rule over fast fashion in its 2018 report, *Measuring Fashion: Environmental Impact of the Global Apparel and Footwear Industries*. The report identified dyeing and finishing, yarn preparation and fibre production as the primary drivers of global pollution within the fashion industry. These processes are energy-intensive and heavily reliant on fossil fuels, contributing to resource depletion and pollution. The report also highlighted the water-intensive nature of fibre production, which has a significant impact on water supplies and ecosystem health. Such a model was likely to become even more problematic to customers and investors, driven by social and environmental factors.

However, to misquote author Mark Twain, as far as fast fashion goes, 'reports of its death have been greatly exaggerated'. It adapted. To take just one example, Swedish giant H&M is still producing vast volumes of reasonably priced, on-trend clothes but has found ways to do so more sustainably. Examples include the increasing decarbonisation of its stores and supply chains, and far greater use of recycled materials to make its clothes (H&M Climate Transition Plan, 2024). At the time of writing, European fast fashion faces a new threat, Shein, a Singapore e-commerce platform with a strong focus on women's fashion. Its direct-to-consumer business model and reliance on low-cost manufacturing in China allow it to minimise costs at every stage of the process, from design and production to distribution and marketing. Not unlike Boohoo, its rapid growth has brought with it increased scrutiny of its ESG claims and performance. In September 2024, the Italian Competition Authority announced that it would launch an investigation into possibly misleading environmental sustainability advertising claims (Reuters, 2024).

Our Research into Boohoo and Financial Value

Using publicly available sources, we analysed the data to gain further insights into Boohoo's experience and how it impacted financial value. While most such research tracks Boohoo's declining share price or market cap, we concentrated on EBITDA. Note how Figure 6.1 shows that, since the scandal, Boohoo's EBITDA has continued to decline, not only compared to previous years but also relative to its peers.

It is interesting to note, given our focus on the link between ESG and financial performance, that this decline in EBITDA continued despite some, post-scandal, improvement in ESG performance, as shown in Figure 6.2.

So, while it seems that the ESG measures implemented by the Boohoo board did improve ESG scores, they did not appear to halt the decline in profitability. This supports our hypothesis that once a company is damaged, recovery from a grave scandal is complicated because the public, media and investors retain a long-lasting memory of the incident. This suggests that investing in preventative measures to monitor, mitigate and manage ESG risks is a wise choice.

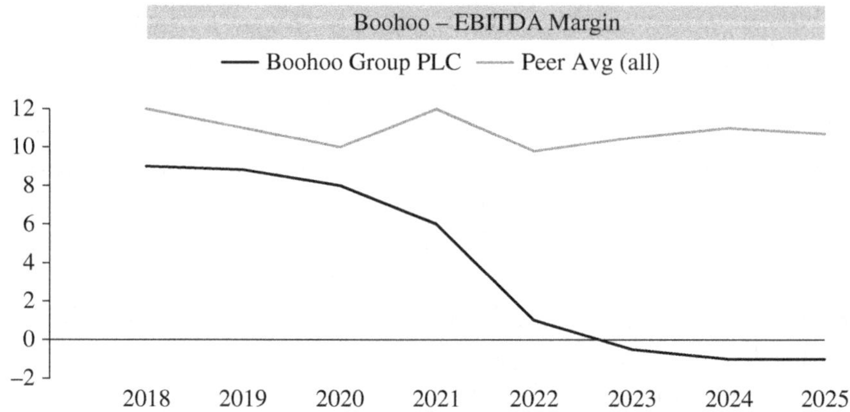

Figure 6.1 Boohoo EBITDA versus peers.

Source: S&P Capital IQ

2020 (ESG scandal)	2021	2022	2023
31.74	41.98	50.86	46.94

Figure 6.2 Boohoo's post-scandal ESG score (the higher the better).

Source: LSEG

Another interpretation is that Boohoo's fast fashion model was under significant pressure from a range of factors, not only sustainability issues but also inflation and supply chain disruptions, all of which hindered the company's ability to restore margins.

Section Summary

- The Boohoo story clearly illustrates the link between ESG failings and the loss of financial value.
- Companies can rapidly lose significant value from ESG controversies, but restoring it is a much longer and harder road with constant scrutiny.
- Any action taken to restore reputation must be communicated and backed up by transparent, practical actions.

- Just because customers are strongly motivated by price, do not assume that is all they care about.
- Sustainable investors should not rely on ESG ratings alone and do their research before investing.
- Fledgling, fast-growing consumer-facing companies that do not incorporate ESG into their operations and supply chains are likely to pay a heavy price sooner or later.

The Palm Oil Story

The subject of this second case study is not a company; it is a crop – palm oil – that is used in everything from chocolate, pizza and deodorant to shampoo, toothpaste and lipstick. It is also used in animal feed and as a biofuel. However, in this case study, we will focus on the role of palm oil in the consumer retail sector, particularly in food products.

How Palm Oil Became Central to Modern-Day Sustainability

In the 1960s, researchers began to warn that the high saturated fat content in butter might increase the risk of heart disease. As a result, food manufacturers started replacing butter with margarine, which is made from vegetable oils low in saturated fat. However, by the early 1990s, it became clear that the process used to produce the oils in margarine, known as partial hydrogenation, created a different type of fat – trans-fat – which was found to be even more harmful to health than saturated fat.

Palm oil proved to be the solution. It not only provided a healthier, natural and animal-free ingredient but was also cost-effective due to its high productivity, delivering significantly greater yields at lower production costs compared to other vegetable oils.

Palm oil also created new opportunities to boost the economies of developing nations and provide income to impoverished communities. Between 1970 and 2020, the world's palm oil production grew by about 40 times. Global output increased from just 2 million tonnes to approximately 80 million tonnes (Our World in Data, 2021).

The Pushback on Palm Oil

Although sustainability efforts initially spurred the growth of palm oil, its very expansion soon became unsustainable. Palm oil was a major contributor to the deforestation of some of the world's most ecologically diverse forests, thereby destroying habitats for endangered species. The loss of these forests, along with the conversion of carbon-rich peat soils, released millions of tonnes of greenhouse gases into the atmosphere.

As negative publicity grew and consumer awareness rose, public opinion began to change. Calls from charities and NGOs to limit the harm caused by palm oil production prompted governments to introduce new regulations. For example, in June 2023, the EU Deforestation-Free Regulation (EUDR) was implemented. It requires that anyone importing or exporting commodities associated with forest degradation into or out of the EU market must demonstrate that the products do not come from recently cleared land or have contributed to forest degradation. Penalties for breaching this ban include the confiscation and refusal of entry into the EU market of non-compliant products, as well as a fine of up to 4% of total annual turnover in the EU.

The Impact on Financial Value

The negative impacts of palm oil production resulted in three main problems for companies using it as an ingredient. First, consumer attitudes shifted away from products containing palm oil, risking revenue and profit margins. Second, regulations limited supplies and exposed buyers to potential fines. Third, once the unsustainable aspects of palm oil became evident, it threatened the environmental and social claims and targets that companies had previously established. Addressing this issue would be challenging, as palm oil remains a cost-effective, adaptable and productive crop, making it difficult to find a suitable substitute.

The Palm Oil Problem and How to Fix It – The Investor Angle

In 2016, Unilever decided to sell its global spreads division, which included many household names and leading brands like Flora, Becel, Country Crock and Blue Band, to an international Private Equity fund (The Guardian, 2017).

Unilever had put the business up for sale, following a review of its assets, which was prompted by the unsolicited takeover attempt by Kraft Heinz (Reuters, 2017). Both Unilever and the Private Equity buyer were aware of consumer concerns about palm oil and were committed to addressing them.

Nevertheless, some deal funding was limited by strict ESG criteria. As a result, potential lenders' credit approval included thorough checks of the target's ESG performance. This is an important point for dealmakers. Even if you do not consider ESG essential in a deal, if your lenders do, then it will become one.

Fortunately, in this instance, we can understand the lender's perspective because their due diligence process and the reasoning behind their investments are disclosed in a publicly available case study (Principles for Responsible Investing, 2018). We included excerpts here as they show how closely the potential investor connects sustainability with financial value.

'Any negative publicity around palm oil sourcing could damage the brands and affect the performance and value of the company. This can cause secondary market volatility in our loans and, more seriously, cause valuation multiples to contract and impair our investment. As with every investment, scenario analysis and consideration of potential risks were modelled. Particular attention was paid to the size of the cost base accounted for by raw materials, with cash flows being stressed for a consequent rise in input prices and a contraction in margins'.

Note here how many of these factors relate directly to those highlighted in Chapter 4, where we found a strong correlation between strong ESG performance and both market volatility (beta) and valuation (price multiples). Note also how, in the final sentence, the materiality of palm oil to margin and profit is highlighted. In the following quote, note how the seller and acquirer's reputation for, and attitude to, ESG is a crucial factor in the investment decision. Please note that Upfield was the name of the spreads business being sold by Unilever.

'Unilever had a strong legacy in sustainability, so it was important that responsible sourcing continued to be a priority at Upfield under Private Equity ownership'.

It is important to recognise that the lender/investor has a comprehensive understanding of the ongoing issues surrounding palm oil and their crucial role in the future performance of the recently acquired company. We will summarise a few additional key points here instead of quoting the original at length. Firstly, the investor finds reassurance in the fact that the Private Equity buyer is 'listed in the US, so is subject to disclosure laws and regulations enforced by the US Securities and Exchange Commission'. This highlights the importance of regulation in supporting investment, as discussed in Chapter 2. Secondly, the case study illustrates how the ESG appraisal does not conclude at the point of investment, with M&G continuing 'to regularly monitor ESG risks and work closely with the management team and key shareholders to identify any weak areas from an ESG perspective that can be strengthened'.

So, what did happen after the deal? Upfield continued to invest in responsible sourcing, with milestones including:

- Sustainable palm oil sourcing policy published in April 2019
- Palm oil 100% sustainably sourced and physically certified since October 2019
- Partnerships established with not-for-profit organisations and satellite operators to support monitoring of palm oil-related deforestation

We included this investor case study because all three parties – the seller, the buyer and the lender – had a strong commitment to sustainability that went beyond the basic requirements of their sectors. However, all three were motivated by financial gain: the buyer aimed for a return on investment, the seller sought to maximise the price and the lender wanted assurance that they would recover their money with interest. Rather than hindering the right decision to sell, buy or lend, being aware of ESG issues related to palm oil is vital for making those decisions. It is also crucial for dealmakers to understand that, regardless of the current political climate around ESG, funders will still scrutinise how ESG factors could influence the price paid and the future performance of the acquisition. Simply put, regardless of trends, when it comes to investing their money, lenders will always assess the risks before acting.

Solving the Palm Oil Problem, One Deal at a Time

By the early 2020s, the writing was on the wall for current methods of palm oil production, and the search for alternatives was already well underway. The solutions could be split into three categories:

- **Palm-oil free:** products which do not contain palm oil.
- **Certified palm oil:** products which contain responsibly grown/sourced palm oil. These were most aligned to the standards set and certified by the Roundtable on Sustainable Palm Oil (RSPO), a global organisation that promotes the sustainable production of palm oil.
- **Palm oil alternatives:** products that would typically contain palm oil, but this ingredient has been substituted with another ingredient.

Examining palm oil usage during this period, in 2023, food and beverage companies accounted for two-thirds (66%) of the $67 billion worth of global palm oil consumption. Personal care and cosmetics were responsible for another 17% of palm oil usage. (Source: Grandview Research, secondary research and company websites). The challenge facing consumer retail products was huge. However, with these sectors comprising some of the largest and most valuable companies in the world, the resources to find and implement a solution were also vast.

With the money and motivation to act, deals soon followed. According to our analysis of publicly available deal data, between 2018 and Q1 2023, transactions valued at just over $10 billion were completed as companies sought to replace or improve the sustainability of the palm oil they used in their products.

As shown in Figure 6.3, most of the investment was directed towards sustainable palm oil production. Between 2018 and Q1 2023, 22 deals worth $ 9.8 billion were completed. Half were M&A, and the remainder were private placements. This mix reflected the strong interest of strategic corporate investors in this space, which accounted for 60% of investments.

In contrast, investment in palm oil-free companies was mainly made by venture capital and Private Equity funds, which accounted for 95% of the investments. Overall, 40 deals were completed during the

Palm-oil free	Sustainable palm oil	Palm oil alternative
\$5m	\$445m	\$5m

Figure 6.3 Average deal size per market segment 2018 to Q1 2023 (rounded to nearest \$1 million).

Source: S&P Capital IQ

same period, amounting to a total of \$199 million. Only two of these were M&A deals, with the remaining being print placements.

A similar story unfolded in the search for palm oil alternatives. Just four deals occurred during the same period, amounting to \$3.7 million. Once again, Private Equity and Venture Capital funds were the dominant players, responsible for 80% of investments in an early-stage, high-risk market.

This higher deal volume and value for sustainable palm oil deals, in part, reflects a consensus within the consumer product and retail sector that sustainable palm oil is the way forward. This approach enables producers to maintain current production methods and enjoy the many advantages of palm oil while addressing the environmental and social concerns associated with its production. It also promised speed and scale.

Consumer Products and Retail (CPR) – Deals Snapshot

Between 2018 and Q1 2023, the CPR sector closed over 65 deals with sustainable palm-oil companies, as shown in Figure 6.4.

Note how activity peaked in 2021 as the sector got to grips with the problem and put their money behind their chosen solution(s). With a 46% share of the total investments (by volume) since 2018, the EMEA region led the overall deal activity in sustainable palm oil. This reflects the fact that Europe is the largest consumer of certified-sustainable palm oil, accounting for 45% of the total global consumption.

Given the financial firepower of the major CPR companies, it is perhaps surprising that strategic M&A is a relatively small part of the picture.

Instead, seed, angel, Private Equity and Venture Capital funds play a significant role. Private placements accounted for 79% of the total deals, as shown in Figure 6.5, with most of the investments being made into angel and seed funding rounds. Nearly half (46%) of the targets

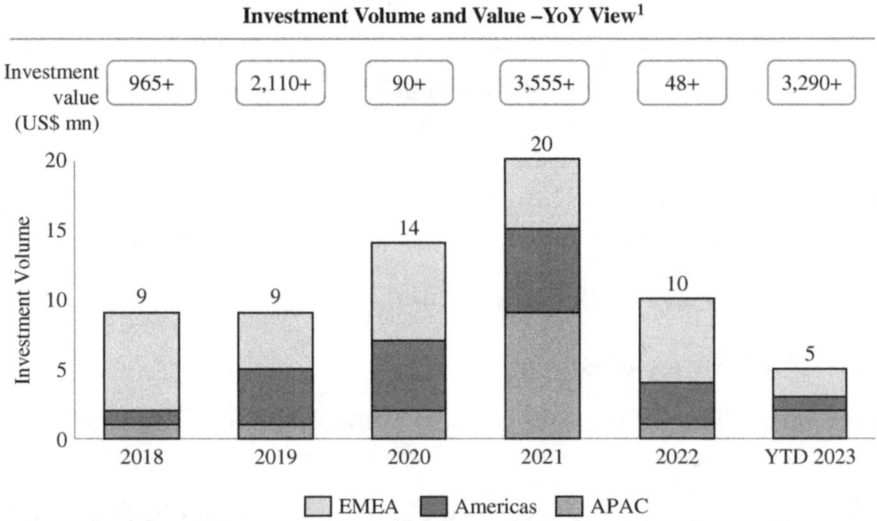

Figure 6.4 Sustainable palm oil investment.

Source: S&P Capital IQ

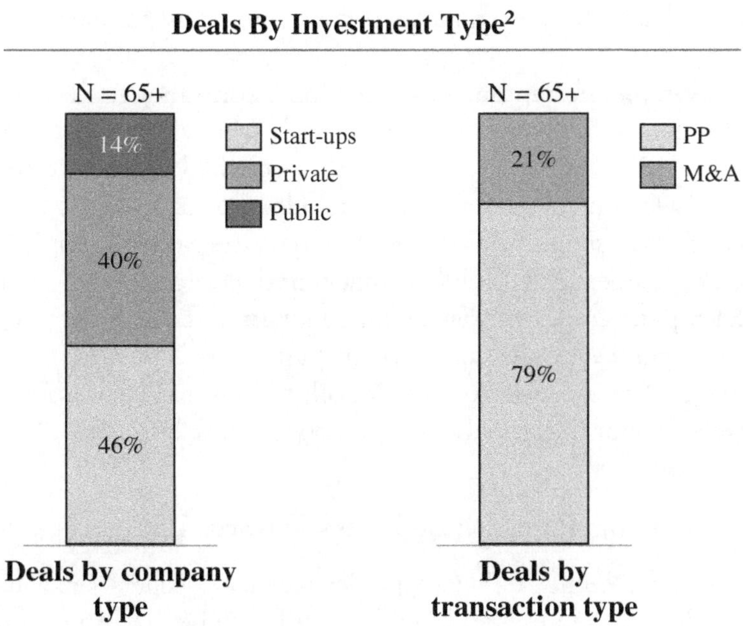

Figure 6.5. Deals by investment type.

Source: S&P Capital IQ

were startups. Like the recycling plastic case study featured in Chapter 4, the need for solutions creates an ecosystem where small, innovative companies – ranging from biotechs to on-the-ground local ventures with palm oil producers – are attracting seed money, partnerships and interest from funds and individuals willing to take a risk on them. Typically, later in the development of these startups, corporates can identify the targets and solutions that are most suitable for partnership or investment.

Key Deal Rationales

Below, we highlight the four key deal rationales for CPR corporates.

Identifying New RSPO-Certified Partners for Palm Oil Sourcing

To ensure the palm oil they buy is truly sustainable, not just in terms of preventing deforestation but also ensuring that there is no forced labour used, or economic harm done to local communities, CPR companies needed to work with partners they could trust to maintain high standards.

For example, in September 2019, global consumer goods company P&G formed a 50:50 joint venture with Malaysian oleochemicals company FGV, which sources RSPO-certified palm kernel oil (P&G, 2019). The agreement also included P&G investing in remediation efforts to support human rights within the palm oil supply chain.

In September 2021, global snack and confectionery company Mondelez partnered with Sweden-headquartered AAK, an international company specialising in plant-based oils and fats, to source traceable and forest-monitored palm oil, to help reduce deforestation and forced labour in the palm oil industry (Mondelez, 2020).

Pushing Existing Palm Oil Suppliers Towards ESG

One of the challenges CPR companies faced was that if they stopped buying palm oil from existing suppliers and switched to more sustainable sources, the harm caused to communities would be substantial. This is because, despite the large-scale operations of palm oil producers, many are small, family-owned farms that depend on the crop for their livelihood. Instead, CPRs began investing in ways to help existing palm oil farmers adopt more sustainable methods. In April 2021, global consumer giants PepsiCo and Nestlé joined and supported a $1 billion scheme to invest in forest conservation across Southeast Asia, aiming to build a more sustainable palm oil supply chain (Thomson Reuters Foundation, 2021).

Satellite Monitoring of Palm Plantations

Ensuring that suppliers in remote parts of the country, thousands of miles away, adhere to agreed standards of palm oil production is a challenge. Therefore, CPR companies also invested in new monitoring methods.

For example, in June 2021, global chocolate and confectionery company Ferrero collaborated with the non-profit organisation the Earthworm Foundation to develop a zero-deforestation verification protocol and utilise satellite technology to trace any deforestation within their sourcing area (Confectionery Production, 2021).

R&D for Palm Oil Alternative Ingredients

Palm oil is hard to replace, particularly at scale and speed, but CPR companies did not give up. They continue to invest in alternatives, capitalising on advancements in biotechnology.

In June 2022, Unilever partnered with US biotech company Geno to launch a $120 million venture focusing on the development and commercialisation of biotechnology-based palm oil alternatives (Genomatica, 2022).

Chapter Summary

We chose this case study because it captures both the benefits and drawbacks of sourcing sustainably, as well as the subsequent impact on financial value. Our key takeaways from the palm oil story are:

- Any sensible investor or lender will consider ESG factors when they have a material impact on the company's current value and future financial performance.
- Innovation, combined with capital, is a powerful way to solve sustainability problems and unlock financial value.

- No matter how green and clean a product may be today, do not assume it will always be so. Constant monitoring and horizon scanning are vital to avoid financial damage and unlock opportunities.

References

BBC News (2020). Boohoo Dropped by Next, Asos and Zalando over Exploitation Claims. https://www.bbc.co.uk/news/business-53327628 (accessed 14 August 2025).

Clarity AI (2023). Measuring ESG Risk: ESG Controversies Lead to a 2% to 5% Stock Underperformance after Six Months. https://clarity.ai/research-and-insights/esg-risk/measuring-esg-risk-esg-controversies-lead-to-a-2-to-5-stock-underperformance-after-six-months/ (accessed 14 August 2025).

Confectionery Production (2021). Ferrero Joins with Earthworm Non-profit Group to Deliver Hazelnut Charter on Sustainability. https://www.confectioneryproduction.com/news/33216/ferrero-joins-with-earthworm-non-profit-group-to-deliver-hazelnut-charter-on-sustainability/ (accessed 14 August 2025).

CSR Hub (2020). Boohoo.Com PLC ESG Ranking. https://www.csrhub.com/CSR_and_sustainability_information/BoohooCom-PLC (accessed 14 August 2025).

Financial Times (2020). Why did so many ESG funds back Boohoo? https://www.ft.com/content/ead7daea-0457-4a0d-9175-93452f0878ec (accessed 14 August 2025).

Genomatica (2022). Geno and Unilever Launch $120m Venture to Scale Alternative to Palm Oil and Fossil Fuels. https://www.genomatica.com/news-content/genomatica-and-unilever-launch-venture/

The Guardian (2017). Unilever sells Household Name Spreads to KKR for £6bn. https://www.theguardian.com/business/2017/dec/15/unilever-sells-household-name-spreads-to-kkr-for-6bn (accessed 14 August 2025).

The Guardian (2020a). More than £1bn Wiped off Boohoo Value as it Investigates Leicester Factory. https://www.theguardian.com/business/2020/jul/06/boohoo-leicester-factory-conditions-covid-19 (accessed 14 August 2025).

The Guardian (2020b). Boohoo Shareholder Sells off Shares in Firm Worth Nearly £80m. https://www.theguardian.com/business/2020/jul/10/boohoo-shareholder-sells-off-shares-aberdeen-standard-investments (accessed 14 August 2025).

H&M Group (2024). H&M Group Climate Transition Plan, 2024. https://hmgroup.com/wp-content/uploads/2024/03/Climate-Transition-Plan.pdf (accessed 14 August 2025).

Manchester News (2022). Black Friday Protest Outside Boohoo HQ in Manchester Against Impact of Fast Fashion. https://www.manchesterworld.uk/news/black-friday-protest-boohoo-hq-in-manchester-impact-fast-fashion-3932003 (accessed 14 August 2025).

Mondelez (2020). Mondelēz International Advances Sustainable Palm Oil Sourcing with Enhanced Traceability. https://ir.mondelezinternational.com/news-releases/news-release-details/mondelez-international-advances-sustainable-palm-oil-sourcing (accessed 14 August 2025).

Our World in Data (2021). Explore Palm Oil Production Across the World and its Impacts on the Environment. https://ourworldindata.org/palm-oil (accessed 14 August 2025).

P&G (2019). P&G to Invest in FGV's Remediation Efforts in Support of Human Rights. https://us.pg.com/blogs/pg-to-invest-in-fgv/ (accessed 14 August 2025).

Principles for Responsible Investment (2018). Case study: M&G. https://www.unpri.org/private-debt/case-study-esg-due-diligence-of-sponsor-and-corporate-in-leverage-loan-market/4083.article (accessed 14 August 2025).

Reuters (2017). Kraft Heinz Bids $143 Billion for Unilever in Global Brand Grab. https://www.reuters.com/article/business/kraft-heinz-bids-143-billion-for-unilever-in-global-brand-grab-idUSKBN15W18Y/ (accessed 14 August 2025).

Reuters (2024). Italy Opens Greenwashing Probe into Shein Website. https://www.reuters.com/business/retail-consumer/italys-antitrust-opens-probe-into-shein-over-environmental-claims-2024-09-25/ (accessed 14 August 2025).

Thomson Reuters Foundation (2021). Big Brands Join $1-billion Forest Conservation Push for SE Asia. https://news.trust.org/item/20210409092535-84x4i/ (accessed 14 August 2025).

7

Financial Value of ESG in Transactions

Lessons Learned and How to Apply Them

We already know from our own experience as transaction professionals that applying an ESG lens to transactions, from identifying the target and conducting due diligence to enhancing performance and exiting, can protect and generate financial value as well as influence the valuation and purchase price.

So, why did we need to write this book? In today's world, it seems there is a disconnect between ESG/sustainability and financial value. This, we believe, is due to several factors, including: the increasing volume and complexity of regulation, the lack of standardisation and sufficient detail for individual transactions across rules and ratings and the politicisation of ESG/sustainability. As a result, the financial value aspects of ESG risk are pushed out of the picture and replaced, to a large extent, by slogans.

The focus of this book is therefore to share with you how and at what level of detail those looking to acquire a business/company should consider ESG factors, and how we think financial value can be identified, articulated and achieved as a result. We then go on to examine some of the challenges, as well as opportunities, that come with this approach, explore how they can be addressed and share case studies that illustrate our thinking.

We believe that if you truly understand your own business from an operational, commercial and financial perspective, the business you wish to acquire, and the ESG value drivers and their financial implications, you will be in a better financial position and, depending on the sector, be able to achieve a lower cost of capital. Put simply, if you miss the ESG opportunity, you will also miss the opportunity to create financial value.

In Chapter 1, we highlight the need for a clearly articulated ESG framework that enables businesses, investors, governments and NGOs to measure progress against common goals. However, with each stakeholder often having different expectations of what ESG entails and requires, and regulations not always aligned, there is currently significant scope for misunderstanding and different interpretations. This poses a particular challenge for businesses. How can they address qualitative imperatives such as 'doing good' or 'saving the planet' in financial value terms? Even when ESG factors are quantitative and measurable – like emissions or water use – it remains difficult for businesses to value these externalities accurately in a way that informs internal investment decisions or creates a sound basis for transaction valuations and decision-making.

The state of play described above, characterised by the lack of a consistent methodology for measuring ESG impact on company performance, has led to a complex and opaque set of ESG-related information being published by companies. In response, regulators intervened by imposing rules on how companies behave and report on ESG factors. As became clear in Chapter 2, the increasing volume and complexity of ESG regulations across regions and countries made it almost inevitable that many companies would come to view ESG primarily as a cost and source of complication rather than as a benefit or opportunity. In addition, the current reporting guidelines do not provide sufficient detail on factors which drive financial decisions from a management board perspective. As a result, the relationship between ESG and financial value becomes almost entirely negative. In this context, it is no surprise that some business leaders started to see ESG as, at best, a drain on their resources, or, at worst, a burdensome obstacle they vigorously sought to remove. This, in turn, further fuelled the ESG pushback and regulatory rollback described in Chapters 1 and 2.

In Chapter 3, we set out to cut through the complexity to highlight for readers where ESG-related financial value is identified and realised in transactions. We revealed how ESG factors not only drive trillions of dollars of value-creating transactions but do so while addressing environmental concerns and meeting customer expectations.

Chapter 4 brought us to the heart of the argument: Does better ESG performance generate greater financial value? We found that, although there is plenty of research correlating ESG performance with positive financial results, it is not specific enough to guide individual investment choices. This is partly due to current ESG frameworks, the limited level of detail articulated by standard setters and other institutions and the fact that ESG rating agencies only provide ratings at an aggregated company level. In contrast, transactions often focus on a business unit within the company. Nevertheless, we acknowledged that ESG ratings, despite their limitations, cannot be ignored because they influence the mindset of investors and because their scoring models are used by banks and financial institutions as a factor in determining the cost and availability of capital. We found a correlation between better ESG performance and financial value, and through our Value Bridge methodology, we developed and measured it at a detailed level. Using the business forecast as a starting point, this methodology adds the capital expenditures and operational costs of a specific ESG initiative, as well as its revenue potential, to the existing business plan to evaluate the impact on cash flows and returns. This approach enables any investor to evaluate ESG strategies based on an ESG-adjusted business plan and cash flow projection, alongside the corresponding cost of capital, to determine the financial value.

In the final part of Chapter 4 and throughout Chapter 5, we discussed how, by moving beyond broad measures and concentrating on company-specific ESG risks and opportunities, at a detailed level investors can identify and unlock financial value by applying ESG due diligence at a detailed level, assessing the materiality, the maturity and impact of ESG on the target company and its financial implications for its valuation and purchase price. We noted how Private Equity, as the leading experts in pinpointing and capturing financial value within a tight timeframe, uses this approach to leverage ESG to their financial benefit.

Key Takeaways for Investors

We hope you enjoyed the journey and found it enlightening. Here are six key points for investors and advisers to consider during transactions:

Focus on the Key Value Drivers

Readers may have already been persuaded that ESG does go beyond risk mitigation and can drive real value. However, as you will also have seen, there are typically hundreds, if not thousands, of ESG touchpoints within an organisation. While a materiality assessment will help to sort the wheat from the chaff, this may not be enough. Use an opportunity and impact assessment across the E, S and G pillars to identify the value drivers which will have a positive financial impact on the business. At the same time, identify and control the potential negative drivers. Carry out the whole process with a value mindset, measuring and monitoring that value in terms of cost savings, earnings and cash flow improvement.

Be Aware of the Advantages and Disadvantages of ESG Ratings

Do not dismiss ESG ratings as they influence the cost and availability of capital, but do recognise their limitations, which include (as previously detailed) a lack of consistency between providers and the broad scope of their single overall company score. Investors, acquirers and sellers will therefore need to adopt their own, more detailed approach during transactions to understand and value the specific ESG-related value drivers and inhibitors for their business case and investment thesis.

Leverage ESG Due Diligence

Proper ESG due diligence employs a thorough and detailed approach, analysing and prioritising the key components in each pillar of E, S and G, and their financial impact on the valuation and business case. By moving beyond a 'hygiene or tick the box' approach to due diligence, dealmakers can identify the ESG factors which are central to the investment thesis. Although risk avoidance is a significant aspect of ESG due diligence, remember that the process can also play a crucial role in identifying and capitalising on ESG opportunities, both from a cost, revenue and cash flow perspective.

Consider Your Time Horizon

It is essential to understand and factor in the status of investments, cost savings and revenue programmes from an ESG perspective when acquiring a company. The time in which these can realistically be achieved will be of paramount importance to all investors. However, as we discussed in Chapter 5 and beyond, timeframes may differ considerably between, for example, a strategic corporate buyer and a Private Equity investor. So, understand the timeline for your investment or investor, but challenge broad assumptions and focus on the details. Consider the organisation's existing ESG structure and maturity, the required capabilities and infrastructure to implement the ESG initiatives, the financial implications on the business case and how it impacts the valuation of the company. Yes, ESG investments may, in general, take longer to bear financial fruit. Bear in mind, however, that not all do. A thorough understanding of the nature and stage in time of all investments, taking into account the holding period and/or expectations of the investor/acquirer, will be necessary.

Have a Strong Story

ESG-value advocates need to have a clear sustainability story, be able to tell it convincingly and understand the audience they are selling it to. That means communicating in the financial language and terminology that investors can understand and providing the data they can use in their valuation/business models. Connecting this to the previous point on time horizon, a strong story is even more critical if the positive value impact is likely to be longer-term. We have seen numerous instances where investors lose patience with ESG strategies because they have not been adequately told and sold the narrative. So, what do investors want to hear? Details on the associated costs and revenue implications of any potential ESG investments and measures, all factored into the business forecast. Please do not shy away from including mid- to long-term impacts like shifting customer behaviour and changes in regulation because savvy investors will understand the risks and opportunities they present.

Be Specific

This is a straightforward point, but perhaps the most impactful. In a world where many regard ESG as too 'fluffy' to invest in, winning the argument requires being specific and pragmatic. Treat it like any other investment in an intangible asset: what are the risks, what are the opportunities and how effectively can both be controlled? Also, understand the preferences of your funding source, especially if it applies its own ESG criteria or, like impact funds, has a particular theme or approach. Finally, keep in mind the regional and sector differences we have highlighted throughout the book, as the appetite for investment and the attractiveness of assets and services will vary accordingly, as will the emphasis on each of the E, S and G pillars.

Key Points for the ESG Universe

Three key takeaways for the wider ESG and investment community:

Make Better Metrics That Meet Market Needs

Since the dawn of ESG, key players have promised improved metrics. Not only have these been slow to develop and often lacked standardisation, but they have also failed to align with the financial language of analysts and investors. Attempts to connect externalities such as climate change or social inequality with financial business performance are almost certain to fail because the relationship between the two (at a single business level) is nearly impossible to quantify. Until ESG and financial metrics align, investment opportunities will be missed or become uninvestable.

Standardise to Add Value

From metrics to regulation, variation and inconsistency obscure the actual financial worth of ESG. A clear example illustrating this broader issue is ESG ratings agencies. Different scoring methods and rating providers reduce public and investor confidence in ESG ratings. Standardising them, perhaps alongside a more harmonised regulatory framework, can enhance their value and offer investors greater reassurance.

Leverage New Technologies

ESG is a data-intensive field, with hundreds of datasets across the E, S and G pillars. The research presented in this book shows that there is still more data to be analysed in the process of identifying, evaluating and realising ESG-related value opportunities. Emerging AI capabilities can help to advance progress, enhance transparency and facilitate a more structured and fact-based discussion on methodologies that determine how sustainability creates value for investors.

Forget All About ESG?

It may seem a strange way to close a book about ESG, but, counterintuitively, the best way to approach it may be to deny its existence as a separate entity and instead see ESG as a regular, integral part of business. Not a standalone category but a key component of standard operational and strategic improvements, from boosting efficiency and reducing risks to identifying new opportunities and adapting to the needs and expectations of customers. As former investment banker John Hoffmire stated in Chapter 1, 'The approach around ESG should be to integrate discussion of corporate environmental, social and governance issues in normal business decision-making. These discussions and analyses should be articulated to the City analysts on a financial basis'. If, like us, you agree with that view, then you may find it frustrating that many discussions or proposals for ESG-related investment face negative sentiment due to misconceptions about its role and purpose, most likely with a dose of political pushback thrown into the mix. Although that can be disheartening, we hope that after reading this book, you will have a greater ability to see through the mist by applying the clear lens of value to spot targets and see the value of transactions. Perhaps you can even reframe the current ESG situation as an opportunity. After all, the more people who are unable to see the whole picture, the greater your chances of discovering and capitalising on creating financial value.

Appendix 1

Materiality, Maturity and Sample Private Equity ESG Due Diligence

Overview of SASB

The Sustainability Accounting Standards Board (SASB) is a non-profit organisation that develops industry-specific standards for companies to disclose financially material sustainability information to investors. SASB standards help companies identify and report on environmental, social and governance (ESG) factors that are most relevant to their financial performance and enterprise value.

The SASB Materiality Map serves primarily as an ESG reporting framework designed to identify the ESG topics that most significantly impact a target's financial value. Beneath the high-level map, SASB offers a more specific framing of ESG issues as they relate to particular sectors or subsectors. For instance, within the biotechnology and pharmaceuticals subsector, 'human rights and community relations' is framed as 'safety of clinical trial participants'.

The tool also presents a valuable selection of metrics to help evaluate performance on each topic, along with a description of why the topic is material to the sector and how it connects to value.

For example, SASB releases a specific Technical Guide to Climate Risks, which maps the materiality of this topic across 77 industry groups. It highlights findings related to climate risk based on research conducted by SASB as part of its standards-setting process.

The bulletin outlines where climate-related risk is likely to be present in a typical portfolio, and what types of risk exist, along with their financial implications.

SASB also publishes a specific Bulletin concerning Human Capital, which discusses the materiality of this topic across 77 industry groups. The bulletin provides an overview of the human capital-related topics within the SASB Standards to assist companies in preparing required human capital-related disclosures. Additionally, the Bulletin emphasises the importance of understanding each company's business model to ensure the correct application of the Standards.

Materiality and Financial Value

A sustainability topic (for example, GHG emissions) is financially material to a transaction when it has the potential to significantly impact the financial drivers of the target company's corporate value, either positively or negatively. This financial impact may materialise in the near term, medium term or long term.

Examples of financial drivers of corporate value include: future revenues; future expenses; future capital expenditures; employee or capital productivity and/or efficiency; market leadership (pricing power and customer loyalty); brand value and corporate reputation (intangible assets); future asset values (stranded or depreciating physical assets; cost of capital (perceived risk by lenders and other providers of capital); access to finance.

Many Private Equity firms employ various methodologies besides or alongside the SASB materiality map and framework. One of the leading ESG rating providers, MSCI, offers the MSCI ESG Industry Materiality Map, which examines ESG risks specific to each industry and illustrates their impact on companies' overall ESG ratings. This can provide an additional valuable perspective, especially if obtaining a higher ESG rating is essential to the investment thesis.

The Three Key Steps

1. Identify the ESG topics that are most important to the target sector by using a recognised framework and supplement or cross-check with other frameworks if necessary.

2. Get specific. Frameworks like SASB should be used only as a baseline for materiality assessments. Most companies have unique business models that involve different risk exposures than those suggested by SASB, and these should be identified and assessed. Factors to consider include:
   - Business model inputs, activities, outputs
   - How many employees are there? Are the manufacturing processes automated?
   - What energy types do they use?
   - Are parts of the value chain particularly exposed to climate change?
   - Geographies of operation
   - Peer and media review
   - Regulatory context and voluntary initiatives
   - ESG maturity of the target and its peers
3. Prioritise. After identifying the most important considerations, evaluate and prioritise the key impacts for due diligence, according to:
   - Likelihood of value impact
   - Magnitude of value impact
   - Company size, sector, customers, product/service, geography, etc.
   - Initial hypothesis on how the target can minimise or maximise value. Over what period is the impact likely to occur?
   - Gain an understanding of potential mitigation measures and how they can be incorporated into the business case
   - Deal structure (minority, majority, asset or entity purchase)
   - Maturity assessment

Maturity Assessments

Essentially, maturity assessments evaluate a business's ability to manage and respond effectively to ESG risks and opportunities. This is crucial because if the target lacks the necessary infrastructure to address any identified ESG-related risks or opportunities during due diligence, its ability to benefit will be significantly hindered.

A maturity assessment examines the infrastructure, governance structures, data collection processes and systems, capabilities, ambitions, procedures and protocols that the target has in place. It helps organisations understand their current ESG status, identify gaps and develop strategies for continuous improvement.

Key aspects of an ESG maturity assessment:

Assessing the Current State: The assessment begins by evaluating the company's current ESG practices, encompassing strategy, objectives, reporting measures and stakeholder engagement.

Benchmarking: Compare the company's ESG performance to industry benchmarks and best practices to identify its strengths and areas for improvement.

Gap Analysis: The assessment highlights the gaps between the current state and the desired level of ESG maturity, pinpointing areas where resources and efforts should be directed.

Action Planning: Based on the assessment, the company can create action plans and strategies to address identified gaps and enhance its ESG performance.

Continuous Improvement: ESG maturity assessments are often conducted periodically to monitor progress and ensure that the company stays aligned with its ESG goals.

Challenges if the overall system is immature:

- There is a greater likelihood of ESG risks occurring and opportunities being missed.
- When ESG issues arise, they will take longer to identify and will not be addressed comprehensively.
- Reputation and the bottom line will suffer in the long term.
- From a transaction perspective, if a company is immature, more investment (in terms of time and money) will be required post-acquisition, which a buyer should consider in the context of the transaction and valuation.

Benefits if the overall system is mature:

- Better positioned to respond to strengthening regulatory environments or more burdensome reporting and disclosure requirements.

- Reduces exposure to risks and reputational damage, while recognising and benefiting from sustainability-related value creation opportunities.
- Gains from a more engaged and productive workforce.

The Power of Benchmarking

ESG benchmarking provides context for a company's ESG performance by comparing it to that of its peers. It employs key performance indicators (KPIs) to achieve this. By benchmarking their ESG performance, companies can evaluate operational gaps, risks and/or opportunities.

Private Equity operations typically build their benchmark in three stages:

Understand the industry through research databases, analysis of market trends of the industry and key sales markets, Confidential Information Memoranda (CIM) documents and relevant news reports about the transaction. Conduct secondary research by visiting company websites and utilising standard frameworks, including SASB and MSCI.

Identify relevant peers from sources including annual reports, sustainability reports, market research reports, broker and analyst reports as well as public and private research databases. Additionally, review the value chain of targets and peers, along with any available client documents and CIM documents.

Select relevant KPIs to benchmark. Choose KPIs based on common frameworks such as SASB and other databases that provide insights into the KPIs relevant for the target company. Ensure that these KPIs are pertinent to the specific industry, sector or subsector, as well as the geographical region of the target and its peers. Next, these KPIs should be harmonised considering factors such as revenue, headcount, geography or production volume to guarantee that like is compared to like.

Focus: Understanding the Business Model

Understanding the target's business model can help identify relevant industry peers for benchmarking analysis. It can also provide valuable insights into market dynamics, the value chain, the competitive landscape, industry evolution, the regulatory environment and sustainability-related trends.

There are multiple approaches to understanding the business model.

1. Research Databases
   (a) Mergermarket:
   Mergermarket is a transaction news and intelligence platform that provides information and analysis on mergers and acquisitions. It also includes databases of deals, news alerts and analytical models that assist users in identifying prospective transaction targets, evaluating market conditions and understanding the scope and rationale of transactions.
   (b) Refinitiv:
   The Deals Intelligence database from Refinitiv offers extensive coverage of global mergers, acquisitions and capital market activities. In addition to transaction structures and values, it provides insights into the industries of buyers and sellers, the parties involved, advisers and other relevant topics.

2. Secondary research
   Company websites/annual reports/and client materials
   Research Databases
   (a) Capital IQ and Capital IQ Pro
   While its primary focus is on financial analysis and investment research, Capital IQ offers various features that aid in understanding the industry landscape. It also provides industry-specific reports, research and market analysis.

(b) Refinitiv
It offers financial data, analytics, tools and additional resources to help you understand the industry. Refinitiv's codes and scheme section delivers detailed industry inputs on business classification.

(c) Bloomberg
Bloomberg offers comprehensive investment research data including investment research, company financials, estimates and pricing data for over 100,000 active and inactive public companies.

Standard Frameworks

(d) SASB standards help define material issues relevant to a specific industry.

(e) MSCI ESG ratings analyse a company's long-term resilience to ESG challenges. The MSCI ESG Industry Materiality Map depicts the current key ESG issues and their impact on firms' ESG ratings.

3. Think laterally

While these tools and sources provide a wealth of financial data and analysis, understanding the industry and business model requires a comprehensive approach. Combining these insights with other industry-specific reports, news sources and qualitative research will give a more holistic view of the industry's dynamics, competitive forces and emerging trends.

Appendix 2

Comparison of Three Global Private Equity Firms on How They Approach ESG in Their Own Firms

Company analysis

Key metrics		Private equity firm 1	Private equity firm 2	Private equity firm 3
Company Overview	Current portfolio companies	162	333	122
	Exits	300	1,197	577
	No. of total funds	114	1712	49
	No. of impact funds	6	2	NA
Investment criteria	Investment range	$1m to $8.5b	$2.2m to $2b	$0.1m to $2.1b
	Enterprise value of companies	$10m to $16.3b	$31.6m to $1b	$10m to $5.3b
	Geographic focus	• USA and Canada • Europe • Asia-Pacific	• United States and Canada • Europe • Asia / Pacific • Latin America and Caribbean • Africa / Middle East	• Americas • Europe • Asia-Pacific
	Investment focus area across sectors	• Tech, media, and telecom • Industrials • Healthcare • Consumer • Energy and utilities	• Real Estate & Finance • Consumer and Retail • Information Technology • Industrials • Energy & Utilities • Health Care	• Tech, media, and telecom • Financials • Industrials • Consumer • Healthcare

Source: Pitchbook, S&P Capital IQ, Industry Research

Sustainability analysis – Environment

Key metrics	Private equity firm 1	Private equity firm 2	Private equity firm 3
Materiality	*Has conducted a materiality assessment for their own company* • Climate change mitigation and adaptation • GHG emissions reduction • Responsible investment • Sustainability products and services in portfolio companies	*Has conducted a materiality assessment for their own company* • Climate resilience • Resource efficiency • Decarbonization	*Hasn't conducted a materiality assessment but applies ESG pre-diligence screening for portfolio companies* • Climate change • Waste and water management • Biodiversity • Responsible investment
Targets	• 2040: 90% reduction in absolute scope 1,2 and 3 GHG emissions • 2027: 100% renewable electricity usage	• 2050: Net zero across portfolio • 2025: Paris-aligned target to reduce Scope 1 & 2 emissions by 75%	• Improve financed emissions and its reporting • Launch climate strategy focused on decarbonization
Initiative	• Renewable energy access • Climate risk management • Innovation in climate tech • Waste management	• Renewable energy procurement Climate scenario analysis	• Decarbonization roadmap creation • Climate data systems upgrade • Fleet electrification • Renewable energy projects
Progress	• 2024: 15% reduction in scope 1 & 2 GHG emissions • 2024:100% renewable electricity usage	• 2025: 93% scope 1 and 2 emissions reduced • 2025: High degree of installed renewable capacity	• 2024: Tailored strategies for select portfolio companies, Climate risk assessment and tracking systems deployed

Source: Company Sustainability Reports, Industry Research

Sustainability analysis – Social

Key metrics	Private equity firm 1	Private equity firm 2	Private equity firm 3
Materiality	*Has conducted a materiality assessment for their own company* • Employee development, health and well-being • Equal treatment and opportunities for all • Employee working conditions in value chain • Employee engagement	*Has conducted a materiality assessment for their own company* • Employee wellbeing • Diversity, equity & inclusion • Career development • Community engagement	*Hasn't conducted a materiality assessment but applies ESG pre-diligence screening for portfolio companies* • Diversity and inclusion • Employee Health and safety • Human Rights • Customer privacy and safety
Targets	• Not more than 60% representation of any gender on board and C-suite • Gender equity in top 20% earners	• 2025: 100% parental leave eligibility for FTEs • 2025: Increase in participation for training in inclusive leadership and ESG seminars	• 2024: Fund non-profits for societal upliftment in line with UN SGDs • 2024: Raise funds via challenge 24
Initiative	• Employee feedback mechanisms • LGBTQ inclusion, Zero harassment policy • Employee well being policy	• Inclusive hiring programs • Leadership development trainings • Equity-pay reviews	• Inclusion strategy • Health and well-being programs • Leadership development trainings
Progress	• 2024: 43% women representation in board, 33% in senior executives • 79% employees reported favourable engagement	• 2025: ESG seminars for portfolio companies • 2025: 57% globally as women employees	• 2024: Funded 5 non-profits and 6 medical research projects

Source: Company Sustainability Reports, Industry Research

Sustainability analysis – Governance

Key metrics	Private equity firm 1	Private equity firm 2	Private equity firm 3
Materiality	*Has conducted a materiality assessment for their own company* • Business ethics • Anti-corruption	*Has conducted a materiality assessment for their own company* • Ethical business conduct, anti-corruption • Transparency & reporting • Board diversity & oversight • ESG-linked compensation	*Hasn't conducted a materiality assessment but applies ESG pre-diligence screening for portfolio companies* • Business ethics and whistleblowing • Cybersecurity • Risk management
Targets	• Reporting year: Zero confirmed bribery or corruption cases	• 2025: Complete alignment with TCFD reporting • 2025: ESG-linked compensation for executives	• Implement climate strategy • Enhance ESG data centralisation and reporting • Host ESG knowledge sharing summits
Initiative	• Anti-money laundering provisions • Whistleblower protection • Industry collaboration for data standardisation and transparency	• ESG-linked executive pay • Enhanced compliance controls • Ethics hotline and whistleblower policy	• Responsible investment policy • Data system centralisation • ESG performance monitoring
Progress	• Reporting year: Zero confirmed bribery or corruption cases achieved	• 2025: Representation of women in board and leadership, 10% higher than PE industry benchmark • 2025: 97% participation in leadership programmes • 2025: ESG-linked financing reached $31.5BN	• Climate strategy implemented • Emission data and enhanced metrics reporting • ESG summits held at multiple locations

Source: Company Sustainability Reports, Industry Research

Index

P

R

S